The Edge of the Law

The Edge of the Law

Street Vendors and the Erosion of
Citizenship in São Paulo

JACINTO CUVI

The University of Chicago Press
Chicago and London

The University of Chicago Press, Chicago 60637
The University of Chicago Press, Ltd., London
© 2025 by The University of Chicago
Published 2025

34 33 32 31 30 29 28 27 26 25   1 2 3 4 5

ISBN-13: 978-0-226-84087-1 (cloth)
ISBN-13: 978-0-226-84089-5 (paper)
ISBN-13: 978-0-226-84088-8 (e-book)
DOI: https://doi.org/10.7208/chicago/9780226840888.001.0001

Library of Congress Cataloging-in-Publication Data

Names: Cuvi, Jacinto, author.
Title: The edge of the law : street vendors and the erosion of citizenship
    in São Paulo / Jacinto Cuvi.
Other titles: Street vendors and the erosion of citizenship in São Paulo
Description: Chicago ; London : The University of Chicago Press, 2025. |
    Includes bibliographical references and index.
Identifiers: LCCN 2024048521 | ISBN 9780226840871 (cloth) |
    ISBN 9780226840895 (paperback) | ISBN 9780226840888 (ebook)
Subjects: LCSH: Street vendors—Brazil—São Paulo—Social conditions. |
    Street vendors—Legal status, laws, etc.—Brazil—São Paulo. | Marginality,
    Social—Brazil—São Paulo. | Employee rights—Brazil—São Paulo. | Informal
    sector (Economics)—Brazil—São Paulo. | São Paulo (Brazil)—Politics and
    government—21st century.
Classification: LCC HF5459.B6 C88 2025 | DDC 381/.18098161—dc23/eng/20241227
LC record available at https://lccn.loc.gov/2024048521

To my mother,
the woman who raised me
and taught me to listen.

I'm a man, not a dog.

PAUL LAVERTY, *I, Daniel Blake*

Contents

Abbreviations

ABRADEF: Associação Brasileira dos Deficientes Físicos
ACP: ação civil pública / class action lawsuit
ACR: areas of commercial restriction
ACSP: Associação Comercial de São Paulo / São Paulo's storeowners association
CPA: commissão permanente de ambulantes / permanent commission on street
    vendors
CPI: commissão parlamentar de inquérito / city council investigative committee
DVA: Disabled Vendors Association
FCC: Federal Communications Commission
FIFA: Fédération Internationale de Football Association
ILO: International Labour Organization
JT: Justice Tribunal
MD: municipal decree
ML: municipal law
MP: military police
PL: projeto de lei / municipal bill
PSDB: Partido da Social Democracia Brasileira
PT: Partido dos Trabalhadores / Workers' Party
SCS: secretaria de coordenação das subprefeituras / district coordination
    department
TPU: termo de permissão de uso / street vending license
WIEGO: Women in the Informal Economy Globalizing and Organizing

Introduction

The phone rang while Valdira and I were having lunch on the top floor of a *shopping popular*—literally, a shopping mall for the common folk—on 25 de Março Street, the commercial heart of Brazil's economic capital, São Paulo. The building's five stories hosted rows and rows of small stands selling knockoffs—from sunglasses to sportswear to cell phones to handbags—both retail and wholesale. Every time we made our way toward the elevators through the crowded corridors of this postmodern bazaar, I could not help but wonder about the fate of anyone standing more than five feet away from the ground-floor entrances if—God forbid—the place caught fire. Metal grids covering the windows on every floor, presumably to ward off burglars, added to the sense of precarious entrapment.

Despite the seemingly chaotic commercial life of its surroundings, the restaurant where Valdira and I ate a couple of times a week ran smoothly. It served a rich buffet of salads, carbs, and veggies, along with a selection of meat, which she relished. The daughter of a migrant from Brazil's impoverished Nordeste, Valdira grew up eating unhealthy foods on the street. She attributed her diabetes to her poor eating habits, the precariousness of her livelihood, and the stress attached to making a living at the edge of the law.

At the time, Valdira, fifty-eight, owned a stall on a sidewalk across the street from the shopping mall where we were having lunch. She sold hats and a variety of other clothing items procured from stores and middlemen, including an Ecuadorian salesman whose Bolivian friends ran a local sweatshop and spared him some merchandise at discounted prices. Valdira's niece Sofia worked at the stall as her assistant. She was the caller. Valdira picked up in a hurry. There were cops at the stall.

Valdira hurried toward the elevators, through the bustling hallways, and rushed out of the shopping mall while complaining that "they"—presumably the cops, perhaps authorities in general—didn't even "let people eat in peace." Crossing the street on red without watching for cars, she arrived at the stall where her niece was waiting for her alongside three police officers in their gray bulletproof vests. Valdira reached hastily for a plastic folder under a pile of clothes at the center of her stall and took out a pack of documents, which she showed to the chief police officer one by one. The officer looked skeptical. Eventually, however, he moved on with his men, leaving Valdira to unwind by her stall. "That last paper saved me," she said when they were gone, letting out a sigh of relief. "Now I need some relaxing." I asked her what the last paper was. It was the copy of a letter signed by the lawyer of a local nonprofit, stating that street vendors with canceled licenses were allowed to carry on trading by virtue of a court order. The ruling had proved a blessing for licensed street vendors in São Paulo—except the court order did not apply to Valdira. Her license had been canceled before the 2012 cutoff date set by the judge.

The Distribution of Rights

Goods and services, infrastructure projects, cash, votes, enforcement, and forbearance are all part of the bargain through which state officials engage with—and govern—informal sector groups. In the gray area of economic informality, where workers enjoy "little or no legal or social protection" and homeowners lack property titles, politics take unusual forms.[1] Numerous studies document the implicit and explicit exchanges at the heart of informal politics, some of which fit the traditional clientelistic mode of government—with its rallies and subsidized group kitchens—while others are more attuned to the neoliberal age, with its fondness for cash transfers and technology.[2]

The problem with the common understanding of politics under conditions of widespread informality is that it glosses over the role and effectiveness of legality at the margins. According to the prevailing view, informality eludes the modern apparatus of statecraft theorized by Max Weber with its reliance on administrative work, codified rules, bookkeeping, and taxation. In the absence of institutional order, informal government takes the form of makeshift arrangements crafted at the margins of the legal framework. Authorities bypass, tweak, subvert, or disregard legal norms in order to extract perks or in their efforts to settle conflicts and implement policy. Without a bureaucratic grasp, moreover, the modern counterpoise to institutionalized power—namely, rights—is in jeopardy. As a result, the politics-of-enforcement framework, which dominates the literature on informality,

focuses on the negotiation of law enforcement instead of the definition, assertion, interpretation, and enforcement of rights. The rights of informal workers exist only on paper, conventional wisdom holds, if they exist at all.

And yet, some informal workers have rights that are set in law. These
rights are, by definition, ambiguous and fragile. But even putative rights such
as those that Valdira claimed on account of a document of dubious legal value
have practical effects on the organization of social and economic life, the distribution of income, and the sorting of life chances. Informal workers aspire
to legal status, and managing their rights and rights expectations is a con-
stituent dimension of the exercise of state power. Contrary to a common view
of informal economies as being governed by "their own political economy,"[3]
legality pervades segments of the informal sector and structures the relationships between their members and the state.

This book is a study of the politics of rights at the edge of the law. It is based
on over a year of field research on streets vendors in São Paulo, Brazil—the
largest metropolis in the southern hemisphere. It depicts a system of government predicated on the promise, granting, withdrawal, dispute, and targeted
violation of rights, which keeps an informal population on edge and in check.
What defines informality, this book argues, is not so much the absence as the
looseness of rights. And the threat of enforcement or the distribution of goods
(and money) are not the only levers that state officials wield. The distribution of
rights in the sense of institutional entitlements to specific opportunities, assets,
or locations plays a structuring role in the government of labor. It breeds what
I call *informal citizenship*—a liminal status at the edge of legality.

THE FIELD OF LEGALITY

Key to the enjoyment of a bundle of rights is ascription into a legal category
such as citizen, refugee, or licensed street vendor. Members of these categories are protected by law. The construction of legality involves the definition
of legal categories and their boundaries—that is, conditions of access or eligi-
bility. It is an institutional process with symbolic underpinnings, as ethno-
nationalist constructions of citizenship illustrate. Perceptions, discourse, and
values interact with official state acts in drawing the boundaries of legality.
Those who fall outside such boundaries—undocumented immigrants, for
example—face state repression and the use of force. Put differently, the law
has a double edge. While acting as a safeguard against abuse of power by those
running the state and third-party injuries, the law categorizes, draws boundaries between and within populations, and legitimizes violent treatment by
the state of negatively designated categories such as "aliens" or "felons."

Informal economies sit at the margins of the legal order and straddle the boundaries between rights-bearers and the disenfranchised. If legality is conceived as a playfield that offers certain guarantees or liberties to players, the most dramatic feature of informality is that the bounds are being erased or (re)drawn while the game is being played—by the refs, the public, and the players themselves. Under draconian administrations, like that of former São Paulo mayor Gilberto Kassab, players who commit minor infractions are expelled. The risk of finding themselves suddenly out-of-bounds, and thus losing their rights, is a defining feature of informal workers' experience.

Outside the playfield, however, the game goes on. Street vendors who lose their licenses go on selling off the books or, like Valdira in the opening story, try to stay on the field of legality by surreptitious means. Lacking rights as workers, unlicensed vendors resort to other tactics, including within-group cooperation and escape—as well as the occasional bribe—in their work routines. Moreover, like most fields, the field of legality is riddled with power relations, and it "traps" those members of the informal economy that have ties to the state. State officials strategically draw on informal workers' ambiguous relation to the law and their fraught expectations of tolerance. The prospect of seeing their rights reinstated after a brutal eviction campaign thus contributed to the submissiveness of licensed street vendors in São Paulo. Beyond this circle, the promise of rights rings (accurately) hollow, and the tightening of laws in a context of economic scarcity encourages more deviant behavior, not less.

Captive though they are, licensed street vendors are not powerless. Informal workers confronted with distorted readings and draconian enforcement of the law develop their own strategies, which, like those of state officials seeking to control or repress them, exploit the blind spots, ambiguities, and moving parts of existing legislation. The tactics used by each side—from enforcement in bad faith to promises of legal status to creative readings of the law and everyday strategies of subversion—intersect in the recursive construction of legality and boundary-making.

Recognizing the effects of legality on informal economies and the condition of informal workers as potential rights-bearers also calls attention to the formal institutions of lawmaking and adjudication, which students of informality tend to neglect. Informal workers occasionally participate in the legislative process. Their participation can be material or symbolic; it can lead to more inclusive or more exclusionary outcomes. Access to justice is costly, sociolegal studies show, but courts also play a part in the lives of the disenfranchised. Beyond the well-documented role of support structures that litigate abuses against informal sector groups, the story of street vendors in São

Paulo shows that judicial processes bring the contested meaning(s) of their rights into play and alter the understanding of these rights in the process.

In short, the distribution of rights is both a method of government that policymakers use for their own purposes and the evolving outcome of multiple processes over which state officials exert partial control. Unpacking its logic sheds a troubling light on the prospects of formalization—that is, the expansion and securing of informal workers' rights—which experts and activists advocate. As a method of government, moreover, the distribution of rights operates alongside and in conjunction with the politics of enforcement, which this book also considers.

The entwinement of lawmaking and enforcement is deeper at the margins of the law, where policymaking toward disenfranchised groups overlaps with their policing, and the boundaries of state authority are often drawn as they are being enforced. Yet the construction of legality is inherent to the broader process of state-making. By considering jointly lawmaking and law enforcement, which together form the system of government that subdues and marginalizes disenfranchised populations, *The Edge of the Law* sheds light on the foundations—and limits—of institutionalized authority.

The Making of Informality

In the mid-twentieth century, rural-to-urban migrants began reshaping former colonial cities across Latin America and beyond, building informal settlements on the hillsides or the outskirts and occupying public spaces in the downtown areas. The sprawling shantytowns in which these migrants settled and their increasingly visible presence on the streets of the "old city" made local elites uneasy, but few scholars concerned themselves with the potentially subversive politics of informality.

One reason for this oversight lies in the Marxist-inspired conception of informal workers as either scattered survivalists or wage workers in disguise, exploited by capitalists who eschew tax codes and labor protection laws by keeping their workers outside the firm or underground.[4] In this view, informal workers lacked the bonds, sense of pride in the product of their labor, and collective shop-floor experience to develop class consciousness—the subjective prerequisite to political action.

There was also an empirical reason, however. Studies that considered political behavior in the 1960s noted that, more often than not, the urban poor voted for conservative candidates, if they voted at all.[5] As Janice Perlman shows in *The Myth of Marginality*, newcomers to Rio de Janeiro were too busy building their homes and securing a livelihood to worry much about politics.[6]

Besides, they found enough economic opportunities to get by and, in some cases, amass a modicum of wealth. In other words, informal workers at the time were part and parcel of a dependent capitalist system that, albeit skewed, was dynamic, with lasting spells of industrial growth that benefited formal and informal workers alike, easing the pressure on the political system. In a context of circumscribed labor market opportunities yet sustained economic expansion, the informal economy provided a cushion against the throes of hunger and unemployment—hence the common description of the informal sector as a shadow welfare state. And while some observers expected the cushion to wear thin as the aspirations of these workers—and especially their offspring—began to grow, military regimes across Latin America dampened the expression of whatever frustration may have brewed among the *informales* in the following decade.[7]

From the 1970s onward, however, economic restructuring gradually transformed relations between labor, capital, and the state, with profound effects on the composition of informal labor. Partly as a result of pressures from business groups to deregulate labor markets, partly in response to reforms mandated by international financial organizations to access much-needed credit lines, and partly as an attempt to compete for foreign investment by lowering labor costs in a globalized economy, governments across much of the Global South laid off public-sector employees, privatized state-owned companies, scrapped barriers to trade and capital flows, and rolled back social protections. The number and share of informal workers increased as a result. The report *Decent Work and the Informal Economy*, published by the International Labour Organization (ILO) in 2002, notes that "the bulk of new employment in recent years, particularly in developing and transition countries, has been in the informal economy. Most people have been going into the informal economy because they cannot find jobs or are unable to start businesses in the formal economy."[8] Even though operational definitions of informal workers vary across countries, estimates for the five Latin American countries for which such data were available at the time—Mexico, Brazil, Colombia, Argentina, and Venezuela—show that the share of informal employment increased in all of them during the 1990s to between 45 and 55 percent.[9]

The trend reflects both the informalization of industrial employment and the shift of a share of the workforce to the informal economy as a result of deindustrialization. In settings ranging from export-processing zones to *maquilas* to the houses of homeworkers paid at piece rate by local or international contractors, the boundaries of formal employment faded. Subcontracting arrangements in global value chains relieved name-brand firms from legal accountability over working conditions and terms of employment at the point of production. Even registered workers saw their rights and benefits shrink. At the same time, Latin American countries compelled to liberalize trade were flooded with cheap manufacturing imports from Asia—especially China—that put formal sector firms, informal cottage industries, and craftsmen out of business. According to Miguel Angel Centeno and Alejandro Portes, in this context, the informal sector became "a place for those escaping the degradation of formerly secure jobs [in the formal economy]."[10] Against this background, the export-led boom of the early twenty-first century fueled by high commodity prices and lavish public spending proved only a respite. It was followed by the worst economic performance for the region in four decades, even before the COVID-19 pandemic shattered the global economy.[11]

In short, the renewed expansion of informal labor in the era of globalization resembles the postwar years of mass urbanization only on the surface. The "new informality" of the twenty-first century, as Juan Pablo Pérez Sáinz puts it, is more atomistic, impoverished, and stagnant than its postwar counterpart.[12] And street trade is perhaps the most visible form of this degraded labor force. Writing on Mexico in the early 2000s, Diane Davis notes, citing Bruno Baroni, that "in the historical central district of Mexico City, alone, the number of street vendors is estimated to be 50,000, a number that has more than quadrupled since the pre-NAFTA date of 1991."[13]

Structural change had political implications that came into relief upon the return to democracy, when the informal sector—later designated by the more encompassing and sometimes pluralized term *informal economy*—became a key player in electoral processes that brought political outsiders with anti-establishment views to power.[14] More recently, the global surge in right-wing populism, which followed a returning Latin American pink tide with its own populist overtones, revived the thesis of an elective affinity between populism and economic informality. The rhetorical identification of populist leaders with the downtrodden—of which the *informales* are the dramatic embodiment—as well as their perceived shared disregard for state institutions and the rule of law support this view. But even if the charismatic authority of the leader fills the gap in the legal-rational authority of the state and helps to stabilize the polity by quelling working-class resentment, populism alone is not enough to defuse the threat that a massive underpaid and underemployed population at the margins of the law poses to political order. Moreover, in the large urban centers of global capitalism, politicians aspiring to executive posts are less likely to run as populists and, if elected, less likely to govern as such. A series of political and managerial constraints and considerations prevents them from doing so.[15] How, then, is this disenfranchised labor force controlled or kept at bay to prevent it from disrupting the economic processes of capital accumulation in a context of deepening inequality and deteriorating livelihoods, where the legal authority of the state is consistently flouted and where the informal workforce can be so massive as to encompass a majority of the economically active population?

WORK AND CRIME

In an effort to draw the analytic contours of informality, Manuel Castells and Alejandro Portes distinguish the legal status of the goods and services being produced and exchanged from the conditions in which production and trade take place.[16] In contrast to criminal markets where illicit goods and services such as cocaine or murder are manufactured, transacted, or delivered, informal economies deal with licit products—for example, haircuts, garments, cab rides—while disregarding norms and regulations such as safety standards, licensing procedures, zoning ordinances, and the like.[17] John Cross sums it up neatly when he writes that "informal economic activity comprises those economic strategies that contravene laws regulating how business should be conducted, but not laws specifying what business may be conducted."[18] Of course, the informal economy remains a gray area. Some goods, like pirated movies or albums, and some services, like sex, are the subject of endless categorization struggles rife with moral claims.[19] Likewise, the difference between formal and informal labor is often a matter of degree, since even corporate actors employ some workers on uncertain legal terms or break certain rules on a regular basis, leading some authors to use the notion of a continuum.[20] However, the distinction between what is essentially a legitimate business undertaken by workers unable or unwilling to comply with all applicable regulations, on the one hand, and criminal enterprises, on the other, matters not only from a theoretical perspective; it explains why authorities are more likely to turn a blind eye to informal economic activities. In fact, the view of informal workers as risk-taking entrepreneurs praised for their grit and self-reliance gained currency in the '80s and '90s, the golden age of neoliberalism. But economic restructuring also made some of these workers undesirable.

As urban centers compete in the global economy to attract foreign investment into high value–added sectors like tech, electronics, or finance, planners revisit the urban landscape along futurist lines. Dramatic skylines and state-of-the-art surface commuter trains convey an open-for-business vibe to international investors while well-paid high-skill workers seek clean, safe, green, welcoming urban spaces. Except for sanitized versions of picturesque, appropriately spaced-out kiosks or trucks usually owned by corporations, street vendors do not belong in this landscape. As Michael Donovan puts it, "Today, the vendors who were so heralded in the past are confronted with a radically different policy environment. Now they are perceived not as agents of innovation, but as anathema to city marketers who claim traders congest streets and create 'broken windows' that generate disorder, blight and crime."[21]

In other words, street vendors, like other informal groups occupying public spaces, are being criminalized.[22] Criminalization entails a series of legal, material, and symbolic measures such as cracking down on formerly tolerated practices, toughening penalties against misdemeanors, or outlawing income-making activities, all in tandem with a branding of informal workers as offenders. The broken windows theory that underpins this movement posits that any sign of public disorder or act of deviance in public spaces, however small, encourages serious crime. In the United States, this doctrine inspired zero-tolerance policies that increased the carceral population and led to the death of Eric Garner, a Black man killed by police in an arrest gone awry, which NYPD officers conducted on suspicion that Garner was selling loose cigarettes on a sidewalk of Staten Island. The same approach is being exported to other countries.[23]

More broadly, criminalization entails a deliberate blurring of lines between informal and illegal activities on the part of state officials, with help from pundits and the media, leading to an equally harsh treatment of those in either group. And, from a legal standpoint, to criminalize is to deprive of rights. Workers lose the right to ply their outlawed trade while their ability to make claims on the state, hence to assert other rights they may hold as citizens or humans, is also undermined.

Legislation, however, is path dependent. While punitive laws may have self-reinforcing properties, protective legislation leaves its own legacy of rights that repressive administrations must grapple with. This book captures the tensions around residual rights at a time of criminalization. It tells the story of how the rights of street vendors came into being and fleshes out the interplay of actors and interests that shaped licensing policies over time. Evicting licensed vendors entailed dismantling these rights and overriding other defense mechanisms, such as clientelistic networks offering political protection.[24] In the legal battle that ensued, the fate of street vendors hinged on creative and contentious readings of their rights and obligations. Like other social groups at the edge of the law, criminalized vendors experienced (and resisted) a troublesome political development characteristic of our time: the unmaking of citizens.

Informal Citizenship

While the concept of citizenship covers a range of realms, including politics and civil life, formal worker status is akin to labor market citizenship.

Formality entails having rights. It signifies belonging on the field of legality, just like being a citizen means having the right to live in a given territory, elect rulers, receive welfare, and so on. Like residents in a foreign country, some informal workers have (some) rights. However, the criminalization of informal workers in public spaces and the blurring of legality make it harder for those on the losing end to maintain or exercise their rights. In conjunction with the political and economic pressures precarious workers and shantytown dwellers are subject to, the erosion of legality produces a fraught kind of citizenship.

The concept of informal citizenship seeks to capture the politics of citizens at risk: people who have had and may still hold certain rights but who are standing nonetheless on the edge of legality, facing both the prospect of disenfranchisement and powerful forces pushing for it. *Informal*, in this context, signifies that their rights are unclear and unreliable. Uncertainty is a well-known aspect of the condition of informality; nevertheless, in the much of the literature, uncertainty stems from the risk of losing merchandise, equipment, or access to a given location—not rights. Yet informal workers bear rights that they see as their own and cling to in the face of adversity. The stories recounted in this book flesh out the subjective experience of dispossession in the field of legality along with the collective and individual dynamics of resistance and subjection that stem from it.

The analysis revisits the political function of rights. In line with the dominant narrative about the making of citizens, conventional wisdom sees rights as a safeguard. State officials hold an array of material, symbolic, and institutional means of coercion; citizens hold rights. According to Norberto Bobbio, there are two types of rights, both of which are defined in relation to the powers that be: those that protect against their evils and those that provide access to benefits.[25] The sociological perspective calls into question the firmness of rights, their shared understanding, and the capacities different groups have to make sure their rights matter. The politics of rights scholarship focuses on movements that seek such recognition and enforcement, with varying levels of success.

By contrast, in the murky waters of informal citizenship, citizens are unsure about what rights they (still) have, what those rights mean, and on which situations their rights may have a bearing. They must assert their tainted rights by any means available as they navigate a fraught and hard-to-read institutional environment. In this context, strategic calculations about mobilization around rights and right claims are never straightforward. Agony and conflict pervade decision-making. Subjects go through painful constructions of the self as a rights-bearer, even as their rights are being repeatedly denied by the state.

That such struggles take place at the heart of cities carries some historical irony. Before it came to mean "a large town," the Latin word *civitas*, from which the word *citizen* stems, referred to a community whose members are bound by the same law. By contrast, in ancient Greek, the term *polis* first designated an urban center, then a body of citizens. To this day, the town and its political heart, the town hall, symbolize the crucible of democratic life. Yet the marketplace also played a role in the early days. In Athens, the *agora* was at once a market and a forum. Institutions operate in and through material settings that shape civic participation. Citizens need a place to meet.

However, much of the urban space in postindustrial cities is hostile, desolate, gloomy, or sterile. From the standpoint of its private makers, on the other hand, the city has become a field of speculation. Unwanted categories ranging from low-income tenants facing eviction to the booming homeless populations of shining US downtowns to the multitude of petty street traders are at once the products of a global system of exclusion and a hindrance to urban development and economic growth. Their criminalization responds in part to lobbying from private actors with outsize influence on urban policy, in part to the concerns of the urban middle classes who embody decency as respectable citizens. Either way, the making of the postindustrial city stalls the making of its citizens.

THE POSTINDUSTRIAL PARADOX

And yet, even as marginality spreads in postindustrial economies, institutional actors in both the public and private sectors must project or uphold an image of tolerance, transparency, diversity, and inclusion. The discourse of modernity sets limits on the criminalization agenda—along with institutional legacies, veto players, and electoral risks. Global players such as the Fédération Internationale de Football Association (FIFA), the world soccer governing body and World Cup brand owner, are particularly sensitive to the public display of such standards, notwithstanding the rampant corruption in its leadership recent scandals have laid bare. In other words, there is a tension between the economics and the cultural landscape of postindustrial capitalism. It comes to light when, for example, a sweatshop tragedy exposes child labor or other objectionable conditions in global commodity chains servicing famous brands. Efforts to mitigate exploitation under these circumstances can be cosmetic or lead to a substantive expansion of rights.

As independent workers, street vendors are not among the groups whose symbolic inclusion pays dividends in normal times. If anything, their unpopularity with the upper strata of the urban economy supports a repressive approach. But exceptional circumstances can bring public and policy attention to their cause. The 2012 Workers' Party (Partido dos Trabalhadores, PT) victory in São Paulo's mayoral elections following a brutal eviction campaign and the hosting of the 2014 World Cup put street vendors on the agenda. World Cup organizers were caught between the economic structure of an event based on the concentration of commercial and marketing rights in the hands of corporate sponsors, on the one hand, and pressures from the streets to do something for vulnerable groups hit by the event, on the other. The solution to this public relations quandary was to grant street vendors shallow, temporary rights to sell a narrow range of products during the World Cup.

The PT also faced the contradiction between the political economy of an aspiring global city that is hostile to street vendors and its reputation as a party with working-class roots that played a leading role in Brazil's transition to democracy. It performed its commitment to democratic values and dialogue through lengthy talks with street vendors that hinged on the—unfulfilled—promise of restoring their rights. And yet, the promise of rights neutralized street vendors. The distribution of rights to disenfranchised populations can thus be material or symbolic. However, it is effective in both its actual and aspirational forms. And it shapes the lives of informal workers.

Street Vending

The streets are the place where poor people who lack the skills, networks, or credentials to find stable employment elsewhere—or who refuse to endure a nagging boss and a stringent schedule—eke out a living. Street trade requires little start-up capital and no formal training. Street vendors do not need to follow a routine or fill out paperwork, which is why street vending is a popular occupation among undocumented immigrants.[26] Compared to most alternatives available to unskilled workers, the sidewalks offer an enticing but deceitful sense of freedom. As spaces of circulating wealth, sidewalks also hold a vague promise of enrichment absent from other menial jobs like working at a sweatshop or cleaning office buildings. The process of economic restructuring led to the disappearance or degradation of such employment alternatives anyway.

As new entrants soon learn at their own expense, however, the streets are a highly contested territory. Storeowners, for one, do not like street vendors. They see peddlers as unfair competitors who lure away customers and avoid paying taxes, rent, utilities, wages, and other operating costs. Lobbying by chambers of commerce or storeowners associations is a driving force behind eviction campaigns. But other constituencies also stake their claim to the sidewalk and regard street vendors as a nuisance, if not a threat. The presence of vendors drives down property values, according to real estate owners and managers. Despite buying from street traders when it suits them, neighborhood residents and commuters—especially those of a middle- or upper-class background—look down on them as a socially inferior and intrusive category, and sometimes fear them. The view of street sellers as a "dangerous class" assimilated to thieves, prostitutes, conmen, and beggars is an old and common stereotype dating back at least to Victorian London.[27] It is routinely revived by media reporting and reinforced by "expert" stances on the matter, such as the broken windows theory.

The informal occupation of sidewalks and squares for commercial purposes does not sit well with urban policymakers, either.[28] The model of the world-class city that inspires planners from Beijing to Johannesburg combines the stereotypical marks of midtown Manhattan—glimmering glass-and-steel skyscrapers, fashion boutiques, and so on—with the folkloric charm of London pubs or art nouveau subway entrances in Paris. By contrast, streets clogged with loud, unruly vendors suggest chaos. And hostility toward street vendors is observable in large urban centers from Hanoi to New York to Mexico City.[29] Even left-wing parties that supported the integration of street vendors into the city in the past, such as the New Communist Party in Kolkata, the PT in São Paulo, or even Mugabe's Zanu–PF in Zimbabwe, turned against them in the age of global capital flows and entrepreneurial urbanism.[30]

And yet, despite the challenges of estimating the size of an informal population that is both geographically and occupationally mobile and whose composition fluctuates according to a host of demographic, political, and economic factors, the numbers of vendors show no sign of abatement.[31] Street trade is one of the largest single occupational subgroups in the informal economy. According to Women in the Informal Economy Globalizing and Organizing (WIEGO), a nonprofit that collaborates with the ILO in statistical measurement of informality, street traders make up 15 percent of total urban employment in South Africa and 11 percent in India and between 13 and 24 percent of informal nonagricultural employment in several capital cities of Africa and 9 percent in Lima, Peru.[32]

The profiles of street vendors—known as *hawkers* in India, *traders* in South Africa, *ambulantes* across urban Latin America, and *camelôs* in Brazil—also vary. Some vendors embrace peddling as a sideline, others as a full-time job. For some, it is a temporary occupation during a time of unemployment. Still others practice street trade for years, even decades, and in some cases their whole lives. The gender composition of street trade tends to be more balanced than for other informal occupations, such as paid domestic work, which is predominantly female, or construction work, typically done by men. As for the products carried by peddlers, they vary widely from newspapers to cheap electronics to garments, music, videos, books, handcrafts, paintings, and all sorts of foodstuffs—fresh, cooked, processed, or packaged.

While the vast majority of street traders are self-employed, work relations in the street vending economy replicate, to some extent, the diversity that characterizes informal employment more broadly. Ray Bromley thus distinguishes ice cream and newspaper vendors who sell products from a single corporate firm on commission—and fit the wage-workers-in-disguise category—from independent vendors who can pick from a range of suppliers and trade in a variety of products. Even then, most of them specialize in one niche and develop ties with a particular supplier, sometimes involving prime vendor contract arrangements.[33]

In this crowded and contentious field, where, when, and how street vendors get to ply their trade depends, among other factors, on their legal status. Most cities run some kind of licensing program that confers certain rights on individual holders. However, "the rights granted by official licenses and permits vary and are often ambiguous," as Alison Brown points out. "In some instances they confer a general right to trade, and in others the right to trade at a particular locality."[34] In São Paulo, as in many other cities, licenses display a designated address where license holders are expected to set up shop. A survey conducted by Bromley in Cali in the 1970s found that "about 80% of street vendors do not have a trading license, and the authorities have refused for several years to issue more than a few new licenses as a measure to control the number of traders."[35] This tightening of licenses is characteristic of the current policy environment, but administrations that embrace a punitive stance against vendors still need to deal with the legacy of licenses from previous administrations.

Organization is a common by-product of licensing. As an identifiable constituency with a clear and specific interest, licensed vendors are more likely to form an association, though associations of unlicensed vendors also exist. In fact, organizations representing vendors vary widely from accredited city-level guilds and international federations like WIEGO to loosely structured local networks or nominal organizations of uncertain membership. These structures serve multiple and sometimes shady purposes. According to John Cross and Sergio Peña, "the organizational leadership can adjudicate vendor conflicts internally, maintain a certain level of control to limit external complaints, and also form a collective front to regulatory agents who are then confronted with a political dilemma, since an organization can mobilize the resources of the vendors to attract public attention to their concerns and appeal to political figures for support."[36] Less commendable functions include extortion, profiteering, or the forceful exclusion of other market participants from a trading area. Such practices are denounced by members and rival leaders or cited by nonmembers as a reason to remain independent. The market-enabling and extractive operations of informal workers associations are not mutually exclusive, moreover; they often go hand in hand. In some places, state officials encourage informal workers to organize. As Calla Hummel notes in *Why Informal Workers Organize*, officials provide incentives, often in the form of cash.[37] From the government's standpoint, street vendors associations can serve a governance purpose. To the extent that the leadership is able to discipline its members both in their occupation of public space and their electoral choices, authorities may be inclined to strike a deal.[38] Transactions of this sort fit the politics-of-enforcement narrative that frames much of the research on the regulation of informal labor in general and street vending in particular.

THE POLITICS OF ENFORCEMENT

According to Loïc Wacquant, the current policies of mass punishment and criminalization are a response to the growth of "desocialized labor" in segregated postindustrial cities.[39] Yet there are both material and political limits to large-scale punitive measures. The ILO estimates that the share of the global workforce in informal employment reached 61 percent in 2018—the last available estimate before the COVID-19 pandemic quashed the global economy, presumably sending the number of self-employed informal workers through the roof.[40] In countries like Egypt, Bolivia, and India, informally employed workers accounted for 63, 83, or 88 percent of the workforce, respectively, before the pandemic.[41] In 2023, estimates based on household surveys put those numbers around 50 percent for Argentina, 85 percent for Bolivia, and 37 percent for Brazil.[42]

The state lacks the resources to effectively monitor and police—let alone incarcerate—so large a population. Under these circumstances, repression shades into what Bromley calls *containment*, a term that captures both the general spirit of policy efforts to tackle informality and the aggregate outcome of uncoordinated policy interventions aimed at preventing its expansion beyond a "tolerable" threshold, which usually consist of a substantive deployment of police forces in upscale neighborhoods and touristic hot spots as well as regular crackdowns on pockets of informal trade.

Then there are the votes. Containment describes the material policy of population control used against informal labor, but it fails to capture the politics. In electoral systems of government, the large-scale repression of the urban poor comes at a political cost. Marginalized as they may be, informal workers have voting rights—unless they are foreigners—and political leaders are aware of the stakes. In the intricate world of informal sector policymaking, therefore, a lack of enforcement does not necessarily amount to an outflanking of the state. Forbearance, as Alisha Holland calls it, is the decision on the part of state officials not to enforce the law against informal workers, knowing (or hoping) that those spared from the heavy hand of the state will return the favor at the ballot box.[43]

If the scope of containment is bound by the repressive capacities of the state, the scope of forbearance is bound by the demands and expectations of other influential constituencies, from name-brand companies pushing for a crackdown on intellectual property rights violations to real estate investors concerned with a decline in property value to, more broadly, local elites and the urban middle classes bemoaning the "invasion" of public spaces.[44] As a result, forbearance is usually limited to specific urban areas (e.g., majority poor electoral districts) and time periods (e.g., before elections) beyond which containment is the norm.

Together, containment and forbearance define the contours of what may be called *the politics of enforcement*. They set the parameters for informal bargaining through exchanges with authorities that allow informal sector groups to keep going. Ethnographic research reveals the myriad ways in which enforcement plays out at the street level, where informal workers obtain leniency from authorities through favors, cash, gifts, votes, haggling, or appeals to human compassion. Authorities, on the other hand, extract favors, cash, and gifts with the threat of enforcement.[45]

As useful as the politics of enforcement literature may be to understand informal labor regulation, it takes the legal framework for granted and fails to consider the legislative process in detail, along with the occasional participation of informal workers in it to claim or defend their rights. Ananya Roy's mesmerizing *City Requiem* shows how Kolkata evolved under the New Communist Party from a populist regime with an inclusive bent toward a loose neoliberal arrangement in which dispossession transits through a patchwork of opaque deals, legal procedures, and clientelistic practices.[46] Building on Roy's insight about the power of ambiguity, *The Edge of the Law* examines how informal workers and other nonstate actors co-construct the field of legality. The writing of rules, the enforcement of penalties, and the definition of rights all occur through a contentious sociopolitical process in a dynamic social and institutional space. Workers have a say on where the line between informal and illegal activity falls, even as the city government tries to narrow the perimeter of legality.

STREET VENDORS IN SÃO PAULO

As the financial and commercial capital of Brazil, São Paulo encapsulates the charms and miseries of an aspiring global city. With over twenty million residents, its metropolitan area hosts one of the largest industrial complexes in Latin America. The city's wealth, matched only by its staggering levels of inequality, has drawn millions of migrants over the years, foreign and domestic, who flocked to São Paulo and Rio, "attracted," in Brodwyn Fischer's words, "not only by the perceived abundance of industrial and bureaucratic work, but also . . . by the promise of citizenship" writ large.[47] The sidewalks became the workplace of those who could not find or did not want other jobs.[48]

Street vending in São Paulo long preceded industrialization, however. In imperial times, upper-class Portuguese ladies had Black female slaves sell pastries or groceries, sometimes displayed on small portable boards (*tabuleiros*), on the streets, and emancipated slaves occasionally practiced the trade on their own. Even then, authorities attached considerable import to the registration and regulation of these trades. A royal ordinance dating from May 4, 1749, set a penalty of six years in Angola or, in the case of foreigners, banishment from Portuguese territories for *mascates* who failed to comply with the law.

The street vending population became more international over the course of the following century in a trend that paralleled the city's gradual transition from sleepy provincial town to the Chicago of South America. A boom in world demand for coffee in the second half of the nineteenth century combined with a ban on slave trade—which caused a labor shortage in traditional coffee-producing areas—benefited those plantations in the hinterland of the state of São Paulo staffed by migrant wage labor from Europe, especially Italians. Many of these migrants took up itinerant trade as an occupation.

Other migration waves, from Japan and Greater Syria, followed the Europeans. To this day, descendants of Syrian-Lebanese immigrants are known as *Turks* because their homeland was under Ottoman occupation until World War I and its denizens traveled with Ottoman passports. Like the Italians before them, many of these migrants took up various forms of peddling, including door-to-door salesmanship and itinerant trade to towns and estates in the countryside. Syrian-Lebanese migration followed a common kin-based pattern of relatives welcoming newcomers, teaching them the basics (especially Portuguese terms of trade), providing them with a stock of goods on credit, and sending them off to the hinterland. As with street vendors today, the dream of every peddler was to become a storeowner or return wealthy to the homeland.

This cultural influx coincided with the rise of a local bourgeoisie made up of enriched plantation owners moving with their families to the city. The urban landscape transformed itself in the process, with downtown storefronts modeled after Parisian boutiques offering imported goods. Where Middle Eastern merchants settled—and especially in the area surrounding 25 de Março Street, which remains, to this day, the main commercial street in São Paulo—the streetscape took on, according to Oswaldo Truzzi, distinctive oriental tones.[49] Descriptions of their influence on the physiognomy of the area point to the bazaar-like appearance of storefronts, with colorful soaps and rich smells, along with the foreign foods and languages that pervaded the street. Orientalism aside, the Syrian-Lebanese brought new commercial practices still observable among fixed-spot peddlers in the area, such as trade credit, and created a vast network of salesmen based on kin.

Domestic migration grew in the 1930s and surged in the aftermath of World War II. By the mid-1950s, São Paulo was the fastest growing city in the world. Between 1950 and 1980, the population of the metropolitan area increased by an annual average rate of 5.3 percent.[50] Migrants were drawn to manufacturing as well as construction and domestic services. They were also poorly paid. As many as 93 percent of migrants working in personal services—that is, mostly domestic workers—in 1970 were paid below the minimum wage.[51] For teenage girls consigned as maids, nannies, or cooks in the homes of affluent households (*casas de família*), street trade was a way out at their coming of age.

At the same time, the economic structure of the city evolved. By 1970, the manufacturing sector accounted for 47 percent of the city's total output, down from 53 percent in 1950. By the end of the decade, the city had 8.1 million inhabitants, more than half of whom were not born in São Paulo, and firms began to face diseconomies of agglomeration. Congestion, taxes, land costs, and organized labor stimulated a gradual relocation of manufacturing concerns, first to the outskirts, then to smaller towns in the state of São Paulo. São Paulo did not become a ghost town, however. Between 1950 and 1970, while the share of industrial activity in the urban economy declined, the share of commerce (merchandise, real estate, stocks, etc.) rose from 20 percent to 26 percent.[52] São Paulo is now a commercial hub where retailers from across

Brazil procure their merchandise. The city is also a financial center hosting South America's largest stock exchange as well as large-scale banking institutions and high-end service firms. The powerful *paulista* business elites are a key force behind efforts to revitalize downtown and—especially in the case of storeowners associations—evict street vendors.

For all its economic power, more than a third of São Paulo's workforce works off the books. Among them are an estimated hundred thousand to a hundred and forty thousand street vendors.[53] According to João Batista Pamplona, in the late 2000s, two-thirds of street vendors were male, almost half did not complete elementary school (versus one-fourth of the workforce), and about 40 percent were born in the Nordeste, a predominantly Afro-Brazilian region.[54] The historical prevalence of Nordestinos and their offspring in the trade has fueled negative stereotypes among local elites who see peddlers as dark-skinned intruders. Following Brazil's economic boom in the early 2000s and the influx of international migrants, a significant number of street vendors came from Africa and Latin America. They were seen as intruders by their Brazilian counterparts.

Street vendors carry their merchandise in backpacks, tarps, or plastic bags. Loose specialization patterns are observable. Africans sell headphones as well as wristwatches and inexpensive jewelry that they carry in suitcases while Peruvians and Bolivians specialize in garments. The vast majority of street traders are unlicensed. They work "on the run" (*na correria*), constantly changing sidewalks and street corners to elude law enforcement agents. While they are spread across the city, they tend to concentrate in bustling commercial areas. Where policing is less intense, vendors sometimes set up improvised stalls made of cardboard or metal grates or push wheelbarrows with fruit, popcorn, and other foodstuffs.[55] When they are caught by the police, hawkers must surrender their wares without resistance. The confiscated merchandise and equipment are normally registered by an inspector (*fiscal*), and vendors receive a ticket that allows them to retrieve their wares after paying a fine—which is seldom worth it. They do not face criminal charges.

A fraction of São Paulo's street vendors have licenses. Licensed vendors own roofed stalls of roughly three by five feet, set up at fixed spots designated by the city (see fig. 1.1). Most licensed spots are clustered on squares or along thoroughfares, but some isolated stalls can also be found in different parts of the city. Some stalls have wheels and can be stored away at night. Licensed vendors with disabilities, who make up a sizable portion of the licensed street vendor population, are allowed to have one or two registered aides working at their stall. Though it is illegal, some license holders lease their stall to other vendors, sometimes registered as aides, and receive rent. There are also a

FIGURE 1.1. A licensed street vendor stall
Source: Univinco.

number of stalls with fake licenses known in street parlance as "cold" licenses or stalls. Other transgressions to municipal statutes stipulating who can sell what products at what location as well as how and where the merchandise is to be procured are routine. Licensed street vending thus sits closer to the informal end of the spectrum.

Licenses are issued by district administrators based on guidelines—and sometimes quotas—defined by a central municipal office, the Secretaria de Coordenação das Subprefeituras (SCS). Before the city tightened restrictions on, then froze, the issuing of new licenses starting in the early 2000s, applicants had to comply with a range of residential, health, and seniority requisites—and sometimes have personal connections or pay a bribe—in order to obtain a license. In 2004, on the eve of a long eviction campaign, there were roughly 5,500 individual holders of street vending licenses—known in Portuguese as *termos de permissão de uso* (TPUs). Licensed vendors are represented by the Union of the Licensed (hereafter *the Union*), the Disabled Vendors Association (DVA), and other district-based associations.[56] The precariousness of licenses creates a permanent tension with the city, and struggles to forestall eviction plans define, to a large extent, the politics of licensed street vending in the era of criminalization.

Overview

Chapter 2 places the struggles of street vendors in the context of a global and historical trend toward the unmaking of citizenship. It traces the origins of a legal and civic status that has both shades and layers, then examines its unraveling against the background of Brazil's social and political history. The chapter also connects the experience of licensed street vendors to that of other marginalized groups facing disenfranchisement as informal citizens. Readers eager to get a taste of life on the streets may skip this chapter.

Chapter 3 is an ethnographic, ground-level depiction of the world of street vending. It fleshes out the tensions, barriers, and boundaries that shape commercial life on the streets. It shows, in particular, the value and significance of a street vending license, at once a marker of status and a legal title, the holders of which struggle constantly to assert their contested rights.

Chapter 4 considers the historical construction of the field of legality in street trade as a bounded field that protects a minority of workers. Their rights originated in a municipal decree and consolidated over time, through military rule and the democratic transition. While the field expanded in the early 1990s, disabled and elderly vendors who had formed organizations and built political networks managed to limit the distribution of rights to other constituencies.

Chapter 5 delves into the contested meanings of informal workers' rights and obligations through the analysis of a mass eviction campaign and the judicial battle that ensued. It shows that the rights of licensed vendors as well as the prerogatives of the city over them—including the right to revoke their licenses—are a matter of fierce legal debate and diverging interpretations. On paper, licenses are precarious titles that can be revoked or canceled by the city on urban planning or administrative grounds, clearing the way for removals. Yet in the case of São Paulo's licensed vendors, other pieces of legislation unexpectedly prompted a judge to stay the execution of evictions. The chapter further shows that legal mobilization in defense of informal workers' rights depends heavily on the intervention of third parties with networks, legal expertise, and a disposition to fight.

Chapter 6 focuses on the strategy of control used by the PT administration, which came to power in the wake of the mass eviction campaign and was compelled to take a stance on the fate of licensed street vendors caught in the legal limbo of the ongoing lawsuit. Contrary to the expectation of vendors who placed their hopes in the party and actively supported it during the elections, city officials exploited the ties binding licensed vendors to the state while dodging every call to reinstate the licenses. They willfully entertained the vendors' anguished prospects of legalization during a drawn-out negotiation process that led nowhere, to the dismay of helpless workers. This chapter thus unveils the subjective and emotional foundations in the exercise of state power with regard to the policy and politics of rights allocation.

Chapter 7 opens with the run-up to the 2014 World Cup. On the one hand, the World Cup, with its extremely tight regulatory framework protecting the exclusive commercial rights of sponsors, is a natural experiment in criminalization. At the same time, public outrage and denunciations of these exclusionary practices and other perceived abuses prompted organizers to launch a program granting a number of—mostly unlicensed—street vendors the right to sell products at official World Cup events. These rights were shallow in the sense that they were not embedded in legislation, came with tight restrictions, and lasted only the length of the tournament. Chapter 6 analyzes the design and rollout of this program. Unlike the promise of license reinstatement that unnerved licensed vendors, the street vendors' participation program during the World Cup gained little traction among unlicensed vendors accustomed to working own account at the margins of the law. Those who did not shun the program altogether subverted it in small ways. The contrast between their experience and that of licensed vendors negotiating the reinstatement of their licenses suggests that the ability of state officials to discipline informal workers through the promise of legalization is proportional to the stakes in terms of the historically consolidated rights that legalization offers.

Finally, chapter 8 examines the strategies of those vendors, licensed and unlicensed, who went on working during the World Cup, defying legal and physical barriers imposed by organizers. It considers the impacts that the tournament had on both categories of vendors and draws the lessons about the limits of criminalization as a governance strategy. Being outside the legal framework enabled unlicensed vendors to take advantage of more opportunities, though their strategies also came at a higher risk. Their challenge to the legal monopolization of rights is, I argue, an act of economic subversion.

The concluding chapter discusses the possibility of going beyond what an interviewee called a "politics of retailing"—that is, the distribution of rights, goods, or favors, including nonenforcement—and the risks of failing to do so. It argues that the thinning of legality is a systemic trend affecting multiple spheres in both the formal and informal economies. Coupled with a policy of criminalization, the erosion of legality creates the conditions for recurrent social unrest and political instability. Yet the alternative of enfranchisement through formalization programs faces political and economic constraints, which this book fleshes out. Caught between an unrealistic norm and a practical imperative, policymakers will likely stick to the cyclical mix of criminalization and retailing while popular discontent grows and a share of the informal workforce slides into actual crime.

2

Unmaking Citizens

Are informal workers citizens? Virtually all Brazilian street vendors in São Paulo had a national registration number and voted, or were entitled to, unless they had been convicted of a criminal offense. Some street vendors had licenses, which means they were also entitled to practice their trade. How they felt about their place in the city—especially in the wake of the campaign to eliminate them—is more of a conundrum. What licensed street vendors experienced in São Paulo is akin to the erosion of a civil order, which leaves formerly protected members of society fearing for their rights. And street vendors are not alone in having such experiences. Economic change undermines institutions that used to infuse citizenship with substance and meaning. This chapter traces the rise and subsequent demise of citizenship in the context of Brazil's sociopolitical transformations and global trends toward disenfranchisement. It conceptualizes the condition of street vendors and other marginalized constituencies with a loose hold on their rights as informal citizenship—that is, a liminal status in which people have (some) rights, though it is hard to know which, and their ability to exercise these rights is always contingent on a set of arbitrary factors.

A Tale of Ascendance

Citizens are made. They are a product of institutions. The difference between humans out in the wilderness and citizens lies in the institutional environment that endows the latter with rights. Not every institutional environment breeds citizens, of course. Some, like feudalism, deprive those at the bottom of their freedom and liberties. And there are shades and layers to the coveted status. In its full expression, citizenship involves membership, recognition, and (self-)respect as well as rights in a host of domains, from civil life to politics to material well-being; it implies access to justice when those rights are violated; it involves education, awareness, and participation; and it means that you are part of a community whose members identify primarily as fellow citizens, are committed to the common good, and regard each other as equals.[1] The foundations of such a comprehensive collective and individual experience stretch far beyond the texts of law and the rights stipulated therein. A right to have rights underpins the citizen status.[2] But legal norms and the political economy governing their making and enforcement either draw on and sanction this overarching right or preclude it along with the concrete rights that stem from it.

In other words, the making of citizens entails the construction of civil and political institutions that guarantee a space of free expression, association, and action to those living under them. Since civic participation shapes political institutions in return, a democratic polity and its citizenry are, so to speak, co-constructed. Thomas H. Marshall's seminal essay introduced the idea of a cumulative if not linear development.[3] Indeed, the modernist narrative sees rights as expanding over historical time. Marshall's well-known reading of this process posits three layers—civil, political, and social rights—the formation of each being loosely associated with a century in British history.[4]

The right at stake in the struggle of street vendors is the right to work in public spaces. Marshall himself noted that "in the economic field the basic civil right is the right to work, that is to say the right to follow the occupation of one's choice in the place of one's choice, subject only to legitimate demands for preliminary technical training."[5] In conjunction with other civil rights, the repeal of the Elizabethan Statute of the Artificers in 1813, which created entry barriers to the guilds, "freed" the labor force by turning a collective body bound by a common status into individual workers fully enabled to enter into contractual relations and sell their labor power to the highest bidder. In this regard, the early development of citizenship served capitalism. The subsequent expansion of political rights in the nineteenth and early twentieth centuries—from the Reform Act of 1832 to universal manhood suffrage and female enfranchisement in 1918—did not threaten the emerging socioeconomic order because newly minted citizens used their rights in line with tradition. It was not until social rights became part of the equation that the capitalist class structure started bending toward equality. Citizenship and capitalism thus found themselves "at war" in the twentieth century; however, Marshall did not predict a crisis or the displacement of one by the other.[6]

Before the dark turn of events that led to the ousting of democratically elected president Dilma Rousseff in 2016 and the rise to power of far-right politician Jair Bolsonaro three years later, Brazil's democratic saga embodied, in a condensed and intriguing way, a similar tale of blooming rights and citizenship expansion. Maria Herminia Tavares de Almeida and Fernando Henrique Guarnieri thus speak of successive "waves of inclusion" in the second half of the twentieth century, which culminated in Brazil's flagship cash transfer program, Bolsa Família, that contributed to lifting millions out of poverty by distributing cash to low-income households while requiring the children of recipients to attend school.[7] In the wake of these changes, a great number of Brazilians achieved a decent living standard and social standing. And labor played a key part in the struggle for citizenship. In fact, according to Gay Seidman, the labor movement "redefined" citizenship in the '70s and '80s.[8] As the country's industrial hub, São Paulo held center stage.

The story begins with what Ruth and David Collier call the incorporation of labor, when "actors within the state established regularized, legal channels of labor relations and made some concessions . . . thereby seeking to take the labor question out of the streets and away from the police and the army and bring it into the realm of law."[9] In a way, incorporation marks the birth of formal labor. In Brazil, however, the process followed a top-down logic, where the "principal goal was to create a legalized and institutionalized labor movement that was depoliticized, controlled, and penetrated by the state."[10] This happened during Getúlio Vargas's first continuous terms in office, from 1930 to 1945.

Vargas established a Ministry of Labor in 1930 and a workers' registration system based on a work card called *carteira profissional* (or *carteira*) in 1932. His administration also issued "reams of legislation" that "offered Brazilian 'workers' considerable material benefits," among them pensions, an eight-hour week, paid leave, workplace accident insurance, and maternity leave.[11] A labor code known as the Consolidação das Leis Trabalhistas unified labor legislation in 1943 and remained the frame of reference for several decades. And yet, despite Vargas's symbolic identification with "the people" (*o povo*) and his regime's exaltation of work as a social value, not every worker had access to these benefits. A majority of workers in Rio and elsewhere still experienced what Fischer calls "a poverty of rights."[12] The rights gap stemmed in part from the legislation itself, which contained narrow provisions as to what workers in which occupations were entitled to the newfound benefits, and in part, too, from the bureaucratic maze of a fledging Weberian state that made it hard to access benefits even for those eligible to them under the law.[13] Hence, the initial state efforts to concurrently protect and regulate labor produced, expectedly, their own share of informality.

Upsetting Marshall's sequential framework, (some) workers in Brazil thus acquired and enjoyed social rights despite lacking political rights, not only under Vargas's authoritarian Estado Novo (1937–1945) but also during Brazil's military dictatorship, from 1964 to 1985. Notwithstanding the systemic co-optation of unions, however, a host of labor actors—including clandestine networks of factory workers and more independent-minded labor leaders—organized campaigns and industrial actions that received popular support and inspired other occupational groups to follow in their footsteps from the mid-1970s onward. Prominent among these leaders was Luis Ignácio "Lula" Da Silva, who became the head of the Metalworkers Union of São Bernado dos Campos—an industrial suburb of São Paulo—in 1975 and embraced a reformist agenda against the expectations of his loyalist predecessor. In 1980, an alliance of independent unions, progressive clergy, and academics founded the PT in São Paulo. They were part of the movement that demanded direct elections at the national level, which Brazilians achieved in 1988. The labor movement also found echoes and allies in the struggles for transportation, housing, and day care among overlapping constituencies in the urban outskirts. Hence, according to Seidman, for participants in the new unionism, "full citizenship came to mean not only the right to participate in politics [at the national level, which was itself a novel demand], but also the right to adequate wages, decent housing, education, and health care."[14]

This narrative of rights as conquests also resonates with Marshall's assertion that citizenship is based on "a loyalty of free men endowed with rights and protected by a common law" and that "its growth is stimulated both by the struggle to win those rights and by their enjoyment when won."[15] However, in this struggle, the informal sector is held to play a marginal role at best. According to dominant historiographical currents, the main drivers behind the advent of political citizenship in Brazil were opposition party politicians and recognized civil society actors, such as unions or the church, who enacted an institutional transformation, as it were, from within. Social movements based or active in informal settlements had an impact—as allies of formal labor organizations in Seidman's account and as potential catalysts in Paul Singer's—but their contribution remained subsidiary.[16] The dominant view thus echoes Partha Chatterjee's conceptual framework according to which informal workers are not part of civil society—which he conceives, provocatively, as the "legitimate" arena of political participation among law-abiding citizens attached to the values, language, codes, and ideals of (stereotyped) Western democracies.[17]

Anthropologist James Holston's theory of insurgent citizenship offers a counterpoint to the conventional perspective on the making of citizens in Brazil. It builds on longitudinal fieldwork in the outskirts of São Paulo, where, as in the outer regions of most Latin American, Asian, and African cities, the original housing stock grew out of the sweat and enthusiasm of the first residents, who built their own houses. These informal settlements hosted a disadvantaged migrant population from other parts of the country. When Holston set his sights on some of these neighborhoods of the *periferia* in the late 1970s, Brazilians were still living under military rule. He followed the lives of residents through the massive political shifts of the 1980s up until the early 2000s, when Lula became president.[18] Holston claims that shantytown dwellers underwent a civic makeover, from marginalized others in "differentiated regimes of citizenship," where "most rights are available only to particular kinds of citizens and exercised as the privilege of particular social categories," to full-fledged citizens, aware of their rights and empowered to use them.[19]

Informal housing residents and the urban poor more broadly achieved legitimate citizen status by insurgent means, moreover. "It is an insurgence," Holston writes, "that begins with the struggle for the right to have a daily life in the city worthy of a citizen's dignity."[20] In fact, expressions like *the right to the city* or *the right to have rights*—the slogan of the prodemocracy movement—frame much of the scholarly debate on the struggles of disadvantaged urban groups, including struggles for services or infrastructure improvements in informal settlements. But even if insurgent forms of citizenship arise from everyday life and the quest to meet basic needs, they take on, in Holston's view, broader political and institutional meanings. "For many of the urban poor, it became a specific kind of demand: a claim of citizens, a citizen right, a right articulated within the framework of citizenship and its legal, ethical, and performative terms."[21]

What Holston describes is a citizen ethos arising not from an institutional process that protects people but from a material struggle in a context in which institutions are explicitly or implicitly biased against the poor—hence the paradoxical insurgent quality of Holston's self-made citizens. His claim that informality in the sense of a loose institutional environment that fails to provide guarantees of basic necessities also creates the incentives for processes of social mobilization through which the citizen self comes about is bold even by the standards of the literature on informality, which acknowledges the resilience and discrete power of informal actors. However, Holston's figure of a self-aware citizen having achieved not only various layers of rights but the subjectivity that comes with the sense of membership in a law-bound community reflects, to some extent, the circumstances of licensed street vendors on the eve of the onslaught. It challenges the dualism that sets citizens apart from the *informales*, echoing older and contested dichotomies.

The Unraveling

How does citizenship come undone? The most straightforward pathway is erasure by the state. A totalitarian regime abolishes not only rights but subjectivities. A totalitarian state based on an ideology of racial supremacy can make a group of people stateless by decree, depriving them of their legal status, then their livelihoods, and finally their lives. The Nuremberg Laws of 1934 thus thrust ethnic minorities "outside the pale of law" and turned them into refugees.[22] The systematic use of torture in military regimes not only aims to deter dissidents from speaking up or taking action; it has a traumatizing effect on the community and, in its most perverse uses, seeks to alter the beliefs and self-image of survivors.[23] Controlling the public sphere wherein citizens create alternative projects is a foremost concern of authoritarian regimes.

Beyond such dramatic episodes, the scholarly discussion on the limits of citizenship has largely focused on welfare recipients and migrants. Under recent policy trends, the treatment that a majority of people in either category receives from the state degrades their personhood and compromises their rights, making their situation akin to informal citizenship. The xenophobic backlash in Western democracies has crystalized into restrictive migration laws that limit access to citizenship and even residency rights. As Ayten Gündogdu puts it, "the normalization of deportation and immigration detention in the last two decades has rendered the legal personhood of asylum seekers and undocumented immigrants precarious."[24] In a context of hostility toward immigrants, states adopt strategies that deliberately blur the lines of legality and favor expulsion, such as the use of "off-shore" processing sites for asylum claims.[25] "International human rights law fails to provide robust guarantee of personhood to asylum seekers and undocumented immigrants," Gündogdu adds. "As a result, their rights remain dependent on highly arbitrary political and legal decisions as well as unreliable sentiments such as compassion."[26] Migrants share such shaky standing and dependence with native-born informal citizens.

Forbidding migration policies intersect with the tightening of social citizenship when access to social benefits is restricted or denied to foreigners in what experts refer to as *welfare chauvinism*. The nation as a cultural form at the center of ethnic-based conceptions of citizenship raises its head under

these circumstances, and citizenship becomes an instrument of social closure in Weber's sense: a way for a group to hoard resources by legal means
and claims of uniqueness.[27] At the peak of their political influence, licensed
street vendors engaged in a similar process described in chapter 4. (In a paradoxical turn of events characteristic of our time, a class of "flexible citizens"
emerged concurrently whose members hold multiple passports—some of
them acquired by investment—and transnational assets to hedge against in-
convenient political twists in their country of origin.[28])

The wave of disenfranchisement is not confined to foreigners, however.
Drawing on Etienne Balibar, Margaret Somers points to the making of boundaries not only around the imagined community of the nation but within it,
through categories of what she calls "stateless citizens"—that is, nationals of
a state who may still have the right to vote but lack any sort of protection or
support from their own government.[29] Historical processes such as colonial-
ism or a legacy of slavery contribute to drawing such internal boundaries and
create second-class citizens. Yet, in the current era, even historically dominant categories become, in Arlie Hochschild's phrase, "strangers in their own
land."[30]

The expansion of the market economy at the expense of social protection and its transnational upshot, globalization, loom large in sociological
explanations of this trend. As market mechanisms spread across the social
body, leading to a deeper commodification of labor and higher levels of inequality, citizenship withers.[31] In contemporary labor markets, a difference
of status arises, for instance, between the salariat, whose members enjoy job
security and a regular income through a mix of skills on high demand and
institutional safeguards, and that mass of casual workers whom Guy Standing
calls "the precariat"—not to mention a small class of rentiers and financiers
for whom labor is not the primary source of income.[32] Informal workers such
as delivery boys or street vendors form the precarious end of the precariat.

Workfare reform, which forces beneficiaries into the labor market, and
the degradation of work and employment in general only account for part of
the current decline in the terms of inclusion, however. The logic of the market and its politics also penetrate the state and colonize civil society. At the
turn of the century, according to Evelina Dagnino, "neo-liberal governments
throughout Latin America [were] bent on achieving a reduced, minimal state
that progressively abandons its role in guaranteeing universal rights by roll-
ing back its social responsibilities and transferring them to civil society, now
envisaged as a mere implementer of social policies."[33] As a result, "previously
guaranteed rights to social services are increasingly viewed as commodities
to be purchased by those who can afford them."[34] Vincanne Adams makes

a similar case in her study of relief and repair efforts in the wake of Hurricane Katrina in New Orleans, where the government outsourced much of the work to churches and private businesses.[35] Dependence on corporate actors or nonprofits for essential services, if available, undermines any sense of community predicated on common rights and obligations.

If legality is understood as an institutional space in which people have rights, the most reassuring myth of citizenship holds that such space is bound to expand or at least hold steady. In fairness, institutionalist scholars have teased out analytic reasons why legal norms and provisions, once in place, tend to "stick."[36] But when structural dynamics chip at the underlying distribution of resources or social values, legal frameworks come under strain. Sometimes structural forces translate into an outright rollback of legal entitlements, as in the case of welfare reform. Sometimes structural forces translate into corrosive social phenomena that undermine the exercise of rights in a different way, as in the case of crime and violence. Susana Rotker and Katherine Goldman's *Citizens of Fear* thus captures the paradox behind the everyday experience of rights-bearers who live in constant fear for their safety and lives.[37]

The structural drivers of disenfranchisement are well known. The suffering it causes is well documented. But the dismantling of citizenship as a process that haunts entire social categories and occupational groups, beyond migrants, still begs inquiry. Margaret Somers's *Genealogies of Citizenship*, Christian Joppke's *Neoliberal Nationalism*, and Loïc Wacquant's *Punishing the Poor* discuss contemporary trends toward weaker social protection and civic engagement from a historical perspective, with enlightening case studies but without any fine-grained consideration of rights and the subjective experience of their piecemeal loss. Between the changing structures of global capitalism and the struggles they unleash stands an institutional layer that shapes those struggles and deserves attention in its own right. Just as the making of citizens involves a fair amount of legislation and paperwork, their unmaking runs through loopholes and into caveats. Even where the letter of the law stands aloof from social praxis, as in the case of informal economies, the unmaking of citizens relies on and acts through the law. At their barest, rights become red tape. But cutting through it stirs emotions and elicits pushback. What street vendors lived through as the rights vested in their licenses came under attack is therefore emblematic of broader struggles marking the end of an era. As disenfranchisement proceeds through brutal or covert steps, it shakes all the dimensions of citizenship, from the feeling of belonging to the material conditions of survival. It also lays bare the ambiguous foundations of state power.

Deconstructing Citizenship

Disenfranchisement is best represented not by a metaphorical fall but as a process of sliding out of the fields of legality. As Aihwa Ong notes, "Newly industrializing regimes, eager to meet capitalist requirements, have evolved . . . systems of graduated sovereignty, whereby citizens in zones that are differently articulated to global production and financial circuits are subjected to different kinds of surveillance practices and in practice enjoy different sets of civil, political, and economic rights."[38]

How do citizens at risk navigate this fuzzy landscape? Proof of personhood such as an official document that bears the name of the holder and shows that they still stand on the field of legality acquires disproportionate value under the circumstances. Its use goes far beyond any administrative function. It becomes an asset and a boundary-making tool, as in the early stages of citizenship, when, according to Fischer, "The *carteira* . . . became a powerful symbol of righteous citizenship—and especially male citizenship—outside the workplace. Police authorities habitually demanded one from any individual suspected of vagrancy, and the document also proved a virtual guarantee that authorities would grant bail to a defendant in most criminal cases. The *carteira* thus evolved into a sort of distinguishing mark . . . that allowed employers and judicial authorities alike to separate those they regarded as citizens from those they saw as *marginais*."[39] Guilherme Dos Santos pointedly called the work card a "civic birth certificate," and its symbolic value has endured over the decades.[40] According to Marcelo Neri, what best symbolized access to the new Brazilian middle classes during the boom years at the start of this century was having a *carteira*, which, by official bookkeeping conventions, amounts to leaving the informal sector.[41]

While ethnonational discourse and supremacist ideologies dominate the study of symbolic boundaries in the construction of citizenship, a granular look at what citizenship means—in everyday life, on the ground, across groups—thus reveals myriad other tools and symbols by which citizens seek to demarcate themselves in order to assert their rights. Like citizenship, (in)formality is a gradient of rights, and similar dynamics play out across the gradient, including on the sidewalks, where street vending licenses become boundary-making tools analogous to the worker's ID, as the next chapters illustrate.

In the absence of a clear institutional demarcation, the payment of taxes also serves as a discursive marker for citizens to set themselves apart from a different class of people. In San Francisco, where the homeless population overwhelmed a stretched nonprofit network following "decades of free-market reforms in which government functions like homeless services were privatized," according to the *New York Times*, some high-end neighborhood residents took matters into their own hands, attacking homeless people, while others condemned the violence but stressed the demarcation: "I definitely would not spray somebody with bear mace," one of them said. "But it's a byproduct of what we're dealing with out here as citizens that pay taxes, that are trying to live through this madness."[42] This othering discourse produces informal citizenship even as the tension between groups leads to a breakdown of the "good citizen" code of conduct among those claiming the higher civic ground. On the streets of São Paulo, licensed vendors turn the argument around and point it to their main enemies, shopkeepers, whom they accuse of widespread tax evasion and who in turn complain about street vendors' paltry contribution to the city's coffers.

Scholars themselves draw boundaries for analytic purposes. Opposite the minority sphere inhabited by proper citizens that Chatterjee calls "civil society," whose idealized members cherish the "civil" ways of democratic politics and obey the law, stands another sphere, which he dubbed "political society"—a realm made up of informal sector groups insofar as they manage to get attention from the state.[43] As marginalized citizens, social actors in political society resort to extralegal means to make their voices heard and get what they need. Clientelism, corruption, riots, threats, and other unseemly forms of politics govern their actions and engagement with state officials. It is noteworthy that not all informal groups "rise" to political society, however. Some, like Bengal's typewriters, toil away their grievances without finding ways, legitimate or not, to invest the political arena.

While Chatterjee's distinction between civil and political society is useful as an analytic tool to capture the social cleavages of unequal postcolonial polities, it conceals the fact that those outside the boundaries of civil society are also citizens, not only as members of the nation—whose definition is itself a matter of intense symbolic struggles—but as legal persons living under the helm of a state. If and when subaltern groups have rights on paper, they will try to exercise them through the official institutions of the state while using other, less seemly tactics at the same time if necessary. In other words, even though Chatterjee's theorization of the "politics of the governed" is more subtle than the transactional model implicit in the politics-of-enforcement framework, the institutional distinction he draws is not as clear-cut in real life as his theory suggests.

Roy nuances the contrast to some extent by showing that administrative procedures are part of the policy repertoire in the gray zone of informality, where those in power deliberately produce uncertainty by bureaucratic means.[44] Focusing on shantytown residents in Kolkata, Roy unveils the strings that bind them to a political boss, Kanti Ganguly. The man, the party, and the state, all of which intertwine to the point of misrecognition, manufacture uncertainty by concealing administrative records, offering land titles—the *pattas*—that never come through, requiring registration at government offices without any clear administrative purpose, and so on. In these bureaucratic entanglements, the struggles of Kolkata's disadvantaged residents echo the travails of São Paulo's street vendors. But Roy stops short of discussing citizenship—or rights. If anything, the strings that Kanti pulls prevent her research subjects from even forming notions of their rights or of themselves as rights-bearers. In other words, informal settlement dwellers lack what sociolegal scholars call *legal consciousness*.

This book tells a different story. It is about informal workers, a portion of whom happen to have legal entitlements. Their rights are written into law, but so are the mechanisms to rescind them. Informal citizens have unclear and precarious rights—rights that can be withdrawn from them on questionable grounds and the content of which is amenable to challenge. Because rights are precarious, authorities can use extralegal means to get around them or even try to cancel them in underhanded manners. And yet, licensed street vendors not only have rights on paper but see themselves as rights-bearers, despite their otherwise informal working conditions and the onslaught they endure. Hence, their demotion from the realm of legality is a problem, not a given.

Moreover, given the path-dependent nature of institutional frameworks, authorities intent on doing away with informal groups and their rights are confronted with institutional safeguards. The rollback strategy is not always available in a clean and clear-cut way. The result then looks more like a tug-of-war. Rights are still *there*—on the books—but their validity is contested by people with the authoritative power to interpret and enforce them. While legal disputes are common in different sectors of civil and economic life, citizenship is at stake when essential rights come under threat, and, upon losing them, people become unable to make a decent living or meaningfully participate in society. Informal citizens live on that edge.

Under Control

If capitalism and citizenship operate on warring principles, as Marshall suggests, and somehow managed to hold (and even grow) together for the best part of the twentieth century, in the twenty-first century, capitalism has prevailed. The surge of the populist right embodies, among many things, an effort to reclaim some kind of social worth through an aggressive assertion of nationalistic ideals among people whose dignity and status as citizens are in jeopardy.[45] Their stances do not sit well with the traditional institutions of democracy. Elsewhere, "citizens tend to withdraw from politics as a consequence of institutional distrust."[46] As institutional frameworks come under strain, the informalization of labor contributes to the informalization of citizenship and raises vexing questions about the functions of rights and the future of politics.

The political history of Brazil offers some hints while underscoring the inherent ambivalence of rights. In Vargas's evolving political project, the extension of rights merged with increased state control. The same legislation that allocated benefits strictly limited the number of unions and the scope of their activities. In other words, the same institutional arrangement that protected (formal) workers enabled the state, in corporatist fashion, to keep them in line. The debate around Brazil's flagship cash transfer program, Bolsa Família, brings out other complexities. Conservative critics decry cash welfare as "handouts" that undermine the recipients' autonomy and self-worth while progressive advocates see cash benefits as important but bemoan the conditions attached to them, which reinforce negative stereotypes of the poor as irresponsible and provide means to control them. In short, rights are not unequivocally empowering.

Drawing on Michel Foucault, recent studies in a sociolegal vein theorize the ambivalence of rights. Their claim is not that the uneven distribution of rights across groups or realms enables the state to exercise control over its population, as Vargas did by granting social benefits while withholding political rights, but rather that rights-bearing has a disciplining influence on the self. As a rights-bearer, the person is made individually responsible for her actions and is thereby discouraged from taking part in or putting forward adversarial claims against the state. As Michael McCann puts it, "the conferral of rights status works as a regulatory discourse that constructs disciplined subjects who internalize imperatives of rational self-governance."[47] In other words, the making of citizens through the allocation of rights also fosters "good citizens"—people who behave in accordance with the prevailing rules and civic norms of society. By contrast, the unmaking of citizens calls for an increase in the use of force, including incarceration. But that is not the whole story. The shakiness of rights, the prospect of losing them, the fear, the angst, and the hope that come with it, along with muddled understandings of what the rights in play are or should be, also account for submission or inaction among groups of informal citizens, as the story of São Paulo's licensed street vendors reveals.

3

The Daily Struggle

The street is like a mother. She'll always welcome her children. But she'll only give what she can, when she can.

STREET VENDOR IN SÃO PAULO

The lives of street vendors are wrapped in plastic. A short distance from the Praça da Sé, São Paulo's dingy central square with its Gothic cathedral and clusters of homeless people and crack addicts as well as lone evangelizers preaching the gospel—but very few street vendors—begins a pedestrianized street called General Carneiro. The street slopes downward over a long single block. At the bottom is a square next to a huge bus terminal at the southern end of 25 de Março Street. Walking down General Carneiro on a weekday morning, against the flow of commuters on their way to their downtown offices, an observer would notice storefronts lining the entire block on the left and a long row of stalls thatched with blue plastic tarps on the right. These stalls belong to licensed street vendors, most of whom are disabled. They offer various goods, including knockoff sports shoes and jerseys, belts, wallets, hardware, T-shirts, and pirated compact disks. The seller is usually an aide or illicit tenant of the license holder; they pack all products in unmarked plastic bags.

Meanwhile, license holders sit in the shade behind the stalls and chat. They talk about life, soccer, politics—especially street vendors' politics—and related subjects. Among them is Gabriel, a Black license holder who is always well dressed and has a vivid sense of humor. He grew up in the countryside, lost his sight at fifteen, and migrated to São Paulo from his homeland in the northeast in his early twenties. His mother had not wanted him to study when he was a kid. "It wasn't even meanness," he said. "Just ignorance." In São Paulo, he got married and had three children.

At around two o'clock on a normal weekday, licensed vendors from General Carneiro start walking in line, holding each other by the arm and led by a sighted colleague, toward a nearby restaurant subsidized by the São Paulo business community for workers in banking and commerce. At the restaurant,

vendors from General Carneiro sit at a large table along with other disabled
license holders from the area and enjoy a copious, tasty meal while talking
out loud and poking fun at each other.

On General Carneiro, when policing subsides, unlicensed vendors enter
the stage. They lay their wares on the pavement in front of the stores, opposite
the licensed stalls (see fig. 3.1). Pedestrians walking up and down the street
thus thread between the rows of licensed and unlicensed vendors. These
workers sell padlocks, plastic toys, socks, umbrellas, and other light items.
They are always on the lookout for an approaching policeman, always ready
to pick up and run. Their ages vary widely, and it is not uncommon to find
aging men or women among them.

Occasionally, a Black man in his sixties passes by, limping and pushing a
supermarket cart. His name is Heloiso, though people on the streets refer to
him by the derogatory nickname of *varrão*, which means "boar" or "wom-
anizer." Heloiso was born in Mississippi to South African parents who later
migrated to the state of São Paulo to work at sugar cane plantations. Though
he spent all his life in Brazil, he speaks a little English. Every day, he fills up
his cart at the wholesale market with fruits such as oranges or mangoes, then
hobbles around downtown selling the fruit by the piece. Because of his age,
his condition, and perhaps his familiar presence in that landscape, the police
don't bother him too much.

Other unlicensed vendors doing business on General Carneiro need to be
wary, however, because at the start of the slope, under a bridge that leads to
the historic site where the city was founded, is the office of Capitão Luis, the
military police (MP) officer in charge of Operação Delegada—a city program
that employs MP agents to police street vending during their days off—in the
25 de Março area. Capitão Luis is a heavy-built but somewhat mellow man
who oversees two overlapping shifts of about seventy-five MP officers from
6:00 a.m. to 2:00 p.m. and from 11:00 a.m. to 7:00 p.m., with about thirty
agents lingering until 10:00 p.m. He knows a handful of unlicensed vendors
by their name. Though his job and status keep him mostly indoors, in his
office or at meetings, sometimes, when he goes out, Capitão Luis does a little
enforcement himself. I asked him if there is tension between the police and
the vendors. He replied: "No, not always. Some bitch, some run. But others just accept it. One day I caught one and he said, 'Fine, take them [water
bottles].' On my way back, I caught him again. 'You again?' [I asked]. 'You can
have them,' he said [handing him more water bottles]. 'I'll fetch more. I need
to work.'"[1] Another time, Capitão Luis caught Felix, an unlicensed vendor,
by surprise, and, as the latter was handing over his wares, told him, "Don't
worry. I'm not working today."

FIGURE 3.1. Street vendors and pedestrians on General Carneiro Street
Note: Unlicensed vendors have their wares on the ground, on the left-hand side. The stalls on the right-hand side belong to licensed street vendors. Photo by the author.

The rumor on the street is that Capitão Luis has a cozy relation with Bruna, the president of the local storeowners association. A street vendor once complained that she is the one calling the shots. "Bruna goes around, calling the Captain. Tells him who to kick out. But who is in charge of the streets? Is it the city government or is it a [private] person?" the vendor asked at a meeting with city officials. Bruna certainly enjoys direct access to the captain and the district administrator. From her office a few blocks away from Capitão Luis's cabin, on a side street of 25 de Março, Bruna solves the problems of her association members, and securing tough enforcement against street vendors is a core part of her job.

One time, a storeowner called Bruna because a human statue in the shape of an angel had set up shop in front of his store. The angel was a young Peruvian street artist named Flavia. Bruna talked to her and later recounted the incident to me in an interview. In Bruna's telling, all she did was suggest that the artist move to a street corner further away from the store entrance. In response, Flavia showed Bruna a recent municipal law on street artists, saying it was her right to perform wherever she wanted. Bruna pointed out that the law forbade structures, and the angel stood on a platform. Hence, Bruna summoned a police officer who did not know her and asked who she was. The officer then said that street artists had the right to be there, and that Bruna didn't understand the law ("To me!"). Bruna had to bring in the inspectors, who ordered Flavia to take down her stall, which they couldn't seize because of the law. After Flavia refused, they attempted to grab her, so she kicked and weltered. They all ended up at the police station.

When this happened, the municipal law protecting street artists had not yet been implemented through a municipal decree. This meant that "by the book," according to Bruna, who had consulted with a lawyer, street artists could not yet rely on it. The following day, she had a meeting with the mayor and his cabinet in which she complained about the proliferation of street artists. The mayor agreed to issue an ordinance (*portaria*) forbidding artists to work on the streets until the decree implementing the law came out.

Bruna also went after some licensed vendors whose licenses were fake or expired. She made more enemies as a result. One day, Capitão Luis told her that a pamphlet signed by the leader of a local street vendors association was circulating. The leaflet stated that Bruna was in cahoots with the captain and that she was trying to get street vendors evicted. She was nervous that upon seeing that pamphlet, any street vendor anywhere in the city would think she was the reason the vendor was not allowed to work. "I'm afraid," she said. "I can't say I'm not afraid. But I can't [show it by] lower[ing] my head."[2]

Bruna's office is located in a nondescript building. A loyal security guard checks out anyone who comes in to look for her and, if uncertain, tells them Bruna is not there. Across the street from Bruna's office is the stall of Altaisa, a woman who, like Gabriel, hails from the Nordeste and became a street vendor in São Paulo. Unlike him, however, she came from a family of relatively well-off landowners. Per local customs, she was forced into marriage with an older man when she was a teenager and left for São Paulo in her early twenties, carrying a reference letter from the wife of the governor of her home state. The letter was addressed to the wife of the governor of the state of São Paulo— who never bothered to meet with her. Altaisa arrived with "lots of money" to a town that was "disgusting, immoral, and illegal." Still, she managed to lead an "almost normal life" working as an embroiderer, making models for sewers and training other workers. Following automation in the 1990s, however, her employment situation deteriorated, as did her mental health. She obtained her street vending license on account of a mild psychiatric condition and sells plastic jewels with help from her children. She noted in an interview that twelve people lived off her street vending business: herself, a sister, another sister who is a widow, two sons, five grandchildren, a daughter who is disabled, and a granddaughter conceived from the rape of her disabled daughter (*estupro vulneravel*). "I work today to eat tomorrow." She has three Chinese providers and a Brazilian one whom she pays three hundred reals (US$135) each day.[3] "Those in the streets, we didn't make it with our sweat," she said, "but with our blood, or rather sweating blood."[4]

Foot traffic is moderate around Altaisa's stall but grows thicker as one approaches 25 de Março, three blocks away, where it suddenly turns into a massive flow of people. The crowd descends like a river from the street on the opposite side, where a subway station is located uphill. A cluster of unlicensed vendors work at the station exit, including Valdira's two brothers, Vicente and Gerardo. (Valdira joined them later, when she lost everything.) Like many street vendors, Gerardo has a criminal record because of a bad deal he made years ago, and he has no retirement plan. Vicente, on the other hand, contributed for years to a social security scheme for independent workers and later lost his benefits when he was scammed by a shady lawyer. They sell umbrellas when it rains, plastic games, and other random products such as pizza dough. Before the economic crisis that began in 2014, Vicente said he was making about four thousand reals (US$1,800) a month.

One Sunday, we met to celebrate Valdira's birthday at a park where she worked on weekends selling hats. Vicente told me that he had "lost" umbrellas, meaning they were confiscated by the police. He felt the seizure was unfair because he had not been working when the confiscation took place.

"But what can you do?" he said. "You can't prove anything. You can't complain."

"Yes, you can," Valdira responded, looking at me. "The problem is that he doesn't know his rights."

"I know my rights, but it's not worth it. It's useless, what are you going to get? You lose a day of work [filing the complaint]. Besides, you can't turn in a cop."

After a while, he added thoughtfully, "It's my fault. I don't have rights."

Like the structure of citizenship with its layers and shades, the field of legality, which creates the institutional framework of citizenship, has scales.[5] The exchange between Valdira and Vicente captures the ambiguity facing those at the margins. In this context, Vincente's assertion that he has "no rights" refers to his position outside the field of legality, given his unlicensed status. As a private citizen, however, Vicente has property rights over umbrellas he had bought, not stolen. Yet the police drew on the ambiguity surrounding his rights to take away his wares, leaving Vicente to wonder and contradict himself.

*

As people exit the subway station through the gate where Vicente and his siblings work and head down toward 25 de Março, they pass by rows of stores like the ones that line most streets in the neighborhood, except for some side streets packed with warehouses. Stores fill not only the front but the inside of buildings, with improvised shopping malls connecting various streets through maze-like corridors and more stores populating courtyards and alleyways. As one vendor put it, "São Paulo is the heart of Brazil, and 25 de Março is the heart of São Paulo." Commercially speaking, he was right.

Many of those stores were owned by the "patricians"—as the Syrio-Lebanese merchants who arrived in São Paulo in the early to mid-twentieth century are referred to—or their offspring. These wealthy landlords subdivided their properties and rented them out to Chinese and Korean immigrants. But Chinese businessmen also own stores, especially in the indoor shopping malls known as *galerias*, which they subdivide into small stands called *boxes*. Electronics are a staple of Chinese-run stands, though they also sell other goods imported or smuggled from China. Garments on offer in indoor shops and at street vendors' stalls, on the other hand, are manufactured at local sweatshops run by Bolivians or Koreans. According to the president of the local storeowners association, the 25 de Março area has the most expensive square meter in town.

As the crowds coming down from the subway station reach 25 de Março and make a left, they enter the most valuable street vending real estate in São Paulo. Two longtime DVA leaders had their stalls on these blocks. One of them, sometimes referred to as the boss of 25 de Março, had been paraplegic since the age of eleven, following a car accident. He worked at a pencil factory at the time, and the owner promised his mother to hire back the boy as soon as he recovered. He did not keep his promise. Back when he had first joined street trade, Artur explained, one had to obtain authorization from the owner of the adjacent store before requesting a spot from the city. A rumor has it that, during a subsequent replanning of street trade in the area, shopkeepers who were not members of or did not pay their fees to the local storeowners association wound up with licensed street vending stalls in front of their stores.

Licensed stall owners on that street have aides who run the business—often their own business. I interviewed a vendor called Tiago who once rented a stall on 25 de Março. At the peak of his business, he was bringing in six or seven thousand reals (US$2,700 to US$3,100) a day, of which about 30 percent was profit. His key asset was access to the Chinese "big boss," who only dealt with the Chinese but made an exception for Tiago and sold him bags at the same price that he sold them to local wholesalers. He had to pay in cash though. "With the Chinese, there's no bargaining, no talking," Tiago said. Eventually, the Chinese supplier raised the threshold to five hundred bags per deal, and Tiago had to go into debt. His case reveals the little secret of business on 25 de Março: most vendors who handle thousands of dollars in sales are also thousands of dollars in debt.

But there were personal reasons behind his setbacks, too, which speak to the lifestyle and psychology associated with a business environment that triggers and thrives on compulsive consumption. While his business was booming, Tiago rented an apartment for himself and a stall for his wife, who was also indebted. In time, she started getting death threats from creditors. Tiago floated more loans. For every thousand reais (US$450) in credit, he paid twenty-two daily installments of sixty reais. Eventually, the business went bust, the couple divorced, and Tiago had to relinquish the stall he was renting.

He became an unlicensed peddler, selling earrings on the run. At first, he sold earrings at the rate of one pair for two reais (ninety cents) and three for five reais. He wasn't selling much, however, so he cut the price by half. "I went from a profit of 1,000 percent to a profit of 300 or 400 percent." He sees this simple move as pioneering, and it paid off. "I began selling like water." Then everyone started selling earrings at one real. At the time of the interview, he was making about six hundred reais (US$270) a week, but "that's not money. For me, that's not money. Only at 25 de Março can you make real money."

Tiago's story captures not only the dramatic swings in the life of high-sales street vendors but also the structural changes to Brazil's economy and labor market following the reforms of the 1990s. Indeed, before becoming a street vendor, Tiago manufactured handbags at his house for ten years. The business was successful, and he employed up to twenty-two workers. He always kept it underground, however. He started as a contractor for two firms, then sold directly to retailers; the transition was not easy. He was ashamed, at first, to enter those big stores. He felt "small" and didn't know what to say. Then he got used to it. At its peak, his business manufactured 1,200 bags—which ran for thirty-five reais apiece—per month, and he made a profit of ten reais per bag.

Then came Brazil's "violent" opening to foreign trade. He initially benefited from Chinese imports. He would buy one and replicate it. Some models would sell for as long as six months. "Can you imagine that?" he asked. "Six months selling the same bag. Now that's not possible anymore. Turnover is crazy in fashion." Then he went bust. "Stores began selling bags at my cost price. And with higher quality raw materials. I couldn't cope." He had to shut down his business and start from scratch as a street vendor. "The peddler never gives up. I know people my age who lost everything and just broke down. Not the street seller."

Soon after I met him, Tiago leased Valdira's stall on 25 de Março for a while, then left because he was not selling and realized Valdira did not have "territorial guarantees." Valdira was not the only vendor with a "broken" license on that street, however. There was also João, whom others said had a valid license but with a different address, and Maria. Like Valdira and a handful of other adventurous street vendors, João and Maria had to negotiate enforcement with officers every time. Once, an officer told João that he was not "on the list." In João's telling, the officer later came back and apologized. "That list is not the same list as the updated list that was recently published," João said to me. "I'm telling you, it's a list that's made in some 'cooking pot' up there" in the district administration. Even in the district of Sé, where the chief of inspectors established an updated record of authorized vendors at the behest of Union and DVA leaders—who complained about interlopers posing as licensed vendors—and the district administration published the record on their website, there was confusion and polemics about who had a right to work. Police officers doing the rounds seemed to use information that did not fully match the official online record. The list—of which there seemed to be more than one—thus became a catchword and a fetish. Once, at the Union's office, after a vendor whose name had appeared on the newspaper of public record showed up to claim his right to a licensed stall on that account, the Union president and his assistant spent some time looking for "the list" before concluding that he was not eligible. "If he's not in there, he can't work," the president said. Meanwhile, there were hustlers who asked for money to add someone's name to the list. Valdira said she was willing to pay, but only if it meant she got her license back (as opposed to simply appearing on the police's roster).

Legality is the space in which people have rights, but that space is elastic and abstract. Drawing its boundaries, in solemn meeting rooms or poorly ventilated offices, is a big part of the making of legality. At the ground level, another basic challenge is to figure out who stands where. Official documents serve that purpose. Because falsification is inherent to the logic of informal economies, other documents, official or not, such as the street vending license or (in the early days of citizenship) the *carteira professional*, provide the kind of background checks that secured, digitalized databases offer elsewhere. As with the street vendors' list, those documents themselves become objects of both manipulation and contestation. Informality thus deconstructs the state. And there are more stakeholders in the blurring of legality than meets the eye. Some interactions I observed in the field suggest that even a representative of storeowners may have had a hand in adding to the list names that did not "belong" while at the same time pushing for the removal of other interlopers.

Despite the precariousness of their position, even unauthorized vendors working with fake or "cold" licenses leased part of their stalls, like many of their licensed colleagues. This created a problem when goods were confiscated, as stalls owners were—informally—liable for the loss. After it happened to Maria, she told me they were going to try to recover her tenant's wares. I asked her if she intended to pay the fine to retrieve them, and she replied, "If you wait for the seal, it can take thirty, sixty days." I asked her if there was a way to get them earlier. "You don't understand," she said. "There's an *esquema* [scheme] for everything, everything."

Part of the confusion surrounding authorized vendors stemmed from a judicial process (described in chap. 4) that shielded some licensed vendors whose licenses had been revoked under the previous administration of Kassab. But even vendors protected by the court order continued to suffer harassment under Kassab's successor. Sephir, a corpulent, warm woman who used a mobility scooter, had a stall at the northern end of 25 de Março, where she sold garments with her son, whom she had registered as an aide. One morning in June, she looked worried and told me about two policemen who had come to her stall. They claimed her aide registration card (*protocolo de auxiliar*) was fake and that it had to be signed by a judge. She said she had almost lost her mind, as she knew what a registration card was. "You register it at the district administration, and it's signed by the clerk," she said, showing me the document in its plastic folder. "Let me explain this to you," she told the cops. The officer said he knew what she was going to say, so she turned to his female colleague. "You think you know better than me?" the officer shot back. They threatened to take her stall. Sephir was so shocked and confused that she hadn't remembered to write down their names. The cops eventually moved on to the stall next to hers, whose owner had an amputated leg. He had witnessed the interaction and was holding his license behind his back to prevent the police from taking it from him on dubious grounds.

Sephir was deeply shaken by what had happened to her and was unwilling to let it slide. She had gone to the Center for Informal Workers (CIW), an NGO working with street vendors, and wrote a formal letter to the mayor to denounce the abuse. When I saw her at her stall, she handed me the letter to read. As I skimmed through it, I noted her assertion that the officers had behaved in a "stupid and arrogant" manner. The female officer had been "rude" and "did not want to listen." I asked Sephir if she really wanted to put "stupid and arrogant" in the letter. She did. "This is not a joke," she said. "This is how I make my living." In a sweet voice, she added, "I'm the mom and the dad in my household. I have debts to pay. I have responsibilities. You can't threaten to take away a peddler's stall just like that, on a whim." She knew she could suffer retaliation. "But you are going to fight for this?" I asked. "I am," she replied. "They treated me like a criminal, a bandit, a hustler. You can't marginalize a person like that. I'm working for a living."

On a previous occasion, when a civil servant seized her license, she went to the police station and filed a report, which she said saved her.

"Why do you say that police report saved you?" I asked her.

"The report proves that they [the city] are to blame, that the crime is on their side. They are the ones who need to provide evidence. Daniel [the civil servant] had claimed he waited for forty-five minutes [for her to show up at her stall]. That's not true." That time, she even paid the fine—"which was illegal"—to recover her license. She paid it to keep working, because each day that she doesn't work "is a loss" (*é prejuizo*).

Sephir saw her struggles through a philosophical lens. She described street vendors as "those little turtles" who face so much trouble and dangers before reaching "quietness" in "the depths of the sea." Before they "find the sea," however, many die of a "nervous heart attack." She told me about a Mexican author she liked, who wrote that utopia is something out there in the horizon, toward which you take ten steps. "And what's the purpose of it?" she asked rhetorically. "Well, that's the purpose, to help you move forward." I asked her what her utopia was. "I have to say there are many dreams that I have had and have had to let go of. Instead of going after utopias, I've had to run away from harm [*prejuizo*]." Valdira put it more bluntly: "If I loved myself, I would not work at 25 de Março."

Sephir has a big heart, and her dream was to do some major social work. The dream of most licensed—and unlicensed—street vendors, however, is to become storeowners. Very few of them make it. Among those who did was Norberto, a friend of Sephir who owns a store across the street from her stall. He started working as a street vendor when he was unemployed. His dad, who worked as a security guard in a building in the area, had arranged for him to rent a stall. The day he made eighty reals, Norberto was in heaven. He felt that he had "touched life." He explained that business was about "conquering" a clientele. "It's about making friends, building trust." He gave goods on credit to people who went back to their home states and told them: "If you don't sell, you can bring it back." Those people brought him clients. "My main merchandise," he said, "is my client."

Despite his success, Norberto kept a humble view on his storeowner status. He considered himself an "elevated peddler." "Other storeowners think of themselves as businessmen," he said. "But they are born that. They don't know what their dad had to do to open the business. They don't know the difficulties." And part of the street vendor's ethos still informs how he runs his business. "The peddler is dynamic. I have to invent merchandise. You saw me when you came in," he said, referring to guidelines he was giving a supplier on the design of a new product he was ordering for the World Cup.

The Thin Gray Line

In the outer regions of legality, where rights tend to fade, the boundary between licensed and unlicensed street vendors matters a great deal. It has an institutional reality. It sets limits—however relative or precarious—to the reach of the state. While the unlicensed vendors are always on the move, licensed vendors sit at their stalls, where, as one of them put it, "clients come to us." For all the threats hanging over them, their world is more stable. In a survey conducted in 2014, less than half of licensed vendors reported ever losing merchandise to confiscations, and it had been over a year since it last happened in most cases. This contrasts with the experience of unlicensed vendors, who, in some areas, suffer confiscations multiple times a week. And those license holders who lease out their stalls enjoy a rent. License holders form a status group with distinctive work routines, politics, and worldviews.

As with other status groups, those on the inner side of the boundary emphasize its symbolic salience. Licensed vendors commonly refer to the unlicensed as "the irregulars," "the clandestine," or "the illegals." A license holder put it this way: "A peddler is anyone who stands on a corner holding a pen [for sale]. That's a peddler. It's not fair that they beat him up or that they don't let him work. But I am a *permissionário* [license holder]. I have my license from the city."

And with that status comes a sense of occupational identity less common among unlicensed vendors. "We are not on the streets because of unemployment," a licensed vendor said. "We are here because this is our trade [*profissão*]. We were here from the start, [even if at first] we did not have [professional] qualifications." A license thus provides a set of practical and psychological rewards, such as comfort and tranquility in the conduct of business, as well as a very relative but genuinely experienced amount of prestige.

The boundary is hard in that it creates a material difference in lifestyles, but it is also thin and fragile. In the criminalization era, a license is almost impossible to obtain; it is not that difficult to lose, however, as the story of Valdira—whose license was canceled after she arrived late to the call for renewal—and thousands of other licensed vendors makes plain.[6] Strangers to the trade or street vendors' enemies may downplay the significance of a license and put licensed and unlicensed vendors in the same bag, while a host of liminal cases populate the border area, from fake or "cold" licenses to people working with expired licenses to illicit tenants and so on.

Each group of workers faces the particular set of challenges that a hostile environment with adverse legal provisions and repressive police forces imposes on their livelihood. Those in a position to assert certain rights negotiate with authorities and deal with those challenges by appealing to the law. Those further at the margins of the field of legality use whatever wiggle room conflicting legislation and murky understandings by state officials charged with enforcing it leave them to try and hold their ground. In this effort, they sometimes rely on legal documents, even documents that do not explicitly protect them. When I pointed out to Valdira that some of the documents she used to weather police controls did not technically grant her the right to practice street trade, she replied, alluding to other street vendors in the same situation: "What we are doing is not right, but it is not wrong, either." After all, the renewal of her license was denied on arbitrary grounds. Aides and tenants of license holders have less to lose, yet they do not escape the angst and exhausting grind of the streets. Finally, unlicensed street vendors—who, as Vicente put it, "have no rights"—focus their efforts on dodging the crushing arm of the law.

Studies of boundary-making tend to focus on cultural processes. Ethnicity is based on stereotypes and discourses that produce identity and otherness. Because traits vary widely within and across theoretical groups, making boundaries takes work. In their review of scholarship on boundaries, Michèle Lamont and Virág Molnár allude to the transition from symbolic to social boundaries—that is, from "conceptual distinctions made by social actors to categorize objects, people, practices, and even time and space" to "objectified forms of social differences manifested in unequal access to and unequal distribution of resources."[7] Gender, race, and class exemplify the latter. Yet they gloss over the institutional dimension in which symbolic differences acquire practical significance—that is, become objectified—as official categories regulating social life. Andreas Wimmer's theory of ethnic boundaries recognizes "institutional orders" as a parameter in boundary-making strategies but considers them only in general terms, at the nation-state level.[8]

A story about ethnicity—or identity more broadly—becomes a story about citizenship when rights are at stake. This is most clearly the case when political entrepreneurs seek to draw the perimeter of legality around a nation defined in cultural terms. Closed regimes of citizenship thus rely on ancestry—a gauge of ethnic membership. In Weber's original formulation, the law was key to social closure as a resource-hoarding strategy. Others, like Charles Tilly, cite the matching of symbolic and organizational categories as a recipe for durable inequality.[9] And Michael Mann evokes the overlap of demos and ethnos as a precondition for ethnic cleansing.[10] To the extent that they consider both legality and representational phenomena, studies of social closure are often based on the assumption that institutions are stable while ethnicity is more fluid and amenable to strategic reconstruction or manipulation.

Preexisting symbolic categories played their part in the making of legality in street trade. The following chapter explores the efforts of disabled street vendors to limit licensing beyond their social group. However, legal status itself creates a sense of distinction and pride, whatever the cultural content of membership. Several claims about the distinctive professional identity of licensed street vendors came from able-bodied licensed vendors, not disabled ones. More intriguingly, even the institutional boundaries governing the allocation of rights are, in this setting, a dynamic construction, and a host of actors will take their chances at claiming a spot on the safe side of legality in an effort to secure a spot in the highly contested physical space of the street.

Work without License

Others will take their chances outside the field of legality. Unlicensed vendors described 25 de Março as both "a cursed place" and "a gold mine." "There's gold here," an unlicensed vendor told me. "But you have to know how to find it." Less ambitious vendors come in search of a livelihood. This was the case with Blondine, a mellow woman in her forties. She started working on the streets when she was pregnant because "when you are pregnant, no one gives you work." She was too scared to go alone, so she asked her sister to accompany her. At first, she felt lots of shame. Now she enjoys it. At home, she gets depressed, but at 25 de Março, there are always people around making jokes, swearing, and gossiping while you work. She has fun—the street is where she feels at home. On the streets, she said, "you live more." And her work as a street vendor allows her to be, in her own words, an "independent mother." Like her friend Tina, who is also a single mother, Blondine lives alone with her child, having had a divorce. However, unlike Tina, who at times brings her teenage son along to help, Blondine will "never bring her son to the street."

Part of what explains Blondine's comfort on the streets is a level of solidarity among the unlicensed crowd on the northern section of 25 de Março. Vendors in that area know each other and get along—for the most part. A dozen of them come from the same neighborhood on the outskirts of São

Paulo. Kevin, whose wife used to work as a street vendor and is now a store employee, brought his brother, who lost his job, and several neighborhood friends to 25 de Março.

When I asked Kevin how he became a street vendor, he told me he had his first run at the trade when he was eight. His father had bought him a bike, which he wrecked on his first ride. He asked his dad for money to get it fixed. Instead, his dad got him a cooler and some drinks. Kevin sat in front of his house and sold enough drinks to fix the bike. In fact, his father also worked as a street vendor, despite having a stable job as a metal worker. When I asked Kevin why, he claimed his dad "didn't like to be bossed over." Sitting next to him, Kevin's wife gave a different reason: "They both like to wake up late." And yet, as a former street vendor herself, she could relate to the pitfalls of being an employee. At the store, "you have to be there every day, and every day the boss gets on your case [*está acima de você*], and colleagues don't help . . . and customers complain." She longed for the streets, where she could leave or rest whenever she wanted. She was considering going back to street vending.

Street trade can be hard physical work, though, especially in that area. One morning, I accompanied Kevin's brother Fred to a store about eight blocks from where he usually worked to buy three twelve-packs of water bottles. Each pack cost seven reals (US$3). As we carried them back, along with the ice, to 25 de Março, Fred complained that some customers still wanted to buy bottles for less than two reals. He also complained about the shopkeeper, who was unpleasant. "Having to deal with the police all day long, and then this guy," he said wistfully.

As soon as we arrived at 25 de Março, Fred took off running. When I reached him, he was watching the police remove his water bottles from the trash bin, where he had stashed them. They took his entire stock; he had not sold a single bottle. "This is like playing bingo," he said. "But you can only lose. The guy knows me. He knows I hide the bottles in the trash. That's how they got me."

Stories of police confiscation fill the collective imaginings of street vendors. Jose still remembers how a municipal guard who confiscated watches he was selling locked the bag in front of him using a zip tie, according to confiscation protocol, but when Jose recovered his wares, the best watches were missing. The trick, as Altaisa explained to me, was to flip the zip tie so that instead of pulling it with the dents facing the ratchet, you slid it the other way to prevent it from locking in. The bag could easily be reopened, then properly fastened after its contents were removed. The worst experience of police abuse Blondine recalled was when a policeman put his hand in her purse to look for merchandise. She thought that was outrageous. She told him to take his "paw" out of her purse. "It's my purse, you know," Blondine said. "I had two items, which I handed him. But I also had my personal things."

Stories of police intimidation and brutality also shape unlicensed vendors' perception of their work environment. Vicente recounted a time when two "bad cops" took money from his nephew, who was helping Valdira's other brother, also a street vendor. The boy came crying to his dad. When the dad confronted the officers, they put him against the wall. According to Vicente, the officer showed his gun and said: "You see this? You see this gun? I'm going to take you prisoner. You are my prisoner. I have a gun." Vicente also spoke of police beatings, which I did not observe. In his telling, one guy was taken to the second floor of a mobile police station and beaten up; he now works close to home. "He never came back to 25 de Março."

True or not, reports of beatings reflect a sense of alienation from state institutions that is widespread among unlicensed street vendors. As I was interviewing João, a licensed vendor, by his stall, a taxi ran into a tall, unusually thin hawker who was carrying a plastic bag with water bottles. As the driver got out of the car to make sure the man was OK, the hawker got up quickly and took off, refusing assistance from bystanders. Another time, Igor, an unlicensed street vendor, fell while he was running away from a cop, was hit by a car, and passed out. A store employee asked him later if he intended to press charges. He said he might file suit against the driver, but not the cop. I asked his friend Fred why.

"It's the fear, you know," Fred said. "That fear. We don't want to admit it, but it's there."

"You mean the fear of retaliation?" I asked.

"Yeah, it could be another cop. It doesn't have to be the same cop. You can't mess with the place from which you draw your living."

Lucas, another young member of the loose local network of unlicensed street vendors, articulated the principle in philosophical terms. "He who seeks justice gets in trouble. You have to accept [the way things are] even if you don't understand. You learn to always obey. And you don't take action afterwards, because you know you can get in more trouble if you do. You need to accept injustice. The police are the law."

The cynicism and sense of alienation from state institutions that unlicensed vendors harbor are not only targeted at law enforcement. Will, an unlicensed vendor, hasn't voted a single time in his life. He claimed to be "against all [political] parties." "None of them helps," he added. "They only make money off the back of morons." His only regret was not having worked as *boca de urna*, distributing campaign flyers on election day, which is illegal.

He said some people do it for rival candidates at the same time. As for the city, it had "never done shit" for unlicensed vendors.

While holding equally cynical views as his coworker, Fred expressed a level of awareness as well as a lack of faith in his fellow vendors' capacity to take action: "I like politics. I'm interested in politics. But you can't organize these guys [unlicensed street vendors]. They don't know what the system is. They don't understand it. They just want to sell and have fun."

"I'm sure they would understand if you talked to them," I said.

"Maybe they would," he said. "But if you start talking about this stuff, they say you are talking too much. They don't listen."

His brother Kevin also noted the difficulties of organizing unlicensed vendors. If you start collecting dues to cover operational costs, "they think you are taking their money . . . they get suspicious. They think you are stealing from them." Will, who had worked as a metal worker in the past, remembered the union as "guys who parked their cars at the factory gates and talked to workers. But at the time I only thought about partying."

The prevailing cynicism reflects a fraught working environment in which state presence takes primarily a repressive form and in which competition among groups and individuals runs rampant. Referring to his time as an unlicensed street vendor, a businessman who managed to transition out of it said: "I did not have life expectations." Lucas agreed: "The street drives you crazy. There's lots of fighting."

Many unlicensed vendors therefore think of escaping. Lucas, for one, hopes to leave the streets. He wants to get married, buy a house and a car. I asked him if he knew many vendors who moved on. He thought about it for a while. "No. I see many who come to the streets, but [moving] the other way is not common." Kevin places his hopes on his son. "Like any dad, I'd like to see him become a doctor or a lawyer." He considers paying for private school so that he doesn't need to pay for private university later. In the meantime, cordiality under pressure is the only viable option. "The smart peddler gets along with everyone: storeowners, guards, other peddlers," Lucas said. "In this job, the less enemies you have, the better." Leonardo, a licensed vendor, echoed that thought: "In this job you have to be on good terms among enemies."

Being a Criminal

There is another line or boundary in the scales of legality; further afield, it separates unlicensed vendors from criminals and outlaws. If licensed vendors are informal workers with (some) rights and unlicensed vendors are informal workers without rights, criminals are, in the view of the public, people who deserve to be punished and upon whom the use of force is justified, for they offend the social and moral orders. The effect of the criminalization policy pursued under Kassab was to push licensed street vendors further toward illegality and many unlicensed vendors out of street trade. Reliable population data on informal workers are hard to come by, but testimonies collected in interviews suggest that the response of a sizable portion of unlicensed peddlers to Kassab's campaign was to exit the field. According to city officials, by April 2011, fifteen thousand unlicensed vendors of the estimated hundred thousand in 2009 had deserted the streets. Those who had the means to move into other trades or areas did so, while others simply fell into destitution and begging. In the words of the downtown district administrator, "At one point there wasn't a single peddler. It was paradise."[11]

Even if the room for negotiating enforcement shrank after the deployment of the MP, a fragile moral economy still governed interactions with MP officers. For instance, it was generally accepted—even expected—that street vendors would try to run if they saw police coming their way and they had an opening. Cops would not blame street vendors for it. However, an unspoken rule posits that, if caught, vendors must surrender their wares without resistance. Experienced vendors complained about neophytes who refused to give up their merchandise and endangered other traders. But a policy of criminalization puts both sides on edge. The repeated confiscation of their livelihoods breeds frustration among unlicensed vendors—even seasoned ones—and increases the likelihood of a snap.

These tensions resulted in violent and sometimes tragic incidents. In the district of Lapa, a young street vendor was shot and killed by a policeman in a scuffle. The victim, along with other street vendors, had surrounded a group of three police officers trying to arrest a vendor. They were pressing for the release of their coworker when the officer's gun went off. On 25 de Março, when Igor stumbled or was pushed while running from the police, fell to the ground, was hit by a car, and passed out in front of his eleven-year-old son, mayhem ensued. Rioting unlicensed vendors destroyed police equipment in the area, including a police watchtower donated by the local storeowners association. Shopkeepers shut down their stores. Licensed street vendors closed shop. Dozens of MP reinforcements flocked to the scene to restore order. Weeks later, in an interview, one of Igor's friends and a fellow unlicensed street vendor at 25 de Março summed up the meaning of their action: "To show them we exist."

The quote is telling, for it alludes to the psychological impact of criminalization, which is profound and perhaps more pernicious at the personal level. A middle-aged woman who sold steamed corncobs at the gate of a hospital said in conversation: "I never imagined, never in my life, that I would be running from the police. I'm going crazy, really. I don't know who I am anymore."[12] Kid, an unlicensed vendor at 25 de Março, attributed his toxic binges to the urge to let go of money that felt dirty:

> The police beats you, insults you. You end up believing what you are doing is wrong, that your money is dirty. I know it's not. I'm not stealing from anyone. But you end up seeing your work through the eyes of the government. And so you spend it. You spend it on drugs, women, alcohol.[13]

The erasure of the *symbolic* boundary between informal worker and criminal—which some street vendors seem to internalize—using discursive practices and the everyday exercise of state violence thus accompanies the institutional process of pushing informal workers into illegality through the erasure of the *legal* boundary between licensed and unlicensed street vending, based on the cancellation of licenses (see chapter 5).

Interviews with MP officers and city officials in charge of suppressing street vendors under Kassab suggest both processes go hand in hand from a law enforcement perspective. Colonel Camilo is the former commander in chief of the MP in São Paulo who signed the renewal of the Operação Delegada agreement in 2011. A top-ranking cop turned councilman, he explained in an interview that, during the 1990s, the MP focused on violent crime. As such crime subsided, the focus shifted to petty crime. Citing Jane Jacobs rather liberally as well as the broken windows theory, he argued that the "ecology of street vending is a factor behind petty crime" because "physical disorder breeds social disorder," and he deemed Operação Delegada a success on every level.[14]

Despite endorsing tough-on-crime policies, Camilo was a well-mannered, soft-spoken politician who refrained from passing judgment on street vendors themselves. This was not the case for other MP officers closer to the front lines of the mass eviction campaign. While some expressed a level of sympathy or at least benevolence toward vendors, others saw them, quite literally, as criminals. Echoing the views of an MP officer on the beat who spoke in positive terms of the military dictatorships of the Southern Cone in the context of a conversation about policing street vendors, a high-ranking civil servant under Kassab said of licensed vendors: "They don't want to work. . . . They are like drug addicts, they don't want to work, they don't want to do anything, they arrive late [to their stalls], they keep suckling. They are all nuts [*tudos zafados*]. I mean, some are decent. They behave like inmates when guards go by. They stop selling [illegal stuff]. As soon as the guard passes, they start selling again."[15]

Seeing members of the target population as criminals seems to be, if not a precondition, a facilitator to criminalizing them. Like others, the official alluded to licensed vendors constantly breaking the rules with practices like the sale of cigarettes or alcohol. (While I witnessed several infractions during my time in the field, I never saw this happen.) He added that they found eighty fake health certificates used by licensed vendors in his district. "The doctor swore they had been stolen from him," he said. "It might even be true." And he claimed that actual crime fell by 85 percent after Operação Delegada was rolled out.

A New Law

At the opposite end of criminalization on the policy spectrum is the expansion of rights, which unlicensed vendors think about as a desirable if purely theoretical possibility. When I asked Will what the city could do for unlicensed vendors, if it cared about them, his answer was "give us licenses." Fred also alluded to it in jest. Pointing to a stall on 25 de Março, he said: "Can't they split it in five and give one slice to each of us?" Amid a freeze on new licenses and a drown-out debate on the reinstatement of old ones, a legislative initiative for the licensing of street trade came from the most unlikely quarters. Councilman Andrea Matarazzo from the right-wing Partido da Social Democracia Brasileira (PSDB) party put forward a bill to legalize the sale of food in public spaces through a system of licenses similar to the one enshrined in municipal law (ML) 11,039, which governs street trade. In contrast to the street vending licenses law, which only authorized processed foods such as candy bars, the new bill permitted the sale of fresh, raw, and cooked foodstuff in food trucks and stalls.

That an initiative of this sort would come from Matarazzo was baffling to many a licensed street vendor. Matarazzo had been a downtown district administrator under José Serra, Kassab's predecessor and coreligionist, when the campaign to eliminate street vendors began. "No one persecuted street vendors like he did," the vice president of the Union said in an interview. The official narrative framed the bill as a law for those who make a living off the streets, an attempt to promote entrepreneurship among the poor. But vendors were skeptical. To think that this bill is meant to help the poor is like believing in Santa Claus, one of them told me.

At an informational meeting, an assistant to the councilman who was clearly not familiar with the situation of street vendors suggested that there was no legal framework protecting them. With this new bill, "there will be spots for everyone—fixed spots," he added. All the official speakers were careful not to touch on the politics of street vending. A talk by the head of Sebrae, a nonprofit for small businesses, was followed by an "expert" talk on what it means to be an entrepreneur. It's not only about having a good product, the presenter explained, but also about price formation and marketing strategy. The expert also noted, quite ambiguously, that there were two worlds—the world of legality and the world of entrepreneurship; he then discussed basic accounting for forty-five minutes. The premise of his presentation was that street vendors did not know how to run a business or keep track of their earnings and expenses. He insisted on the need to separate the firm's budget from personal wealth while at the same time agreeing it was sometimes hard to do. The goal, he said, was to "professionalize ourselves." Even though many of his teachings were part of the street vendors' natural lore—or perhaps for that reason—the audience would relate to his statements and comment "I did this" or "I have this issue."

For all the efforts organizers made to steer clear of thorny political issues, politics came up with a vengeance in the Q and A session. Luiza, the wife of a licensed vendor, requested the mic and took Matarazzo's assistant to task:

> First, we do have a law. It's ML 11,039, the law of street vendors. We've been fighting for a year to go back to the streets. And now you are trying to open them for McDonald's. Those guys don't need a spot, they already have their restaurants. But we won't let you roll over us. We are going to fight.

When Luiza spoke, Giovanni, the young lawyer and assistant who had implied there was no previous law for street vendors, looked down with an air of contrition. Another assistant intervened to point out that the meeting was not about politics, only for technical questions. (Valdira would later wonder: "What does 'technical questions' mean anyway?")

It was not the first time that the councilman had come under fire from street vendors in connection with his bill. At a city council hearing, a licensed street vendors' leader publicly called him the "biggest persecutor of street vendors" during his tenure as district administrator. Matarazzo defended himself, claiming that at the time he was part of the executive branch: "I never intended to exterminate peddlers. I met with all of them and showed much respect. But I was forced to enforce the law, to follow orders. I was not a councilman at the time."

Antagonists of street vendors were also puzzled, however. It was rumored among them that fancy restaurant owners and chefs seeking to set up food trucks to expand their clientele were behind the initiative. The promoters of the bill were aware of the suspicion, pervasive among street vendors, that "the big guys" would use the law to "flood the city." They argued that the bill capped the number of spots for license holders at two for that reason. A closer reading, however, suggested the total was three: one main spot and two franchises. Whatever lobbying restaurant owners may have done, electoral motives likely played a role as well. A few months after passing the bill, Matarazzo made a bid for mayor, which was cut short by his loss in his party's primaries.

From a historical perspective, the fact that a former nemesis would put forward the only bill of substance that granted street vendors some rights was a sign that the leadership of licensed vendors had lost the leverage it once held and that the city government no longer saw the expansion of rights as a profitable strategy. After failing to secure the reinstatement of licenses from the PT administration, Union and DVA leaders seemed reduced to defending, by any means available, the fraction of licensed vendors protected by a court order. According to the Union's vice president, the leadership had "done its part" by presenting the draft of a municipal bill to Tristan, a PT councilman who was the political patron of organized licensed vendors.[16] At the same time, the street vendor recognized that the councilman "could not help much" because he had "other commitments." He mulled that the only way to regain some traction would be to get a licensed street vendor elected to the city council.

Yet political habits die hard. During a visit I paid to the president of the Union toward the end of my fieldwork, he showed me a draft of a bill to reform ML 11,039 that he was working on. The first version of the draft was the work of Artur, a disabled street vendor leader whom Tristan had praised in public. The Union president was working hard on fine-tuning the language. He felt that the verb *decrees* did not fit in the enacting clause, and a more suitable verb had just slipped from his mind. I suggested *determines*, but he was not convinced. Unfortunately for him, Tristan's chief of staff, a lawyer, did not have time to look at it.

Place in Perspective

The description of street trade in São Paulo has so far focused on 25 de Março, which holds a mythical status in the collective imagination of street vendors across the city. It is an outlier in terms of the volume of trade and the intensity of policing. But the categories of street vendors and the dynamics of street trade are not radically different from elsewhere in the city. To be sure, smaller marketplaces exhibit some traditional traits reminiscent of the bazaar economy described by Clifford Geertz in his classic study of Sefrou that are foreign to a mecca of informal capitalism like 25 de Março.[17] For example, at a subway station on the outskirts where a small group of street vendors gather in the evenings and on weekends, an honor code prevents vendors from inquiring about their coworkers' "source," meaning their main supplier. And it is expected that the "source" will not sell to another street vendor, lest shortages arise.

As in the *souq* of Sefrou, however, trust remains an important asset on 25 de Março, at least for fixed-stall vendors. The story of Norberto—the street vendor turned storeowner who sold on credit to build a clientele and ensure the long-term viability of his business—makes this clear. By contrast, in the fluid economy of unlicensed street trade, trust is absent from the dealings with customers. In the case of search goods such as plastic toys, quality is assumed to be low. When selling experience goods such as cheap electronics, unlicensed vendors sometimes offer an on-the-spot demonstration that the product works, but they largely depend on the credulity of buyers who will never see them again. Chances are the battery-powered razor will stop working by the time the customer gets home. The anonymity of the parties involved in these one-off, cash-based transactions thus creates opportunities for vendors who set the price according to "the face of the client." A hawker from 25 de Março who, in the evenings, worked at the subway station near his house, tapping the flow of commuters returning home, said that the pen drives he sold there were real ones, unlike the ones he sold at 25 de Março. On the streets, as Fred put it, "the dumb guy eats a cold meal. That's the law!"

While tensions over the occupation and division of space are inherent to street trade wherever it occurs, the ethnographic study of a consolidated marketplace like 25 de Março misses the process by which space is originally consigned to street trade and parceled out. Elsewhere, street vendors sometimes have to take collective action so as to "conquer" space and set up an informal market. Hence, Luna, a street vendor from the eastern neighborhood of Itaquera whose two dreams were to raise a parrot and fly in an airplane, felt pressured to take part in a collective attempt to set up stalls near a subway station. And the pressure she felt was tied to her occupational identity. "Otherwise, [other street vendors] will say: 'This one is only a peddler when it comes to selling.'" The parallels with the struggle for informal housing, which also relies on collectively enforced takeovers of land or buildings, are striking. Finally, places with less policing are less profitable, but they afford street vendors more leisure time, especially when some kind of protective arrangement is in place. A friend of Valdira who worked as a street vendor at a park said she enjoyed her job: "When I'm not selling, I talk about Jesus."

In short, the informal economy of street vending is unequal not only with regard to income and location—a proxy for income—but in terms of legal status, which defines the relationship to the state and the material conditions of doing business. Street vendors do not have equal rights. A form of social closure mirrors the broader logic of citizenship, which, in terms of policy, more often takes a path of definition by exclusion than the fostering of community and civic participation cherished in classic texts in political philosophy. In this case, the right at stake is the civil right to work—the first layer of citizenship, according to Marshall's framework. Some vendors have it, others do not. What makes the case interesting from an analytic standpoint is that even the institutional boundaries of legality are open for negotiation. And the battle for legality intensifies with criminalization.

At one level, citizenship is a straightforward matter: a person either is a member of a nation-state, recognized as such by its sovereign, or she is not. At another level, which considers the layers and shades discussed in the previous chapter, citizenship presents itself as a gradient or a set of roughly concentric, overlapping fields. Each field represents legality in a particular sector, such as street vending, and determines who has what and how many rights. Unlicensed vendors stand outside the field of legality in their sector, even though most of them occupy, as Brazilians, the space of legality on the broader field that grants them the right to vote, live, and work in the country.

This intricate architecture adds nuance to such terms as *second-class citizens* by mapping the various realms in which citizenship is strained. Moreover, analyzing dynamics around a particular boundary sheds light on the tensions surrounding the definition of citizenship more broadly. It shows that those on the inner side of legality give meaning and value to membership irrespective of other identity-building processes—which, in the case of citizenship *sensu stricto*, typically take ethnonational overtones. They do so even though—or, perhaps, especially because—the boundary is blurry and shaky. Finally, street vendors are clear-eyed about the structure of social inequality underlying the architecture of citizenship; they called out the new law as an effort to extend the rights of those who have plenty (i.e., restaurant owners) and grant them access to a territory, the street, that is being denied to its rightful tenants.

4

The Rights of Time

In early 2012, on the eve of a de facto ban on street vending, the downtown district of Sé, where commercial activity is concentrated, had 116 street vendors with a valid license. Of these 116 street vendors, 94 percent were classified as disabled (see fig. 4.1). Two years later, as the legal battle to reinstate licenses dragged on, about two-thirds of authorized vendors citywide were disabled or elderly, and around 95 percent of licensed spots on 25 de Março Street—the "sweetheart of all peddlers," as one of them called it—were occupied by the disabled and the elderly. Disenfranchisement is a selective process.

Among the members of what a rival vendor once described as the "aristocracy" of street vendors was Felipão, a blind man in his late sixties who sat by his stall with a battery-powered, racket-shaped mosquito killer in his left hand and a piece of wire tucked between the fingers of his right hand. He would rub the wire against the racket in a repetitive, circular motion to give himself small electric shocks. Felipão's son studied at a private Catholic college in the United States. A couple of stalls down the block was Artur's, the so-called "boss" of 25 de Março, whose childhood injury left him paraplegic for life. As a bonus perk in the district of Sé and in that district alone, disabled and elderly vendors were allowed to leave their stalls by 1:00 p.m. while letting their assistants look after business.

Disabled vendors did not always rule the streets, nor did disabled vendors benefit from inclusive policies at the national level. Brazil recognized disability rights only partially and belatedly. Gabriel, the blind license holder who arrived in São Paulo over forty years ago, and Sephir both complained about the lack of opportunities and the discrimination they faced as disabled workers. The default occupation was to become a beggar, and relatives encouraged

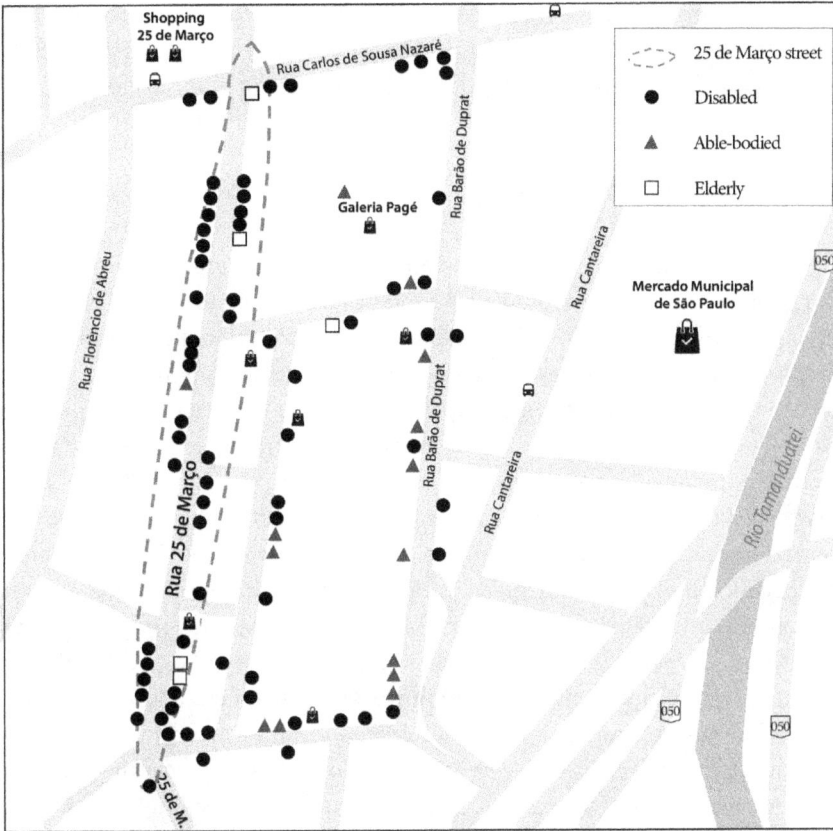

FIGURE 4.1. The distribution of licensed stalls in and around 25 de Março Street in 2014
Data from the city of São Paulo downtown district administration (*subprefeitura da Sé*). Map: Isabelle
Renneson.

them to take it up. Why were disabled vendors overrepresented among the
licensed few before and in the wake of the mass eviction campaign?

The rights of disabled and elderly street vendors are enshrined in municipal
legislation. ML 11,039 allocates a third of licenses to "seriously disabled" vendors, another third to disabled and elderly vendors, and the remaining third
to the able-bodied. But the advantages enjoyed by the disabled and the elderly
preceded this statute. In fact, the adoption of ML 11,039 in 1991 both consolidated the rights of the disabled and took away their monopoly over legal street
trade. The history of licensing among street vendors in São Paulo sheds light
on the unequal distribution of rights over time. It shows that groups protected
by institutional barriers build up material and immaterial assets that allow

them to secure a legacy of rights during critical junctures. In the process, they shape the contours of legality. And in desperate times, when rights themselves come under threat across the board, the discrete payoffs of social closure, such as networks and political capital, offer an edge to longtime insiders.

Making the Rules

Upon his inauguration as mayor of São Paulo in 1953, Jânio Quadros set out to regulate street trade following a period of relative neglect.[1] He was driven, in part, by pressures from storeowners who have traditionally regarded peddlers as unfair competitors and an urban nuisance. During his first year in office, Quadros issued six municipal decrees (MD, *decreto municipal*) on street vending. The first of these decrees, MD 2201, banned street vending from the downtown area, the commercial heart of São Paulo. By the same token, MD 2201 established the rules for the allocation of spots beyond the central region.[2] Despite a campaign pledge that only disabled people would get permits, they were only given preference, followed by the elderly, those with numerous offspring, married people, and finally bachelors staying with host families. While the initial distribution of rights favored the disabled, it did not create a monopoly, as any adult worker was still eligible for a permit.

Probably in response to supply problems resulting from the downtown ban, subsequent decrees created exceptions, first for sellers of lottery tickets, then for mobile fruit vendors.[3] A later municipal decree subdivided the city into sectors (some of which impinged on the foreclosed downtown area) and established a system of rotation among licensed vendors, limiting the occupation of each spot to two weeks in an effort to spread the benefits of centrality more evenly. The last of the six decrees exempted the disabled from the rotation system, thus guaranteeing them a stable hold on their spots.

These measures laid a legal boundary along a social boundary. Indeed, the distinction between the disabled and the able-bodied is a social construction that exerts a stable influence on resource distribution, according to Lamont and Molnár's criteria, usually in favor of the able-bodied. While reaffirming this social boundary, the Quadros decrees sought to upend the unequal access to resources by allocating (more) rights to the disadvantaged side.

The legal boundary thus drawn was not steadfast, however. Albeit significant, the advantages achieved by the disabled and the elderly were relative insofar as other social groups could also hold a license or ply their trade downtown. Moreover, they were precarious: MDs are lower-order regulatory instruments that can be easily overturned by other MDs at the discretion of subsequent mayors or overridden by MLs.

Under Quadros's successor, pressures from storeowners against street vendors intensified. Using their political influence inside the city council, storeowners associations pushed for a bill that banned street vending for *all* groups in the downtown area. It was approved by the council in 1957.[4] That same year, the city council passed ML 5,440, put forth by the mayor himself. Claiming it would be "inhumane" to remove disabled vendors from the downtown spots they already occupied, the bill called for an exception for this group while granting them tax exemptions.[5] Charitable feelings aside, it was rumored that the mayor's wife received under-the-table payments from disabled vendors. Given the preeminence of MLs over MDs, this law became the overarching norm for policymaking toward street vending. In short, it was not through a single, authoritative distribution of rights but rather through a series of path-dependent legislative steps mixing interests and values that the disabled came to monopolize legal status in downtown street trade.

In 1964, a coup placed Brazil under a military dictatorship. Draconian law-and-order legislation adopted across the country restricted freedom of movement and outlawed the "unproductive" occupation of public spaces as "loafing" (*vadiagem*). In state capital cities like São Paulo, the military regime itself appointed the mayors. Policy oscillated between the cancellation of licenses and efforts at sharpening and tightening regulations. On the whole, however, the framework established by ML 5,440 prevailed, guaranteeing a legal monopoly over licensed trade to disabled and elderly vendors in the downtown area. Even though licenses had to be periodically renewed, MD 14,396, issued in 1977, introduced a seniority rule by which street vendors with the most time on the streets had priority in the selection of spots during renewals. And military rule stifled demands for broadening access to street vending rights.

The distribution of street vending rights in the postwar era thus followed, for the most part, a top-down logic. Successive governments drew the line between potential rights-bearers and those who, under prevailing rules, were forced to work at the margins of legality and in the shadows. As it happened, the process favored a specific social group: the disabled. Contrary to the conventional storyline of a symbolic boundary solidifying into a social boundary then being enshrined into law, the field of legality, which initially encompassed a more diverse population, "shrank" as a result of political pressures to ultimately dovetail a bounded social group. As an unintended consequence, these licensing rules created a political constituency that developed the ability to shape legislative policy.

Indeed, the rights granted to the disabled and the elderly led to their organizing into an association, the Associação Brasileira dos Deficientes Físicos

(ABRADEF), formed in the early 1960s. The ABRADEF later branched out into another association, the DVA. According to a longtime leader of disabled licensed vendors, the official function of the now-defunct ABRADEF was the same as the DVA at the time of fieldwork—namely, to assist the city government with the selection of street vending spots (*marcar os pontos*) and to solve issues of control and inspection.

When a working group was established by mayor Mario Covas in 1983 to design a lasting policy for street vendors, representatives of disabled peddlers were invited to the table. Not surprisingly, the decrees that came out of the group reserved fixed spots in the central district to "seriously disabled" street vendors while authorizing spots beyond that area for other disabled and elderly traders. The able-bodied were only allowed to circulate on the outskirts with so-called human-propelled carts. Despite a continued tug-of-war between the city and the peddlers, this arrangement held under the second administration of Quadros, following Brazil's return to democratic rule in 1985.

Hence, the participation of informal workers in the making of rules did not lead to a significant expansion of the field of legality. On the contrary, as insiders, disabled and elderly vendors defended a status quo in which the able-bodied had to work on the outskirts and on the move. Their action echoes both the politics of social closure, where protected groups seek to keep entry barriers high, and the recursive logic of institutional development, according to which groups that benefit from a particular institutional arrangement invest part of their returns in sustaining it.[6] The fact that São Paulo is a conservative polity where interest groups opposing street vendors wield substantial influence favored policy restraint, as did the authoritarian character of the regime until the mid-1980s. The situation was to change dramatically, however, following the election of Luiza Erundina, the PT candidate for mayor of São Paulo, in 1988.

EXPANDING BOUNDARIES

As a national industrial hub, the city of São Paulo has attracted a large inflow of rural migrants from the poor, predominantly Black northeastern region of Brazil known as the Nordeste, and street vending has long been a niche for Nordestinos who could not find or gave up on factory work. As predominantly dark-skinned outsiders in a marginal trade, these migrants still face hostility from the notoriously conservative local elites. In this context, the unexpected coming to power of Erundina, a social worker hailing from the Nordeste herself and belonging to the leftist PT, gave rise to two diverging interpretations among the public.[7] For the socioeconomic elites, it meant chaos.

For the poor, and especially her fellow Nordestinos, it meant freedom. And so, in a climate of nationwide expansion of civil liberties coupled with high unemployment rates and economic depression, the streets "exploded" with vendors.

As recounted by Aldaiza Sposati, the top public official in charge of street vending policy at the time, the PT leadership was worried about potential attempts by conservative sectors to sabotage the government and brand it as incompetent.[8] The two strategic areas where a boycott was expected were trash collection and street vending. In both sectors, city officials were aware of the need to impose order and show results. At the same time, it did not take long before demands from groups of able-bodied vendors working without licenses on the outskirts of the city made themselves heard, and these demands found echoes among radicalized groups within the ruling coalition.

The absence of an established framework for urban governance compounded the challenge facing city administrators. Brazil adopted a new national constitution the year before, and the division of powers across different levels of government had yet to be defined and implemented. In fact, the so-called General Law of the City (Lei Geral das Cidades), which establishes the prerogatives and duties of city governments, was not signed into law until 1990. As one district administrator put it, "the rules of the game were still in the making."[9] At the local level, the norms of urban governance had to be "invented" in a context marked by improvisation and firefighting. When it came to street vending, "We were just trying to figure out what the hell was going on," Sposati said. "Trying to avoid chaos."[10] All the ingredients of critical junctures—from change of leadership to a sense of crisis and institutional indeterminacy—came together in those turbulent days.

The first step taken by the new administration to stem the rising flow of street vendors was to distribute tickets to all traders found on the streets on the fourth day following Erundina's inauguration. Ticket holders could then register with the city and apply for a license. As it turned out, the distribution of tickets occurred during a holiday period, when many longtime vendors had gone back to their hometowns in the Nordeste. Their complaints prompted the city to issue a new call by which licensed *and* unlicensed vendors who could produce proof of their longtime involvement in street trade (notices of confiscation, testimony from reliable witnesses, etc.) would be added to the database.

Tickets did not amount to licenses, however. The purpose of distributing tickets was to take stock of the growing population of street vendors. After this information was collected, legislation had to be crafted to determine who could sell legally, what, when, and where. Various stakeholders were invited to the table, including representatives of the long-standing organizations of disabled and elderly vendors as well as informal leaders of able-bodied vendors who emerged spontaneously at the time to voice their demands. This marked a shift from the previous era, when "only the disabled were able to talk to authorities, because they were the legal ones."[11]

Negotiations carried on through a series of heated meetings. Sposati recalled one of them: "One of the able-bodied would say: 'We are all equal. We all have the right to work.' A furious disabled man would reply: 'Oh yeah, you think we are equal? Why don't you come here, let me poke out your eye, let me break your arm . . . Let's see how equal we are.' . . . That meeting ended at the police station."[12]

Paraphrasing Tilly, the outrage that this disabled vendor felt reflects the pains of "unmatching." Even though the legal boundary surrounding disabled vendors originated in a chain of political contingencies, by the time of the intended reform, the "myth of rights" had taken root.[13] In the worldview of disabled street vendors, there was an intrinsic link between their bodily condition and the right to a license. To this day, according to an able-bodied licensed vendor, "the disabled cannot conceive that an able-bodied [license holder] would occupy a better location than them."

Perhaps more intriguingly, authorities themselves recognized the legitimacy of these claims. As Sposati pointed out, the disabled and the elderly "had been there [on the streets] for a long time. They had that right, and they saw themselves as entitled to that right."[14] Her stance on the matter is especially telling considering that, as a social worker, she saw the streets as the "worst place" for the disabled and the elderly to be, given pollution, traffic, and related health hazards. Hence, the social and symbolic legacies of the long-standing match between disabled and licensed would condition efforts to expand the legal boundary and widen the distribution of rights in spite of the newfound political will to enfranchise street vendors as a whole.

In the telling of an old-time member of the licensed street vendors' leadership, disabled vendors understood, for their part, that things were about to change. The question was how big a share of the licensed market they would have to surrender. As it happened, this was also a matter of heated debate within the ruling party. Following a month of negotiations and internal debates, state officials settled on an arrangement encapsulated in MD 27,660, issued on February 22, 1989. Two-thirds of the spots would be given to the disabled and the elderly while one-third went to the able-bodied. The disabled and elderly were also given priority in the selection of spots, and the seniority rule was maintained.

In the midst of this urban drama, storeowners did not sit idly by. Having lost their influence over the executive branch, they resorted to the city council. In 1989, councilman Bruno Feder, whose party, the Partido Liberal, represented the interests of commercial elites, put forth a bill aimed at setting limits to what Feder described as "urbanistic terrorism"—that is, the massive spread of street vendors across the city.[15] While drawing largely on the decree issued by the Erundina administration, the bill introduced a two-year expiration date for licenses and established the mandatory requirement of having lived in São Paulo for seven years to be eligible for a license. The bill, which prompted mass protests by street vendors, was vetoed by the mayor; however, the city council approved it with the absolute majority needed to override the veto. ML 11,039 thus became the new legal norm governing street trade. In response to the new law's restrictive provisions, organized street vendors' leaders drew on their political influence and pressured Feder into submitting another bill "correcting the previous one," as a politically influential old-timer put it.[16] The second bill, which was also approved by the council, reestablished the seniority rule, rescinded the requirement of seven-year residency in São Paulo to obtain a license, and abolished the limit on the number of renewals.[17] The prerogatives held by the disabled and the elderly remained intact.

In short, at the end of Erundina's administration, the able-bodied had gained access to the category of licensed street vendors, entering the realm of legality. Echoing the well-known process of political incorporation of labor, when workers came to be represented in government, this transition was a form of legal incorporation.[18] The legal incorporation of the able-bodied in street trade was contentious, however, as it upset a time-honored institutional arrangement with its attendant system of symbolic representations. Legal incorporation was also selective, and selectiveness consolidated over time. Through the reform process, the disabled and the elderly secured their relative advantage in terms of both tenure and location: they still enjoyed the privilege of legality through quotas on licenses, and they preserved the privilege of centrality through priority rights in the selection of spots as well as the seniority rule, which allowed them to maintain their dominance in the much-coveted downtown area. Organized business opposed the expansion of rights, but they were not the only ones. Active efforts by the initial beneficiaries of the licensing program to retain their advantages also explain why, at a time of expansion, other groups did not access the benefits of legality as widely as some reformers had intended. Such feedback mechanisms account for the "stickiness" of legal boundaries and the skewed distribution of rights over time.[19]

Rights on the Ground

Legal norms have implications beyond their common treatment in the literature on informality as either abstract structures or elements of background.
In particular, formal rules draw the edge of the law—that is, the line that
separates potential rights-bearers from virtual outlaws, around which many
symbolic and material struggles unfold. Hence, the vagaries of lawmaking are
not foreign to the politics of informality. At the same time, a spotlight on the
formal processes of legality should not conceal the gap that defines informality between the law on the books and the daily practice of business. Nor are
legislative processes independent from the politics of implementation and
enforcement.

In São Paulo, after the new legislation was in place, the focus of the struggle shifted to its implementation. Despite the quotas for licenses established
in the new law and the consultative role granted to the Commissões Perma-
nentes de Ambulantes (CPAs, Permanent Commissions on Street Vendors),
the power of issuing and canceling licenses was left in the hands of district
administrators who delegated such tasks to their subordinates. In the downtown district of Sé, where the most profitable spots were located, the struggle
to define the who, the when, and the where of street vending was particularly intense. The limited staff could hardly cope with the mass of unlicensed
vendors, and suspicions of corruption hung over inspectors from previous
administrations.[20]

Access to officials with decision-making powers became a key asset for
street vendors in this context. For their part, city officials were looking for
civil society partners to help them police the streets. As Cross notes, resource-
wanting state authorities tend to rely on leaders of street vendors organizations to implement their policies.[21] In the recollections of a city employee,
the larger the number of street vendors that a given leader could mobilize,
the more the city would be willing to engage in negotiations with her. Many
associations of street vendors emerged at the time, some of which had but a
handful of members. Once again, in this landscape, long-standing organizations of disabled and elderly peddlers had an edge. As legitimate interlocutors
with a large and established following, leaders of these organizations briefed
local officials on attempts by other groups to "take over" the streets. "In order
to evict the newcomers, we had to ally ourselves with the established ones," a
district administrator explained.[22]

The bias toward organization—which is itself a product of time—is not
the only bias at work in the distribution of rights through the implementation process, however. The period that followed Erundina's tenure reveals

the dark side of the discrepancy between the books and the streets—namely, extortion. The power to extract resources unlawfully from informal workers is usually associated with enforcement. Legal norms provide law enforcement agents the perfect tool to blackmail economic actors whose livelihoods stand, by definition, at variance with the law. A closer look at the "mafia" that ruled São Paulo in the 1990s shows how interconnected rule-making, implementation, and enforcement can be, however. Racketeering loomed large, but so did other corrupt practices involving high-level policy decisions and new regulations—all of which played a part in keeping disadvantaged vendors at the margins of legality.

A CORRUPT MIX

The day after Paulo Maluf, a fixture in *paulista* politics and a longtime fugitive on Interpol's wanted list for money-laundering and other white-collar crimes, took over from Erundina as mayor of São Paulo, police forces carried out a raid—known in Portuguese as *blitz*—in the downtown streets. Gilberto Monteiro da Silva, one of the street vendors working on the iconic bridge of Santa Ifigênia at the time, said at a hearing that he quickly understood what the raid was about: city officials were putting pressure on street vendors to raise the ante. Organizing vendors and collecting bribes to pay city officials, as he had done, were the only way for vendors to stay in business.

Collecting bribes to turn a blind eye on infractions was not the only way in which state officials monetized the uncertain legal status of street vendors, however. In the district of Lapa, where a councilman was raising funds for his brother's campaign for a seat at the state legislature, and in the downtown district of Sé, district administrations sold licenses.[23] In Penha, another district where corruption ran rampant, officials stopped short of peddling licenses but offered to add the names of prospective food vendors to the roster used by inspectors, for a fee. A street vendor caught by the police collecting bribes, who was married to a municipal inspector, charged for information about impending raids. Officials also asked for money from licensed vendors to let them engage in other infractions, such as setting up stalls larger than regulation, running multiple stalls, changing locations, and so on. Confiscated merchandise was itself an asset to be squeezed, either by requesting a kickback to return it to its owner, by embezzling it, or, as a witness in the second of two investigative committees (CPIs, commissão parlamentar de inquérito) set up in the city council to probe the bribery networks testified to everyone's dismay, by sending it to the house of the councilman who "owned" the district for private use at his parties. And the same politicians who received under-the-table cash payments (and checks) from street vendors would raise illegal campaign money from storeowners with the promise that, if elected, they would rid the streets of vendors, as Afonso José da Silva (a.k.a. Afonso Camelô), the historic leader of street vendors in the neighborhood of Brás, once made public on live TV.[24]

The collusion between the executive and legislative branches had an institutional basis, so to speak. Because mayors depend on support from the city council to carry out their agenda, they are prone to cut deals with council members who are elected through a system of proportional representation. Leaving aside instances of blatant vote buying through direct under-the-table payments—in which Maluf's anointed successor reportedly engaged to save his political skin—the standard arrangement consisted of bestowing individual council members control over a particular administrative district. The political "owners" of the district would indicate a person loyal to them, whom the mayor would appoint as district administrator, along with other employees tied to the council member. By these means, the boss of the downtown district of Sé, who was eventually impeached, put his brother-in-law at the helm of the district. In Pirituba, a former councilwoman placed her own brother. The CPI investigations revealed that, in those places, district administrations would operate as money-making schemes based on the extortion of a variety of businesses or private citizens requiring or lacking some kind of official permit, street vendors among them. According to José Eduardo Cardozo, the PT councilman who presided over both CPIs, the biggest innovation he observed between the first, established in 1995, and the second, set up in 1999, was that local district inspectors—known as *fiscal* in singular and *fiscais* in plural—were more prone to designate a street vendor to collect and deliver the bribes instead of doing the rounds themselves.[25]

The political economy unveiled by the investigative committees on the so-called inspectors' mafia calls into question the viability of policy prescriptions that urge governments to simply extend or enshrine the rights of unlicensed vendors. The formalization agenda, which rose to the status of conventional policy wisdom following the publication of Hernando De Soto's bestseller *The Other Path* in 1986, posits that recognizing the informal rights of disenfranchised workers and entrepreneurs through property titles has the potential to unleash a virtuous cycle of investment and growth.[26] Contrary to De Soto's fantasies, however, a formalizing spirit cannot descend on the streets of Bangkok or Harare and deliver to each vendor a bundle of enforceable rights that they will exercise in neutral fashion. Resistance from formal businesses or organized labor is not the only obstacle to enfranchisement, moreover. The political game feeds off the gray zone of irregularity and limits the scope of efforts to expand the field of legality. As the rather extreme case of São Paulo shows, vested interests within the legislative body had a grip on the law and used it to their advantage.[27] The power to make, enforce, or circumvent the rules gave authorities, including lawmakers, the power to extract money. They even monetized legal incorporation by selling licenses. And they created rules that suited their purposes. The highest-ranking official in charge of street vending policy under Maluf's successor, Celso Pitta, was found guilty of compelling licensed vendors to purchase stalls from a particular company, whose owner confessed to paying bribes to the official's subordinates, on pain of seeing their licenses revoked.[28] The stalls were lavishly marked up and, as it turns out, unfit for disabled vendors.

MARGINAL POWERS

There is no evidence that the old guard of disabled licensed vendors played an active part in the scheme—or *esquema*, to use Brazilians' favored word for organized corruption—of the inspectors' mafia.[29] In fact, some of them testified against city officials in the CPIs. But licensed street vendors had lost the power to make the rules. The findings of the first CPI inspired its chairman, Cardozo, to work on a municipal bill in concert with licensed street vendors associations. By then, the association representing the disabled peddlers, the DVA, had allied itself with a group of licensed, able-bodied downtown street vendors and founded the Union of the Licensed. The Union achieved legal recognition and became the official representative of licensed street vendors in the city, even though the DVA—and especially its longtime leader—remained highly influential. Not surprisingly, the crafters of this new bill left untouched the rights associated with seniority and disability. Among the proposed changes were the right to receive another spot in case of revocation, the right to transfer the license to a close relative in the event of death, and the right to use the stall for advertisement. Organized licensed vendors never gathered enough support to pass the bill or even bring it to the floor, however. Their legislative influence is conditioned by a constellation of interests that are sometimes aligned with their demands—especially when it comes to limiting access to licenses for other vendors—and often opposed to them.

The process behind the bill sheds some light on the thorny politics of street vending nonetheless. Three city council members, including two from the PT, were working on separate bills. It appears that Aldaiza Sposati, then a PT councilwoman, worked with representatives of another street vendors' organization, the Sindicato de Trabalhadores da Economia Informal de São Paulo (SINTEIN). Her proposal built on social economy principles. At city council hearing in which the three political actors came together to work out a joint bill, Sposati suggested letting street vendors cooperatives or associations manage licenses themselves, collectively—as opposed to the current system in which the city granted nominal individual licenses. The idea found its way into the bill.

While each politician was probably courting votes and enlisted street vendors' leaders as partners to that effect, the minutes of the hearing also convey an intent to bring some order and stability into the street vending economy—to the benefit of (established) street vendors. Cardozo said it was time to stop treating the street vendor "like a beggar, like a thug. The street vendor has to be treated like a citizen."[30] The text thus included provisions for the training and certification of inspectors who are not "dealing with a cat, with an animal," Cardozo added. "[They are] dealing with people (*gente*)." To be respected, inspectors had to treat street vendors with respect. Then again, the bill never reached the floor. (Cardozo, on the other hand, would go on to become Minister of Justice under Lula and Dilma Rousseff's attorney during her impeachment trials, thanks in part to the visibility he gained as head of the first and second CPI in São Paulo).

In Retrospect

Rights are a product of history. They arise from political arrangements that grant certain groups institutional access to resources and that, by the same token, create constituencies prone to defend "their" rights. Since property rights are exclusive by definition, the distribution of property rights—including time- and use-limited rights vested in licenses—draws a line between haves (rights) and have-nots. A range of players have a stake in where that line falls and exert influence on it. Hence, street-level exchanges between cops and vendors or hands-off approaches at higher levels of government make up only a small part of the web of conflicting interests and dubious political strategies that govern, and profit from, informal economies. Vested interests surrounding the regulation of street trade reach well within the political body in charge of making laws—without whose support any large-scale policy to bring unlicensed vendors under the helm of legality is doomed—in patterns far more complex than the exclusion of small players by big business or formal labor. And upsetting such patterns carries risks.

Monteiro Da Silva was one of the first street vendors to come forward during the hearings of the second CPI. He described his role as a bribe collector as "hell." He said he had no choice but to take it up and later felt trapped in it. "On the streets," he said, rather ominously, "you either take part in the

esquema or you die. . . . There is no way out."[31] His agony is telling. It implies
that the disciplining power of the state extends to those at the margins of the
law and feeds off their marginality. Exposing the corruption scheme was apparently liberating for the vendor, who later celebrated the publication of a
book by a journalist on the case. Inspectors themselves showed relief during
hearings, when they finally opened up. However, like Afonso Camelô, the
street vendors' leader who denounced corruption on TV, Monteiro Da Silva
was later targeted by gunmen and paid with his life. Disabled vendors also
suffered retaliation under Pitta, Maluf's successor, who took revenge against
accusations of corruption by canceling licenses. According to a longtime disabled vendor, several of his disabled colleagues and friends died from stress-
related health problems as a result. Pitta then took the opposite route of issuing a call that let anyone with a disability apply for a street vending license.
His term ended in disgrace before he was able to carry out his plan.

✶

Whereas the previous chapter fleshes out the meaning and value of the
boundaries of legality in street vending, this chapter examines their making
as a historical process. In a corrupt political economy like the one governing São Paulo from the mid- to the late 1990s, exclusion is not only a way to
gather votes or political support by claiming to fend off "intruders," as some
of the locals see street vendors; it is also a means to extract revenue from
outsiders—in this case unlicensed street vendors—by charging them to let
them work. But licensed vendors suffered, too, from the threat of demotion.
As informal citizens whose rights are, by definition, ambiguous, they fell prey
to a range of extortion and intimidation tactics. The definitive loss of citizenship is rare, as governments only pursue it in extreme cases, but citizenship
is understood here as a gradient in which a country's residents or visitors,
having less rights, occupy the shaded regions, and the power of removing
their status is often used by authorities, if not for revenue, for disciplining
purposes. Licensed street vendors are never free from this threat.

   Not all administrations were as corrupt and baleful as those of Maluf and
Pitta, but even council members from opposition parties, like the PT, were
prone to strike deals with organized street vendors, if not for money, for votes,
and political representation of informal workers' interests is inevitably partial
and biased in this regard. The return to power of the PT in the early 2000s
did not fundamentally alter the game. Policing was relaxed, and unlicensed
vendors proliferated, but only a fraction of the more than 22,000 applicants
registered in the call issued under Pitta were granted a license. Downtown,
according to the final report of a third CPI, "the executive branch assigned,

very timidly, only 1,244 spots for [licensed] street vendors in the district of
Sé [despite receiving] 5,000 applications."[32] In an area of downtown called
Centro Novo, only the "upper crust" (*a crema*) of licensed vendors remained
on the streets, according to a representative of storeowners and fierce op-
ponent of street vendors. In other words, licensed vendors managed to "hold
the line" through their connections. Disaffected street vendors complained
that by sitting in the CPAs and having access to city officials, the "aristocracy"
of licensed vendors were able to punish nonaffiliates or dissenters and benefit the ruling clique. The PT state official in charge of street vending policy
at the time himself acknowledged that the Union and DVA leadership, with
whom he had built personal ties, had a "conservative" agenda. The stability in the distribution of rights across regimes and administrations makes
it all the more perplexing that even the consolidated rights of disabled and
elderly vendors came under threat, in dramatic fashion, after the PT failed to
secure reelection in the mid-2000s, ushering a dark era for São Paulo's street
vendors.

5

The Right Narrative

Ideas about where the limit of legality runs and who is or should be protected flourish on both sides of the line—or lines—as well as within the government bodies in charge of makings laws and enforcing them. Collective or individual, these beliefs shape legality on the ground. According to critical legal scholarship, the law itself is nothing but a set of institutionalized beliefs. The *unbearable lightness of rights*, as McCann calls it, comes from them being at once fundamentally abstract and very real.[1] Rights are what we think they are, or, in case of a dispute, what judicial authorities say they are.

In its most common and intuitive form, a policy of disenfranchisement involves stripping members of a given group of their rights. When changing the law to that effect is not politically viable, creative strategies emerge that get at the essence of rights, their meaning(s), and, by extension, the boundaries of legality. If contested, these strategies unleash interpretative struggles within and around the institutions of justice. This chapter focuses on efforts to undo street vendors and deprive them of any legal status as well as on the implications of the ensuing struggle for our understanding of the margins of legality. Toward the end, the personal story of Valdira fleshes out the travails of those who go through an expulsion from the field of legality while clinging to their rights or the memory thereof.

A Wave of Repression

Even by the standards of the crackdown on street vendors, squatters, and other informal sector groups that swept across the urban Global South at the turn of the century, the onslaught experienced by street traders in São Paulo from 2005 to 2012 was fierce. Street vendors' leaders referred to it as "a massacre" and an "attempt at extermination."[2] It began in early 2005 with the inauguration of Serra, a right-leaning politician with close ties to the *paulista* business elite, as mayor of São Paulo. His election marked a shift in urban policy toward a more punitive, law-and-order approach that consolidated after Serra stepped down in 2006 to run for governor and was replaced by his vice mayor, Kassab. Kassab was vice president of São Paulo's main commercial association: the Associação Comercial de São Paulo (ACSP). Soon after becoming mayor, he launched a program called Clean City (*cidade limpa*) that forbade advertising in public spaces. The removal of street vendors was not an official item on the agenda, yet pressures on street traders intensified.

In 2009, the Kassab administration signed an agreement with the chief commanding officer of the MP, a police corps under the helm of the state government. By the terms of this agreement, known as Operação Delegada, which was renewed for three years in 2011, 3,900 armed MP agents in uniform were to patrol irregular street vending activities in their off-duty time. Until then, the policing of street vending was the preserve of the Guarda Civil Metropolitana, a police force denounced as brutal, venal, and unprofessional by vendors in interviews. The professional training and corporate ethos of the MP made it harder for vendors to negotiate enforcement with individual agents. Kassab also staffed the city government with MP officers. Unlike some of his predecessors' impulsive acts of political revenge, which backfired, Kassab's methodical elimination campaign made sure to circumvent legal safeguards by abiding by procedural norms and targeting vendors one by one, over a long period of time, in its effort to strip them of their rights and titles. It was a surreptitious policy of planned disenfranchisement. Its goal was to extinguish legal status in street trade. How did licensed vendors survive?

Political Resistance

Given its legal precariousness, informal trade is heavily dependent on politics. Clientelistic arrangements by which groups of vendors plead allegiance to a political patron who, in return, protects their freedom to work are common in the Global South.[3] In the case of unlicensed vendors—a more volatile and porous population—arrangements of this nature can be tacit, with rulers simply foregoing their law enforcement duties in poor-majority districts while expecting votes in return.[4] In circumscribed spaces such as parks or squares, a more explicit political bargain with a more or less stable group of unlicensed vendors is possible if they are organized.

Licensing, on the other hand, creates a bounded, identifiable constituency that is vulnerable enough to still require protection but whose contours are precise enough for it to be mobilized—and monitored—by its leadership come election time, even when it is spread across a wide geographic area. In São Paulo, Tristan, the PT councilman, was the political patron of licensed street vendors, especially disabled ones, and the Union and the DVA acted as his electoral brokers. According to the DVA vice president, the relationship with the PT originated in a "personal link" to a councilwoman who, as a member of a policy commission in the early 1980s, supported street vendors. The councilwoman introduced them to Rubens Possati, a party member and activist, who then introduced licensed vendors to Tristan, for whom he worked as an assistant. The tightness of these ties was palpable. Possati described the Union vice president as the "brains of the street" (o intellectual da rua), and the Union vice president later returned the compliment by describing Possati as "the man who knows everything . . . [who] is not moved by someone crying [and] works within the law." Their connection was strong enough that Possati recalled how, while working in the city government, he once contacted the vice president of the DVA and told him to "get [his] people on the streets" and stage a protest. The leader "brought two thousand street vendors [in front of the district administration building] and that's how the problem got solved."

One of the reasons eviction campaigns often fall short of their stated goals, according to Cross, is this reciprocal dependence of informal economies on politics, the other reason being that mid- and street-level bureaucrats have stronger personal incentives to accept bribes than to enforce the law.[5] If the mayor or his staff start to persecute vendors too aggressively, the political patron intervenes to defend his electoral basis, be it at the top or with mid-level officials. A street vendor leader cited the hypothetical example of a councilman making a phone call to a district administrator and asking her to leave "that street vendor by the flower shop alone" because "he's my friend." Cross uses the term state integration to refer to the level of alignment in the interests of state officials at different echelons of government to pursue a given policy—usually one of repression.[6] High levels of state integration are rare.

By staffing the city government with MP officers while deploying the ranks against street vendors under Operação Delegada, Kassab achieved such unity of purpose. Indeed, Kassab appointed retired coroneis (i.e., the highest-ranking officers in the MP) to the head of all but one of the thirty-one administrative districts (subprefeituras) that made up the city. Another retired MP officer was placed at the head of the SCS, the administrative department in charge of coordinating policy implementation—including the regulation of street vending—across districts. A number of lower-rank MP officers filled mid-level positions within district administrations citywide. As an NGO worker put it, Kassab "militarized" the city government. In so doing, he insulated the administration from political pressures emanating from the city council. As the campaign proceeded, Tristan and his staff lobbied the city administration officials but only managed to delay evictions on an individual basis.

Framing the Law

Kassab went after both licensed and unlicensed street vendors. According to ML 11,039, street vending licenses are "precarious, onerous, individual, and non-transferable."[7] Precariousness is thus written into the law; the rights associated with license holding can be rescinded without much trouble. In fact, licenses can be terminated in two ways: through revocation or cancellation. Revocation refers to the withdrawal of licenses from a group of street vendors with stalls at a particular location, such as a street or a square. It can be enacted unilaterally by the city government in the name of a loosely specified "public interest." Additionally, a license holder who incurs three violations may face cancellation of her license. Either way, the person loses the right to trade in public spaces.

The city government set out to revoke licenses in various street vending concentrations—known as *bolsões*—while cancellations of individual licenses increased dramatically based on ruthless sanctioning practices. Inspectors would visit the same stall two or three times a day (up to six times in one account) and sanction minor infractions that had theretofore been tolerated, such as the hanging of products from the corner of the stall's thatch.

In its efforts to increase cancellations, the Kassab administration went further. Its strategy consisted of implementing a rigorist interpretation of the law that altered not just the spirit but the meaning of norms. This restrictive interpretation made it compulsory for license holders to remain at their stalls at all times during opening hours and to keep their stalls open throughout the day. It turned a right into an obligation. Remembering those years, vendors alluded to draconian policing practices such as the sanctioning of stall owners who had temporarily left their stall to use the restroom. The goal of Kasab's legalist approach was to dismantle whatever legal protection licensed vendors enjoyed and clear the way for evictions.

When a license is canceled, vendors can dispute the infractions leading to the cancellation or plea for a pardon from the district administrator. Oftentimes, however, street vendors only found out about the cancellation of their licenses after the deadline for administrative dispute had passed. Those who launched administrative proceedings requesting a review of the decision came up against the same authority that had sought the cancellation in the first place. In this regard, the appointment of MP personnel to administrative offices ensured the enforcement of the mayor's hard line. Insights into these administrative processes obtained through interviews and consultation of documents attest to an adamant posture on the part of administrators who systematically rejected appeals by street vendors.

This approach had a disarming effect. Before a public defender and an NGO lawyer filed the lawsuit that led to the preliminary injunction that ensured the survival of licensed street vendors as an occupational group, several individual vendors sought judicial redress on their own. Most of these efforts fell through, however. In fact, some of these cases landed on the dockets of the same judge who later granted a preliminary injunction to licensed vendors as a group. As the judge pointed out in an interview, individual lawsuits had little chance of succeeding because the law favors the city. "They have no rights [*não tem direito a nada*]," she said, referring to street vendors. "If [the city] follows the procedure, they have no rights."[8]

A lawyer who represented individual street vendors noted that "it's hard enough to obtain a preliminary injunction [to prevent an eviction], let alone win a case. For every five injunctions you get, you only win one case."[9] The same interviewee further noted that refusals by judges to grant individual preliminary injunctions under Kassab, which increased over time, often did not address the plaintiff's claims but simply cited the legally embedded "precarious" character of the licenses and the right of the city to unilaterally revoke them. This rationale was questionably extended to instances of license cancellation, which result, in theory, from an accumulation of three administrative infractions by the license holder. And even when they had a case, poorly represented street vendors sometimes used the wrong legal instrument. Instead of requesting a preliminary injunction, which examines the merits, they requested a writ of mandate (*mandado de segurança*), which is meant to safeguard civil liberties and only takes procedural aspects into account.

Not surprisingly, in this context, many street vendors chose to not take legal action at all, even when they believed that their licenses had been unlawfully canceled. In the neighborhood of Brás, where licenses were revoked in 2009, an employee of the local association said that they did not file a lawsuit because "the outcome was predictable." A vendor in Jabaquara said she did not join a class action because she knew it was "not going to work." The costs of launching a judicial process can be substantial, moreover, and many street vendors cannot afford them. The feeling that the city was enforcing the law—however distortedly—contributed to a lack of challenge. "He [Kassab] struck

us down by the book [*cassou dentro da lei*]," an interviewee said. It helped
Kassab's cause that the rights of street vendors are tenuous and that the justice
system was stacked against them.

The licensed population shrank as a result. In 2004, on the eve of Serra
and Kassab's coming to power, there were an estimated 5,500 licensed vendors
in São Paulo. By 2009, more than a third of the licenses had been revoked or
canceled. Downtown, the numbers went from 1,222 licensed vendors in 2005 to
744 in 2006 and 550 in 2009. Another 1,930 licenses were terminated across the
city over the next two years. Then, on May 19, 2012, the incrementalist approach
suffered a twist: Kassab revoked all standing licenses by municipal decree. Every street vending zone was declared forbidden, and the remaining licensed
vendors across the city were given thirty days to clear out. In the view of a
particularly insightful leader of licensed street vendors, this was an attempt to
"finish the job" after Kassab realized that the time window was closing; the end
of his term approached, and he had little chance of winning reelection.

THE LEGACY OF POLITICS

Unlike previous historical periods, when the struggle of licensed street vendors revolved around defining the contours of the legal framework or shaping
its implementation, the era of criminalization, which started under Kassab,
ushered a scramble for survival. Fear and helplessness dominated street vendors' daily experiences. Some, like Valdira, went into unlicensed vending or
related trades after losing their titles; many reportedly died.

While the big picture of the run-up to the lawsuit and preliminary injunction is one of overwhelming defeat, a closer look brings out some nuances in
the timing and impact of license terminations and evictions. Informal politics in their traditional, clientelistic version failed to reverse the course of the
eviction campaign, but it delayed the outcome for some vendors. After the
Serra and Kassab ticket won the mayoral race, Possati went on to work as
an assistant to Tristan. In that capacity, he sometimes lobbied city officials
on behalf of street vendors. In an interview, Possati complained that city officials from the Kassab administration paid no heed to the street vendors'
pleas. "We would arrive there, tell them what was going on, and they would
tell us: 'That's not possible. There must be a mistake. We'll look into this.'
Then, the next day, they did the same thing worse."[10] On the other hand, the
former downtown district administrator under Kassab said that he obliged
representatives of licensed vendors with numerous concessions. "They would
come and ask for favors," he said. "The number of times that I broke the rules
so they could get a vendor here, transfer him there, when by law I should

have canceled his license." In fact, this official developed friendly relations
with both Tristan and the president of the Union. He also claimed that he
"preserved the disabled until the end . . . for social reasons. Out of compassion I let guys work who were not within the rules. They had done things that
were wrong, but I gave them another chance."[11] Charitable feelings aside, it is
likely that the councilman and his staff's requests for leniency with the district administrator concerned disabled vendors above all—Tristan's primary
constituency among street vendors.

Sephir, another disabled vendor with political connections—not to
Tristan, but to a state congresswoman, Celia Leão, who was herself disabled
and a champion of disability rights—used those connections to recover her
license. It had been taken from her by the downtown chief of inspectors, who
claimed that Sephir had leased her stall, which is illegal. The congresswoman's office called the city official. The first time, he didn't answer. The second
time, Celia's lawyer made the call, and the official agreed to return Sephir's
documents but didn't. The third time, the lawyer "went tough on him," and
the civil servant relented. It may have helped that Leão belonged to the PSDB,
a right-wing party allied with Kassab's party at the time.[12]

Then, on May 19, 2012, following the ban, every licensed vendor lost the
right to practice street trade. And yet, buying time, as some licensed vendors
had managed to do, serendipitously enabled them to preserve their right to
work in the long run. Indeed, the preliminary injunction issued the following month, on June 4, set a cutoff date of 2012, meaning only those vendors
whose licenses were revoked or canceled that year could legally carry on with
their trade. About fifteen hundred vendors fell in that category, among them
a higher proportion of disabled vendors and their leaders, as noted in the previous chapter. Although the evidence is circumstantial, it suggests that their
connections to Tristan and their organization may have allowed this group of
vendors to put off cancellations and evictions until 2012.

The bigger mystery, however, is that a court order protecting the rights
of workers without rights had been issued. According to the Union president, the injunction saved street vendors as an occupational group (*salvou a
categoria*). It was perceived by some as something of a miracle. As with the
administration's unconventional rationale for cancellations, the reinterpreta-
tion of the law and of the rights of street vendors played a fundamental role.

The Road to Court

It is unusual for a dispute between the state and informal workers to wind
up in a court of law. Part of the problem lies in the many hurdles preventing

marginalized social groups from accessing justice. Another issue is informal workers' shady relation to the law itself. After all, street vending licenses are revocable, and both licensed and unlicensed vendors engage in a host of ir-regularities that can easily be used against them in court. Instances of judicial decisions favoring street vendors are unsurprisingly rare.

A common ingredient in stories of legal mobilization is the role of support structures and civil society actors bringing cases on behalf of disadvantaged groups.[13] In *Courting Social Justice*, Daniel Brinks and Varun Gauri empha-size for their part the receptiveness of courts.[14] In São Paulo, it took both, plus a good deal of commitment, cooperation, and willingness to fight the odds. The depth of coordination between state and nonstate actors calls into ques-tion, once again, common views of civil society.

In Somers's theory of citizenship, civil society is a dynamic arena that hosts a variety of groups. At its best, it informs the public debate and holds the state to account; at its worst, it becomes an appendix of the state or the market. Its independence is therefore key to its public interest function.[15] By contrast, Salo Coslovsky stresses the links between civil society and government bodies pur-suing social justice goals, such as the Ministério Público or public defenders.[16] In São Paulo, the office of the public defender, which provides free legal assis-tance and litigation services to indigent citizens and underprivileged (*hiposufi-cientes*) social categories, arose from joint efforts by government attorneys and "scholars, social activists and representatives of social movements, progressive religious groups and NGOs" to create a more effective judicial service repre-senting disadvantaged constituencies.[17] In their daily workings, "channels of mutual influence . . . include a number of informal connections between public officials and outside agents that can be quite consequential."[18]

What stands out in the case at hand regarding the collaboration of a public defender and an NGO is not just the joint filing of a class action lawsuit that bore some fruits against all odds but the outlining of a narrative upon which the rights of street vendors were provisionally restored. In contrast to the hidebound reading of legal norms pushed by the city government to justify evictions, the rationale for the protective court order broadened the under-standing of street vendors' place in the city while breathing new life—and meaning—into their rights.

A NEW ALLY

Upon realizing that their efforts to forestall the looming extinction of their constituency through politics as usual fell consistently short, the Union and DVA planned a protest in early 2012. For this protest, the leadership of licensed vendors extended an invitation to participants of the Street Vendors' Assembly, a forum founded in 2010 by an NGO—the CIW—as an arena to debate inclusive policy and promote the empowerment of street vendors. This moment of unity notwithstanding, tensions between both camps ran high. The CIW employees—among them lawyers, researchers, and social workers—looked down on the traditional leadership of licensed street vendors as active members in a sectarian, clientelistic system. In fact, the Assembly established by the CIW gathered street vendors and vendors' leaders from different parts of the city, most of whom had become alienated from the leadership of the Union. On the other hand, the Union and DVA leaders saw the CIW as a novice outsider impinging on their turf. Hence, the DVA and the Union boycotted a subsequent demonstration organized by the Street Vendors' Assembly by, according to a CIW employee, giving the order to their members not to attend the event.

Concurrently, however, the CIW was studying strategies to counteract the mayor's elimination policy. As part of a separate project on issues of access to housing, the CIW hosted a legal services unit that had worked closely with public defenders. In Brazil, public defenders are entitled to file class actions on behalf of disadvantaged groups, especially when the damages inflicted or foreseen are regarded as affecting the public interest. A class action filed on these grounds is called an *ação civil pública* (ACP).

Drawing on their legal expertise and networks, CIW workers reached out to various members of the judiciary, including two public defenders, to probe the possibility of launching legal proceedings against Kassab's evictions. While none of their initial contacts agreed to get involved, one of them pointed the CIW to Bruno Miragaia, a public defender who, in March 2012, had filed a class action on behalf of a cluster of about two hundred street vendors whose licenses had been revoked by the Kassab administration in the district of São Miguel Paulista. On May 25, the lower court judge assigned to the case, Judge Carmen Teijeiro, issued a preliminary injunction compelling the city to suspend evictions in São Miguel. The injunction cited a procedural flaw in the revocation process: authorities had not convened the consultative body known as CPA, which, according to the municipal ordinance regulating street trade, has to be heard on matters related to the relocation of street vendors or the revocation of their licenses.

The decision by Miragaia to request an injunction for the vendors of São Miguel was not a matter of course. Other members of the judiciary, called on to take action, had declined. At a rally, Tristan, the political patron of licensed vendors, complained that the Ministério Público, a judicial institution akin to the ombudsman, bailed on them (*se omitiu*). According to Tristan, the *promotores*, as its attorneys are known, told him: "It's legal [what Kassab is doing]. The city regulates street trade. There's nothing we can do." Teijeiro herself reported getting pushback when she issued the injunction in favor of street vendors, both from some of her colleagues who did not agree with her decision and on her Twitter account, with messages like "Why don't you put those peddlers in your doorstep?" What motivated Miragaia to file the lawsuit was, in his telling, a personal sympathy for street vendors fueled by childhood memories of shopping in the neighborhood with his mother and interacting with them.[19]

As it happened, Miragaia had worked for another public defender with close ties to the CIW. According to one of the NGO workers involved in the process, this common acquaintance facilitated trust and cooperation. And so, after the judge granted the first preliminary injunction for the vendors of São Miguel Paulista, Miragaia and the CIW began working together on a new class action encompassing licensed street vendors in the city as a whole. The second class action insisted on the "deliberate" and "systematic" policy pursued by the Kassab administration to eliminate street vending across the city as well as on the absence of any urban planning criteria governing the process. By virtue of a provision to avoid contradictory jurisprudence, the lawsuit was assigned to the same judge, who granted the plaintiffs another preliminary injunction staying evictions citywide for street vendors dispossessed of their licenses in 2012.

The judicial decision lays out the rationale, which draws on the plaintiff's arguments. The devil is in the purpose behind the license cancellation and revocation measures. If the purpose was to enforce the law, then cancellations could only be disputed on merit, and the odds were stacked against vendors. If, on the other hand, these measures fit into a broader urbanistic project—"a city without peddlers," as a street vendor once put it, referring to the image São Paulo sought to project to international audiences—then they entered a different realm of law, known in Portuguese as *direito difuso*, where group rights are in play. In granting the *liminar* (preliminary injunction), the judge recognized that such was, indeed, the intent of the city. Echoing the claims of the lawsuit, the rationale for the court order built on a stepwise reasoning according to which: (1) the expediency, frequency, and scope of the revocations and cancellations denoted a general intent by the city administration to eliminate street vending; (2) such a project transcended administrative functions and impinged on the realm of urban planning; (3) by virtue of a set of constitutional provisions, urban planning had to be carried out in a democratic and participatory manner; and (4) the city administration failed to engage diverse social constituencies forming the urban environment, including street vendors themselves, despite having at its disposal the institutional tools to do so (e.g., the CPAs). Underlying the legal analysis and interpretation is a clash between a view of the law as a tool to enact a given conception of the city from above and the participatory principles enshrined in Brazil's constitution, which the judge affirmed. Articulating their bearing on the case was a challenge in which civil society played an important and creative role.

The conventional view of civil society actors in instances of legal mobilization on behalf of disadvantaged communities is that of brokers. Stuart Wilson thus describes the role of a nonprofit in Johannesburg as simply "link[ing] slum dwellers up with competent legal assistance."[20] In São Paulo, the NGO connected street vendors with the public defender, but its contribution went far beyond that. It helped craft a new authoritative reading of the city's actions that stopped the disenfranchisement of vendors in its tracks. In the absence of any public statement belying their intentions, which officials in the Kassab administration were careful not to make, showing intent or simply seeing the pattern behind individual cases of license cancellations scattered across administrative districts and courthouses was not a given. The NGO was able to map the trend, and, in so doing, build the case, thanks to its numerous ties to street vending. A team of workers from the NGO was set up to collect newspaper articles as well as announcements and reports from the city's newspaper of public record. Concurrently, CIW employees asked street vendors' leaders to submit paperwork, such as the fines and notices of license cancellation, attesting to the lack of proper administrative procedure and motivation. According to a CIW worker involved in the process, "it was easy to obtain those documents thanks to the trust relations [with street vendors] already established in our biweekly meetings [of the Street Vendors' Assembly]."[21] The process echoes Coslovsky's argument that interconnections between government bodies like the public defenders' office and civil society create "a form of distributed intelligence that gives formally autonomous agents direction and thrust."[22]

Yet the judge's receptiveness to these efforts, despite the pressures and backlash, was also key. Her distancing from other members of her profession in her view of street vendors shows that individual dispositions mattered more, in this case, than the overall inclination of the courts, which ended up supporting street vendors on appeal but had proven impervious to their plight until then. Beyond the courts themselves, the existence of the office of the public defender, which had both the competence and the function of bringing class actions against the state on behalf of disenfranchised groups, increased the receptiveness of the justice system, even if a personal inclination and sympathy toward the group were what got the public defender involved in the first place.

At a deeper level, this struggle shows that the rights of informal workers are a matter of interpretation. When they exist, those rights are fragile, even on paper. Instead of changing the law, Kassab enforced a literal reading of the rules. It was a subtle strategy aimed at extinguishing the rights of street vendors by removing them from the field of legality one by one, or in small groups, while adhering to the letter of the law. The result was a massive loss of rights and a vanishing of legality as a protective space. The judge's decision to bring a new authoritative reading of rules and rights to bear on the case reestablished the boundary and saved a fraction of workers. It did not go unchallenged.

Politics Enter Justice

Kassab had, as a lawyer put it, "instrumentalized the law to political ends." His legalism violated the spirit of the law in pursuit of a political agenda. Instead of sending politics back to the usual arena of day-to-day negotiations between street vendors and the state, however, the lawsuit imported the politics into the justice system. The injunction unleashed an unprecedented sequence of moves and countermoves—a battle in which the boundaries of judicial competence were considerably stretched.

Using a legal prerogative inherited from predemocratic times, the city government filed a stay of execution—known as *suspensão de liminar*— against the preliminary injunction issued by Teijeiro. Such a request is automatically assigned to the president of the Justice Tribunal (JT)—the state's highest court—who ruled in favor of the city government, thus overturning the injunction and clearing the way for the coercive removal of stalls by the initial June 19 deadline. The move was legal, if high-handed. According to Teijeiro, the fact that the arbiter is known in advance to be the president of the JT, in contrast to another recourse instrument that would have assigned the matter to a panel of three randomly selected JT judges, makes the *suspensão de liminar* more akin to a political tool.[23]

The public defender and the CIW lawyer who authored the class action responded by filing an appeal against the decision from the president of the JT. The appeal was to be ruled by a special committee of twenty-five JT high magistrates (*desembargadores*) scheduled to convene on June 27—eight days after the eviction deadline. Alleging that there was an "imminent risk" of "irreparable damage" if evictions were carried out before the date of the vote, the plaintiffs also requested another preliminary injunction against the JT president's stay-of-execution order. That injunction was granted by a high magistrate on June 21 but revoked by the president of the JT himself the following day. This tug-of-war was unprecedented and extremely controversial from a legal standpoint. According to Teijeiro, only the special committee had the authority to overturn the stay of execution from the JT president. And yet, the borderline move helped delay evictions.

Finally, on June 27, the special committee members upheld the initial court order by a vote of twenty-two to three, which meant the city was barred from carrying out evictions at least until the lawsuit was ruled or settled. Beyond the judicial parrying, securing a favorable ruling by the special committee required what the public defender described as extensive "fieldwork."[24] During the week that preceded the vote, he and the CIW lawyer who cosigned the lawsuit requested meetings with all twenty-five members of the committee. Twenty-two of those magistrates agreed to meet with them. At those meetings, according to Miragaia, the duo tried to raise awareness of the needs and predicament of the street vendors.[25] Again, in a hostile environment, personal dispositions mattered as much as, if not more than, institutional features.

Meanwhile, street vendors began to stage regular protests. When the possibility of large-scale evictions materialized, the Union and the DVA abandoned their conservative stance. On June 18, seven Union affiliates, including six blind men, chained themselves in front of the mayor's office, asking for talks to be resumed. On June 20, another protest took place with members of the Street Vendors' Assembly in attendance. Finally, on June 27, the day of the vote, more than three hundred street vendors gathered in front of the JT and celebrated the decision. The city subsequently appealed the special committee's judgment at a federal court of appeals, but the court upheld the ruling, which remained in force until the election of a new administration and its inauguration in January 2013.

The unexpected successes of the class action—first the injunction itself, then its upholding by the JT—despite what looked to many to be a lost cause prompted some political actors to try to jump on the bandwagon by having their names added to the lawsuit after the fact. Some, including Tristan, were traditional leaders of licensed street vendors, while others had nothing to do with street trade. The judge did not allow it ("It would have made a mess"), and the public defender said in an interview that he explained to them politely that the lawsuit was a judicial process, not a political one.

In a way, the court battle redefined not just the boundaries but the content of legality. Street vendors participate in the everyday construction of legality through the distinctions they draw and the claims they make. But the judicial process recast the field on a different level by adding a new layer to the interpretation of their rights. The view of street vendors as an organic part of the city and of the city as a legal entity protected by the constitution was foreign to street vendors. Yet it served to uphold the rights of a vulnerable group in the face of a brutal campaign to eliminate it.

The judicial decision redrew the edge of legality. It restored the right to work for about fifteen hundred street vendors while leaving the other four thousand or so whose licenses were revoked or canceled before 2012 high and dry. When I asked the judge why she chose 2012 as the cutoff, she responded: "Based on the information that I received, I felt that was when it started. Besides, neither the public defender nor the CIW set a date in the lawsuit, and they didn't complain afterwards. I had to set a date. I couldn't leave it open."[26] In the gray area of informality, where laws are always subject to interpretation, enforcement is negotiable, and information is murky, even a parameter as straightforward as the cutoff date created painful uncertainty for some and new opportunities for others.

Among those affected in uncertain ways was a man who walked into the office of the president of the Union one day claiming that he had spoken with Tristan before coming there. The city inspectors all agreed that there was no reason to confiscate his stall, but the MP lieutenant ("and, you know, lieutenant is above sergeant") said that he would seize it regardless. The man looked distraught. He was carrying a mountain of documents. His problem was that he had been working legally until 2012 thanks to a *liminar* he had obtained through a lawsuit that he had filed on his own, but that *liminar* had expired (*caiu*). Hence, the lieutenant had given the order to remove his stall. But in 2012, he was still working legally and therefore should have been protected by the *liminar da juiza* (the judge's injunction). The public defender had told him as much, but he was afraid to set up his stall.

The Union president told the man that they had recently met with Tristan and were planning to meet with the new SCS secretary as soon as he was nominated. The leaders would bring him the Union's proposal to reinstate the licenses, and if he didn't accept it, they would "take to the streets." When the street vendor pressed him, the president agreed to write a letter to the district administrator saying that the vendor should be allowed to work.

The vendor's problem was not unique. Informal economies are rife with liminal cases. Another vendor paid a visit to the Union after he had been to two lawyers and then to the CIW, who had written an opinion about the *liminar*. He had written letters to the SCS and to the downtown district administration, to no avail. He was desperate. His name had been published in the newspaper of public record, which meant he was entitled to work. However, he did not show up on the list of authorized workers used by the MP officers to check stalls. The Union president listened to him and offered reassuring words, but no solution.

As distressing as the judicial process was for those who felt they qualified for legal protection under the injunction yet found themselves unable to exercise their rights, with authorities giving them the go-around at every turn, it was even more painful for those who, having lost their rights in an arbitrary fashion, did not qualify for protection because the incident took place before 2012. Still, the judicial process opened a window of opportunity for some of them to work—so to speak—in the shadow of the injunction. One of them was Valdira. Her plight captures the pain of informal citizens whose rights can be canceled without recourse and whose lives revolve around asserting them among skeptics and trying to recover them against the odds.

The Story of Valdira

Valdira lost her license in 2006, in the early days of Kassab's mass eviction campaign. She missed the first call for the renewal of her license and arrived ten minutes late to the second and final call. In the past, this had never been an issue. On this occasion, however, the official in charge reprimanded her for wasting his time, saying "Do you think I'm a clown to sit here waiting for you?" and refusing to renew her license. Valdira had been a licensed street vendor for more than ten years. During the tumultuous years of the Erundina administration (1989–1992), when the city launched a program to register street vendors as a first step toward issuing licenses, she managed to secure a coupon signed by a city administrator, which allowed her to obtain a license. "My God how I pestered him," she said with a smile. She went to his office day after day, until he finally signed the ticket on his lap. When the city employee refused to renew her license in 2006, she told him: "You are taking away bread from my mouth [*você está tirando o pão da minha boca*]." She lost her status as a licensed vendor, her job, her livelihood, and her dignity all at once. At the time, however, the long-term consequences of this administrative decision were hard to predict, even for her.

After this happened, Valdira fell into depression. She took up various gigs, including one as a "puller" (*puxadora*), a worker whose job is to bring customers from the street into a store, usually through a mix of shouting and enticing. She also found a source of income at a large park near her house on the outskirts of the city. There, vendors who had been working on the run for a long time, selling toys, drinks, and snacks on crowded weekends, had organized, formed a cooperative, and made a deal with the park administration

FIGURE 5.1. Valdira (left) and her sister selling hats at the park
Photo by the author.

to be allowed to sell at fixed spots. After joining the cooperative, Valdira was able to set up her stall in the park during the weekends. She showcased and sold the same merchandise she used to sell at her licensed stall on 25 de Março—that is, hats (hip-hop and baseball caps, fedoras, broad-brim women's chapeaus, berets, etc.), most of them made in China (see fig. 5.1).

The other source of comfort that helped Valdira endure much of her trying routine was her faith. She had not always been a believer. Back in the days when she was living the good life as a licensed vendor, God was seldom on her mind. But then, around the time when, as she liked to say, "the street shut its doors and the park opened its arms," Valdira found Jesus. She found him at an evangelical church near her house, where she went every Sunday after working at the park and on most weekday evenings. The contrast with the streets, as she saw it, was total. "On the streets, no one is a friend of no one. At the church, we are all brothers and sisters."

During services, she lauded God with fervor in chants and hallelujahs. She also volunteered, doing favors such as cleaning the church bathrooms, and, of course, paid the dime. For all her strenuous efforts, she had not managed to convert her sister—nor me, though I accompanied her once to the service. Pointing at me with his finger, the pastor uttered some prediction about "a problem in your life" soon to be resolved thanks to His intervention. Vague prophesies marked the tenor of his sermon: "Tomorrow things will be different. Tomorrow things will work out"; "You'll get what you are waiting for. What is yours is yours." Valdira fully embraced the view that everything that happens to us is a deed of the Lord and a reflection of His will while constantly invoking God as the single force behind the ever-forthcoming solution to her problems: the reinstatement of her license.

THE RIGHT TO WORK

Even though her license was canceled in 2006, the injunction issued by Teijeiro offered Valdira a chance to go back to street vending downtown. By law, the injunction only covered those whose licenses were terminated in 2012. Yet, in the gray area of informality, the existence of a court order protecting licensed street vendors, regardless of its actual purview, combined with the inauguration of a new administration in 2013, meant an opening. After paying a bribe to some shady characters who claimed to have leverage inside city hall, Valdira set up her stall at "her spot" (*meu ponto*) on the northern end of 25 de Março Street, where she used to work before her license got canceled. Initially, the move paid off. She enlisted her niece as an aide and was even able to sublet half the stall to another vendor, a practice that is forbidden but common in the trade.

The situation was stressful, however, for every inspection by the MP raised the specter of confiscation, if not eviction. The interaction with law enforcement described in the opening paragraphs of the book was nerve-racking. During another encounter with law enforcement, she mentioned that her late brother had served in the MP, which was true. The officer expressed sympathy and went on with his round without giving her trouble.

Eventually, however, Valdira was forced to take down her stall. The officer told her he would walk down the block, and if the stall was still there when he came back, he would have it seized. However, her subletter, Reginaldo, was dragging his feet. The officer came back, and Valdira had to argue with Reginaldo in front of him and all the onlookers. Their run-in was humiliating, and she didn't want to deal with that anymore. Later, Reginaldo discounted a whole day from the weekly rent of nine hundred reals he paid her, even though the incident happened at 1:00 p.m. "He takes advantage of him being a man and me being a woman," she said. "He knows I don't have a husband and my brothers won't intervene. He wants to do as he pleases." When I asked why it made her so mad, she replied: "You know that feeling when you don't control what's yours?" After pointing out randomly that she had never been to the theater, she added, "That's my life."

When things got really tight at 25 de Março and the prospect of reclaiming her spot was in serious jeopardy, Valdira told a friend: "Thanks God I have the park." However, at the park, relations between the leadership of the cooperative and its members had been difficult for a while. Nora, one of the leaders who had played a critical role in organizing vendors and negotiating with the park administration, was now insisting that vendors should incur several expenses that to many felt unnecessary, if not suspicious, such as paying for the laying of gravel at each spot or purchasing tents for the stalls "to look nicer." The leadership alleged, as usual, that it was a request from the park administration, but Valdira believed it was just an easy way for them to make money, as they could charge a lot for little work. There were also rumors that the leaders had benefited from allowing the "big guys" like Nestlé and Coca-Cola to have their own stands at the park. And the notion that the requested "improvements" were yet another instance of "peddlers extorting peddlers," as Valdira once put it, was not far-fetched. At a meeting of the cooperative, Nora's daughter, a teenage leader in the making, reprimanded the audience: "You claim that you don't have money to pay your dues and then we see you on Saturday having a beer at the bar. If you have money for a beer, you can pay your dues!"

A PEDDLER'S LIFE

Being on the edge of the law had its own subjective consequences for Valdira. One of them was her penchant for spending. She owned a collection of more than eighty shoes and a microwave that sat idle in her kitchen for seven months. One day, as I walked into her house, I stumbled upon a brand-new sofa that took up most of her narrow, improvised living room. She had bought it on credit, along with a new kitchen table, even though the old sofa and table were still in good shape. After I pointed out the precariousness of her financial situation and questioned the wisdom of spending money on expensive items under the circumstances, she explained that the new furniture was a "fruit of her labor" and that she felt proud having it and looking at it. "I don't go out, I don't travel, I work Sunday to Sunday, I don't do anything. I feel I have a right to buy things that I like. I'm proud of this table, I bought it through my work." As for the sofa: "I need it. It cuddles my ego."

It should not come as a surprise that Valdira's ego needed some cuddling. The streets are tough on the self, sometimes irreparably so. But they are also a refuge. Talking about her childhood, Valdira once shared: "I never had a dad. I mean . . . a dad who loves you and hugs you and looks after you. He only beat me up. When I was a child, I worked for a long time at a house [*casa de família*]. I remember my dad was always there at the end of the month to pick up my pay. The first thing I bought for myself was a watch. When he saw it, he gave me another beating. 'Now you are going to eat that watch for a month,' he said."

Beatings were not the only threat she and her sister Marta faced in that abusive environment. Valdira was almost raped once, at a vigil, and then a second time. Her sister was sexually assaulted by a relative. Eventually, Valdira ran away. "I went from getting beaten up at home to getting beaten up in the streets," she said. But she did not take up street vending right away. She started working at a thread factory on the outskirts of São Paulo, where Marta found her. "I would have liked to be a schoolteacher," she told me. "[But] my life was besieged. I kept fleeing. My mom died when I was seven. I was beaten with broomsticks, with belts. I felt revolted all my youth. I didn't have any will to study."

Her life as a street vendor was not entirely devoid of gratifications. Before her license was canceled in 2006, she made good money and spent it lavishly. With a female friend and fellow street vendor who had political connections, she would attend cocktail parties and other social events. In the late 1990s, she was living the high life. "I'm telling you, we used to change clothes in the cab," she said. She never imagined that life could come to an end. "I thought I was . . . how should I put it? . . . significant." On a different occasion, her take on those days was gloomier: "My life was hell. I suffered a lot. That's why I drank and partied."

Partly as a result of her runaway life and partly due to bad luck, Valdira did not manage to build a stable household. She never had children, and while she did marry Jorge, her reasons for doing so were not romantic. Valdira fell in love in her early twenties, for the first and only time in her life, with João, her boyfriend at the time. They would travel "everywhere" during his holidays. They would stay together from Friday night to Sunday evening or even Monday morning, before he went to work. It was a delight, until someone came looking for her one Saturday at the hostel where she was staying, even though none of her relatives or friends knew the address. The person looking for her was a woman who was eight months pregnant and claimed to be João's wife. He had sent her there. Valdira promised this woman that she would never hear from her again—and she never did. Several years later, when she was working as a street vendor, her ex once walked by her stall. He was accompanied by his son, Guilherme. "I met you in your mother's womb," Valdira told him. That's when she decided to marry Jorge, as a form of revenge.

Jorge began selling with her at the park after he lost his job in photo development to the rise of digital photography. They separated when he developed a heavy taste for alcohol and she discovered he had homosexual preferences. She maintained kind feelings toward him nonetheless. "Not love, but something," she said. "I ask God to take it away, but He hasn't." Following their breakup and his moving out of the house that they rented together, Valdira enlisted the help of Marta. She paid her sister about twenty reals to sit with her by her stall at the park, mostly to keep her company. At the end of the day, they would gather for snacks or a meal at Valdira's house, a few blocks away from the park.

Unlike Valdira, Marta had responded to their childhood traumas by seeking stability all her life, opting for a nine-to-five registered job at a hospital where the pay was low but stable. She stayed in that position during most of her work life, contributing toward retirement—which she now received—and saving for a house that she built and owned. In one of our conversations at Valdira's stall, Marta and I concluded that there were two types of people: the street vendor (*ambulante*) and the factory worker (*operária*). One is a risk-taker who plays fast and loose with the rules and loathes authority; the other is tame, obedient, and law-abiding. She placed herself squarely in the latter type. "I could not live the way she lives," Marta once said about her sister. "I don't know how she can stand it."

Over time, Valdira's life began to unravel. Her stall at 25 de Março, which she had set up again, was confiscated on her birthday. "I went to church and cried." The family from whom she rented her house wanted it back for an aging parent, so Valdira was forced to move out with her three dogs. She found another place, which cost twice as much, though, by that time, she was living mostly off her savings. She could not find anything cheaper where she could keep her dogs, she said. At her previous house, she kept two of them in the narrow alleyway and the third one in her small backyard. Every day, when she came home from work, she cleaned up their waste, washed the floor with soapy water, and fed them. Valdira loved her dogs more than anything in the world. She also reprimanded them often, sometimes for no apparent reason. Watching her, it occurred to me that these were the only beings over which she had, or could pretend to have, a semblance of authority.

A few months later, after she was unable to make rent, Valdira moved to her sister's house, where she could stay with her dogs. We had discussed this possibility in the past, but she had been reluctant, as she worried about tensions with her sister's children, who might see her as intruding. Unfortunately for her, those fears came true, and her relationship with Marta soured, but she had nowhere else to go. In the meantime, the park shut down due to a yellow fever outbreak. Deprived of her license, her stall, and her lifeline, Valdira started working on the run as an unlicensed vendor. She stopped selling hats, a product that she saw as a sign of taste and glamour and that had become part of her identity—"they call me *a Val dos chapeus* [Val the hat seller]," she told me once—opting instead for lighter, more portable goods, such as foldable laundry bags. She went on working during the COVID-19 pandemic despite being high-risk due to her diabetes.

As with so many vendors exposed to the stress, the weather, and the violence on the streets—where the sun "eats your skin" all day long—Valdira's work had taken a toll on her body. Like many other street vendors I met, she suffered from diabetes. She realized she was sick one day when she was cleaning the bathroom at the church and started sweating profusely. She had lost eight kilos in the previous weeks. While I was in the field, she was also diagnosed with a huge calculus. Then her hair turned gray and began to fall out, as did her teeth, and she had frequent headaches. A tumor on her left side, which turned out to be benign, caused her constant pain and disrupted her sleep. Surgery was too risky, however, because of her diabetes. I had once asked her if she had considered other occupations. "What would I do?" she asked. "Work as a nanny?" I inquired again when life got really tough. She pointed out that no one would hire for a nanny a toothless old lady with no previous experience in the job.

Throughout her ordeal, Valdira kept saying that she would get her license back ("*meu TPU vai sair*"). God had arranged for it. She pursued every avenue, however unrealistic, and knocked on every door requesting its reinstatement. After it became clear that the CIW, despite having filed the lawsuit, was unable to do much for workers who lost their licenses prior to 2012, she pleaded with politicians and public administrators. She wrote a letter explaining what her license meant for her and how much she had suffered, which she delivered to the office of the downtown district administrator. Using a common strategy among workers at the margins of the law who try to build up some form of legal capital in the hope that they can later somehow transform it into a title—in her case, a license—she paid a fee at the district administration using her old license number. Even though her license had been canceled, the number was still in the system, and the clerk accepted the money. She then let the chief of inspectors know that she had paid. "Well, that's because you want to," he replied. Meanwhile, at her church, the pastor said he knew a councilman to whom he would bring her case.

At first, Valdira related this news with enthusiasm, as if blind to the adamant posture of the city against reinstating licenses and the hopelessness of her efforts. In time, her enthusiasm wore off. She had moments of anger. She wanted to put an end to the false leads, the rumors, the gossiping on the streets and from authorities. "I can't wait to get back my license so I can shut their mouths with it," she said once. Faith, love for her dogs, and the lack of any imaginable alternative kept her going, until one day, on the phone, when she expressed dismay. She said she could not make sense of everything she had been through and confessed to having lost, at times, the will to live.

Two Edges

Valdira's story exemplifies a radical form of legal dispossession—being stripped of personhood. What could come across to an external observer as a common, almost trivial event—the administrative act of denying the renewal of a street vending license—condemned her to years of material uncertainty, accelerated physical decline, and existential struggle. The dramatic stereotype of those on the receiving end of criminalization policies as young men "on the run" or behind bars glosses over the many other casualties who, like Valdira, see their lives fall apart without drawing attention.

But Valdira's story also hints at the informal opportunities that emerge in the shadows of legality, when judicial intervention restores the rights of some among the targeted workers. Thanks to the court order and a change of government, Valdira was able to return to her spot for a while. It is the essence of what Nezar AlSayyad refers to as the "informal way of life" that those who practice it will make the most of any situation and work through the cracks.[27] In fact, there were reports that, in the wake of the preliminary injunction, local authorities in some districts were allowing vendors whose licenses were revoked or canceled in 2011 to work as well, based on a misunderstanding, honest or self-interested, of the scope of the ruling. That even a judicial process intended to enforce the formal rules of the game would produce such externalities is telling. It speaks to the fluidity of the margins of legality, where street- and high-level politics shape the field. At the same time, many of those who, like Valdira, found a sliver of hope in an injunction for whose protection they did not technically qualify ended up trapped in an endless (and hopeless) bureaucratic maze trying to recover their rights—and growing restless about it.

By contrast, some of those who received the right to go back to work thanks to the injunction saw the experience of street vendors in a different light, especially after the dust had settled and the threat of eviction seemed behind them. Hence, a licensed vendor told me: "What Kassab did was to moralize street vending. Before this was a mess, you couldn't even walk. Now it's much better." Echoing complaints voiced by Gabriel, another licensed vendor protected by the injunction, she alluded to licensed vendors "breaking the rules, wanting to expand their stalls all over the place, for example." Gabriel's take was more nuanced, however, as he noted that in the process of disciplining street vendors, Kassab "forgot the human being."

From a sociolegal perspective, Kassab did more than that. Disregarding customary practice and established arrangements, his administration decided to enforce the law to the letter and, in so doing, turned workers into outlaws. It is noteworthy that, even under these circumstances, the selectiveness continued to operate, surreptitiously, as attested by the comparatively better fate of (some) disabled and elderly vendors who likely benefited from access to information and favors from state officials. Like the politics that shape the institutional framework, the politics that enact legality are not one-sided, and some street vendors had enough connections to buy time.

Kassab's reading of the law also challenged the meaning of their rights. His administration transformed the right to sell on the streets, which defines licensed street vendors' trade and identity, into a contingent entitlement subject to technical review. In doing so, Kassab compromised not only their right to work but, at a more fundamental level, their right to have rights. Beyond its discursive appeal, the right to have rights conjures the certainty that one will be recognized and treated as a person—able to claim, debate, and defend one's rights when necessary.[28] Informal citizens do not enjoy such existential certainty.

Another implication of Kassab's policy of extinction was that street vendors were denied their status as members of the city. Even before criminalization, the ideal of membership at the heart of the notion of citizenship, with its reference to community, had lost ground in the neoliberal era. Save for nationalistic ideologies that spur an emotional sense of belonging at political rallies, the exercise of citizenship had drifted away from the collective construction of a common world toward isolated acts of participation by individuals whose ties to politics and to each other feel increasingly hollow. It is hard to imagine a democratic polity made up of citizens who go bowling alone, as Robert Putnam put it.[29] And Kassab's approach to urban planning, with its heavy reliance on the MP at every level, had a strong top-down flavor antithetical to civic engagement. In an unexpected way, the rationale for the court order rehabilitated the idea of membership by recognizing street vendors' right to participate in the making of the city.

Though it proved providential for (some) licensed street vendors, the court order was a temporary measure adopted in response to an imminent threat of "irreparable damage" on a vulnerable group.[30] It was, moreover, a politically controversial measure, as the backlash experienced by the judge made clear. The judge was candid about her feelings: "My hope is that they will reach a settlement. I really don't want to rule on this matter. And I know it wouldn't solve anything."[31] The return to power of the PT in 2013 had made those wishes possible. It had also stirred up the hopes of licensed vendors who were caught in a legal limbo, yearned for the full enjoyment of their rights, and understood that the lawsuit had simply stemmed the bleeding.

6

The Politics of Hope

MARIA: Leonardo told me it's going to be nice. The stalls will have a roof. You don't even
  need to worry about having to be there all day long.
ME: Where is that?
MARIA: In heaven.

In the summer of 2012, while licensed vendors were still reeling from the ban that came close to destroying their trade, the electoral process to appoint the successor of Kassab was gathering steam. The two front-runners were both center-right candidates with ties to the *paulista* business elite. One of them was Serra, the former mayor whose decision to run for governor brought Kassab, his vice mayor, to office. Coming a distant third in the polls, with only 7 percent of the vote intention, was a little-known former minister of education and professor of political science at the University of São Paulo named Fernando Haddad. Haddad was the PT candidate. He had the full endorsement of then president Rousseff and the party's historic leader and icon of the Latin American Left, Lula.[1] The elections were scheduled for November 7. Street vendors understood that even if the courts had offered them a respite, their future was a matter of policy hinging on a political decision. Vendors pinned their hopes on the election of Haddad, for whom they campaigned earnestly. They hoped that a PT administration would put an end to the nightmare they had endured under Kassab.

By 2012, however, the PT was not the same party that launched the large licensing program of the early 1990s, when radical alternatives were still prominent in the political debate. The PT had evolved from the teeming coalition of radicalized groups of its beginnings—leftist intellectuals, radical clergy inspired by liberation theology, and dissenting trade unionists—into an institutionalized political force. Like the views and values of many socialist parties in the West, those of the PT leadership had veered toward the center, away from the staunch redistributive stances of the party's early days.[2] Wendy Hunter describes the PT's "moderation" as a strategic adaptation to the neoliberal zeitgeist of the 1990s—when Brazil entered the global economy—and

the hard realities of electoral politics.[3] In 1989, Lula advanced to the presidential elections runoff on a socialist platform, and Erundina's own government
in São Paulo embodied the "revolutionary" aspirations of the Left. Yet Lula
did not win the 1989 elections and, in the following decade, lost twice to the
candidate who implemented the economic policies of austerity, privatization,
free trade, and deregulation.

Urban management itself calls for pragmatism, and the political economy
of Brazil's financial capital—where white-collar workers make up more than
half of the electorate, the service industry accounts for 80 percent of gross
municipal product, and local elites hold massive wealth and influence—did
not leave much leeway for populist policy, especially toward street vendors.
In an interview, the president of the DVA explained that, had Kassab gotten
his way, the ban would probably have lasted since none of his successors,
regardless of their political affiliation, would have dared to "take such a controversial decision as bringing the filth [sujeira, meaning street vendors]—as
they would put it, back to the streets."[4]

Against this backdrop, Erundina's experiment on the eve of Brazil's embrace
of globalization was an anomaly, and the party's retrospective assessment of
it was rather self-critical. Haddad still benefited from historical working-class
support for the PT—including among street vendors—and Lula's popularity,
but he ran on a platform of economic and infrastructural development fostered
by technocratic governance. He won the runoff against Serra and took office on
January 1, 2013. His administration inherited the lawsuit.

This chapter recounts the negotiations for a settlement between representatives of licensed street vendors and the party they had supported for more
than two decades, which was reluctant to reinstate their licenses. It shows
the leverage that the promise of legalization affords authorities over those at
the margins of legality. Conflicting emotions and utopian aspirations kept
street vendors in check. Granting rights to a narrow subgroup of informal
workers—the self-reinforcing policy of São Paulo's city government toward
street vendors for decades—or quashing them, as Kassab did, are only two
prominent tools in the repertoire. Withholding or even dangling rights is another powerful lever in the government of informal labor.

From a historical perspective, this episode captures the disenchantment
and alienation that traditional constituencies on the Left felt as their leaders embraced a more business-friendly agenda. As a concept, neoliberalism
signifies both a promarket ideology and a set of regressive policies that hurt
(mostly) the poor.[5] Critics denounce the term as implying a conspiracy of
political and economic elites while its adepts sometimes use it abusively, as
an abstract force accounting for every social ill. However, the term's implicit

reference to a political economy underlying adherence to market orthodoxy is salutary. What corrodes or corrupts the institutions of citizenship, directly and indirectly, is not markets as such but the political forces acting within and around them, including dominant market players whose ways often run counter to the very precepts of free-market competition they extol. Whether or not the PT took a neoliberal turn at the start of the century is a matter of endless debate, including among well-versed scholars, but even in the absence of an ideological conversion, there is no doubt that the Haddad administration faced the constraints of a global policy trend. What makes this case unique is that the lawsuit repeatedly brought the two sides face to face, in a room, over several months. Street vendors had the opportunity to express their anger and frustration directly to party officials. Instead of providing answers, however, policymakers stalled. They entertained the hopes that licensed vendors harbored of seeing their rights reinstated while tapping the divisions, conflicts, and fears among their representatives. In other words, city officials exploited the emotional dimensions of informal citizenship.

The Setting

In March 2013, three months after his inauguration, Haddad met with the leaders of the Union and the DVA thanks to the intercession of Tristan, the PT councilman. In April, he met with the NGO workers who had filed the lawsuit and, according to one of them, told them that the only thing he could commit to was dialogue.[6] Then, in May, the NGO team and the head of SCS—the department within the city government that defines guidelines on urban policy citywide and oversees the implementation of municipal policy by each district—agreed to seek a settlement. The judge, who was hoping not to have to rule on the case given the pushback she had experienced after issuing a court order in favor of street vendors, sanctioned the settlement initiative. Talks began at the end of May, with a deadline set for November.

A negotiating group made up of representatives of the parties in the lawsuit as well as other stakeholders met every two weeks between the end of May and early November 2013 in a large rectangular room on the thirtieth floor of the downtown skyscraper where the SCS is located. During the last month of negotiations, meetings occurred weekly as time was running out. The group convened fourteen times in total; I attended the last nine meetings. I also interviewed eleven participants separately.

Participants fell into three categories:

1) *Representatives of the city*. The chief negotiator on behalf of the city, who also presided over the meetings, was Rigoberto, a mid-ranking SCS employee. The blueprint of the negotiating group listed representatives of nine other government bodies as well as six administrative districts with licensed street vendors. Officials representing departments seldom attended, however, and districts tended to send mid-ranking officials. Occasionally, other government employees showed up, including a police chief and a former political broker. The head of SCS—officially referred to as the *secretary*—never attended.

2) *Representatives of street vendors*. Six representatives of street vendors were listed in the official blueprint, along with six substitutes. Four of the main representatives were attendants of the Street Vendors' Assembly (hereafter the Assembly) set up by the NGO that filed the lawsuit. The other two were the vice presidents of both the Union and the DVA, who were said to be more influential than the presidents. The latter were listed as substitutes but also attended the meetings. Other street vendors who found out about the meetings sometimes showed up, along with the substitutes for the Assembly participants, some of whom led their own neighborhood-based associations.

3) *Representatives of civil society*. The representatives of civil society on the roster included Helena—the NGO employee who represented the plaintiffs, since one of her colleagues at CIW had filed the lawsuit—as well as an academic, a trade unionist, a social activist, and a representative of São Paulo's association of storeowners. The storeowners trade association declined to send a representative, however. Aside from Helena, who played a prominent role in the talks, civil society representatives seldom attended or participated. The public defender who cofiled the lawsuit was also present at some meetings.

Rigoberto sat behind a desk at one end of the room. One or two other key negotiators on behalf of the city sometimes sat next to him. Facing them were all other participants—including representatives of other government agencies—sitting on several rows of foldable chairs split by an aisle. The leaders of the Union and the DVA (presidents and vice presidents) were usually the first to arrive and sat in the front row on one side of the aisle as well as on a single row of chairs to the left of Rigoberto's desk. On the other side of the aisle, high- or mid-ranking city officials usually occupied the front-row seats. Other attendants, including Helena and the public defender, filled the seats immediately behind them. Other leaders of neighborhood-based associations of licensed vendors as well as other street vendors, representatives of civil society, lower-ranking city officials, and a researcher sat in the rows further back on both sides of the aisle.

Because attendance by some participants was irregular and some stakeholders who were not on the roster (e.g., licensed street vendors wanting to "see for themselves") showed up at certain meetings, turnout varied considerably. An average of twenty to twenty-five participants filled the room during meetings.

At the beginning of each session, Rigoberto briefed the audience on decisions that the city had made since the last meeting and laid out the order of the day. Attendants often interrupted him to ask questions. Eventually, a list of speakers was drawn, and those who signed up would come forward in turns to ask a question or make a pitch. As a rule, speech did not follow a logical sequence from one speaker to the next—and sometimes within each pitch. Depending on the speaker and the point they were making, the background noise of cell phones and chatting grew or faded.

The government's agenda transpired early on in the talks. The city wanted a settlement while reinstating the fewest possible licenses. In theory, representatives of street vendors advocated for the reinstatement of all licenses terminated by the Kassab administration. Yet the leaders belonged to the fraction of licensed vendors protected by the court order, which put them at times in an awkward position. Moreover, they were interested in new regulations that could be adopted within the negotiating group, as part of the settlement. Finally, the agenda of Helena and the NGO she represented was to promote inclusive, participatory policymaking that enhanced the rights of all informal workers, licensed or not. Her sheer lack of pragmatism raised suspicions among other participants about underlying conflicts of interest, however.

The Talks

The dynamics of the meetings were characterized by two mirroring, paradoxical attitudes. The city used delay tactics probably aimed at forcing their counterparts to accept a minimal offer toward the end of the negotiation process, under the pressure of time. Although buying time is a common political strategy, the city's stance stood out as distinctively brazen. I call it blatant inaction. The response from street vendors and their representatives was anger coupled with repeated threats to abandon the talks, which never materialized. I call it futile outrage. Divisions among them and conflicts of interest also played a role in what looked at times like an absurdist play.

THE ART OF DIVERSION

Ruling party officials faced the difficult task of denying rights to one of their constituencies—rights that its members had held for a long time. They had to perform dialogue. To keep the conversation going without making any commitment, the city used various tactics. One of them was to bring up for discussion issues that street vendors cared about in the daily conduct of business.

Both the NGO and the Union saw the negotiating group as an opportunity to make changes to the legal norms governing street trade, beyond the reinstatement of licenses. The Union had submitted a proposal that consisted of a list of specific changes to the municipal decree regulating licensed street vending. The NGO had submitted its own proposal on behalf of the Assembly, an ambitious step-by-step plan to define a citywide policy along six pillars (policing, legislation, etc.), each of which contained itemized lines of action. Rigoberto would print these documents and distribute them to attendees at the beginning of a meeting, then go over the items in each document one by one. Thus, even though there was no official timeline for the reinstatement of the licenses, debate raged about the number of aides each vendor should be allowed to have or the right to transfer the license to the offspring upon death of the holder.

The proposal to make the Union dues mandatory for all licensed street vendors spurred heated controversy:

HENRIQUE (SCS OFFICIAL): I don't believe it's legal. Let's have the [city] legal services take a look.

ERIVALDO (RIVAL STREET VENDOR LEADER): If that's legal, it's immoral. The union tax [sic] is pure hustle.

RIGOBERTO: This is like asking payment of union dues to get employment.

MIRAGAIA (PUBLIC DEFENDER): You are linking an administrative act to the union's statutes. I would just leave that out.

DVA VICE PRESIDENT: The union dues are [mentioned] in ML 11,039. It's illegal for associations to charge [their members, but not for the Union].

UNION PRESIDENT: What's indecent is to do what some do on the streets [i.e., collect informal taxes]. We are within the law.

UNION VICE PRESIDENT: It's in the law. Doesn't the Union pay stationery, doesn't it pay for [other expenses]? And then the [member] doesn't want to pay [her dues].

Even the mores of vendors were a subject of debate. The DVA vice president suggested a statute requiring "good moral conduct" (bons costumes). "I'm sick of seeing vendors snuggling up at their stalls," he said, causing an outcry. "You are giving the city more grounds to repress you," the public defender pointed out. Diversion had repeated payoffs. At the beginning of each meeting, Rigoberto would provide a recap of the previous session, laying out the items on which there had been agreement and those on which there had not—sparking renewed debate.

Hence, despite the evasiveness of their stances, city officials managed to entertain the illusion among street vendors' representatives that they were shaping the law. It helped that street vendors were attached not only to their status as license holders but to the various rights and benefits that stemmed from it. By steering the conversation toward such piecemeal rights, officials turned attention away from the more fundamental rights at stake—namely, the right to work as a street vendor—and avoided taking a stance on the number of licenses they were willing to reinstate until two weeks before the deadline. It was as if, because of their political habits of discussing regulations, licensed street vendors forgot they were at risk of expulsion from the field of legality.

The idleness of some of these issues was not lost on other participants, however. Once, after a speaker suggested that "morbid obesity" be added to the list of disabilities granting priority access to a license, I heard a street vendor in the back comment: "They haven't solved the issue of the revoked licenses and they are discussing obesity." But the authors of each proposal, who were also the main spokespeople for street vendors, took each point of their respective programs to heart. And when, on one occasion, Helena pointed out that they were discussing "trifles," she offended the vice president of the DVA while failing to reorient the debate. Rigoberto sat silently watching as they squabbled. In fact, during most of the talks, Rigoberto kept a steady tone and a poker face, even as he was being lambasted by other speakers, and lost his calm only once.

WIELDING THE LAW

The city also used other tactics. One of them consisted of outlining improbable but alluring relocation plans, such as transferring vendors who lost their licenses to an informal marketplace under renovation known for its massive commercial turnover. Street vendors' leaders seemed enticed by the idea and tried to sell it to other vendors—as Maria suggests, with some irony, in the chapter's opening quote—even though they were not willing to make the move themselves. Uncertainty about the expected returns in a new and contested environment added to the fragile legal status of the marketplace. Contrasting the legal instruments that regulated the enclosed market and the streets— hence the security of the attendant rights—the DVA vice president told a civil servant: "[You want us] to abandon a municipal law and go under a municipal decree, are you nuts?" ("*Sair de uma lei para entrar num decreto, tá doido?*").[7]

The most sophisticated stratagem relied on the city's ability to shape the legal framework. On August 9, without prior notice to participants in the

negotiation group, the city issued an ordinance calling for vendors with licenses terminated in 2012—that is, those protected by the court order—to submit to their respective district administrations proof of administrative or legal
flaw in the cancellation procedure for a review of the decision. Ordinance 38,
as the edict was called, gave the interested parties a thirty-day window to act.
This move by the city put licensed street vendors and their leaders in a bind. If
they attended the call, they legitimized the process and, in doing so, validated
the city's foreseeable claims that the licenses of those who did not attend the
call had been lawfully canceled and that those who attended the call but could
not produce evidence of a flaw should be evicted. On the other hand, if the
leaders tried to sabotage the process by telling members not to attend the call
(as they did), they still ran the risk that a sizable minority of licensed vendors
would not listen to them, compromising both their strategy and their authority as leaders. Faced with a crushing dilemma, the leaders' best bet was to try
to compel city officials to rescind the ordinance, which gave the officials additional leverage in the negotiations. Moreover, by targeting exclusively cancellations made in 2012, Ordinance 38 underscored the potential rift between the
street vendors protected by the court order and those left out. The rescinding
of Ordinance 38 thus became one of the street vendors' main demands, along
with the reinstatement of licenses. At one meeting, Rigoberto said he would
discuss the demand with his colleagues. (It was apparent that city officials who
did not attend the talks occasionally met with Rigoberto behind closed doors
to make strategic decisions.) At the following meeting, Rigoberto stated that
the ordinance had not been rescinded while offering no explanation.

Instead of making a baseline offer on the reinstatement of licenses or sta-
bilizing the boundaries of legality to allow street vendors to figure out who
was in and who was out, city officials were conniving to narrow the scope of
legality while adding confusion to its outline. By introducing ad hoc procedures to ascertain membership in the world of legal street trade, as they did
with Ordinance 38, they created tensions within an already fragile group of
people whose legal status the state had called into question, under a previous
administration, and who were still reeling from it. The city's strategy was not
(only) to divide and rule; it was to create new rules and pretend to revisit existing ones to confuse and divide a population whose relationship to the law
was fraught to begin with.

FUTILE OUTRAGE

Street vendors were not fooled by the city's stalling strategy. They complained
about it vociferously. At the first meeting I attended, the first person to speak

was the president of the Union. He cited "people enduring hunger" (i.e., street vendors whose licenses were canceled and who were unable to work), recalled the hopes placed on Haddad, and lamented how little street vendors were listened to. "This is like talking sex with angels," he said, sparking chuckles among the audience. "People [street vendors] are calling me, from all districts. They want an answer. They feel lots of frustration. We want you to restore the licenses . . . and devolve decision-making powers to district administrations. There's a lot of sadness in this situation. It's really bad. We don't know what the city wants. There's a lack of decision [from the city]."

When street vendors' representatives met with Helena to draft a common proposal, a street vendors' leader commented pointedly: "We are playing the role of fools in this process." And, two weeks before the end of the talks, after the city circulated its proposal for a settlement suggesting that all issues on which the negotiation group had not reached an agreement be referred to a yet-to-be-established street vendors council, a representative of street vendors said: "We've understood what you [the city] are doing with this council. You are just using it to put off all the decisions you don't want to make." Claudia, a combative licensed vendor, was less diplomatic. "You are laughing in our face [*zoando na nossa cara*]! What about Ordinance 38? You said it would be rescinded? Why hasn't that happened?" Participants also slighted Rigoberto to his face: "We've all understood what his role is. His role is to take the heat [*levar porrada*]."

There was more to the street vendors' anger than the feeling of being denied their rights—or rights they felt entitled to—and the city's obvious duplicity. It was also a reaction to the breach of an unspoken contract. Ethnographic insight into clientelistic arrangements nuances the relevance of the quid pro quos linking patrons to their clients or brokers. A web of meanings signifies their relationships in ways that conceal or downplay each party's material interests while inspiring followers to attend political rallies and give to or work for their patron.[8] However, an interruption in the flow of goods and services from the party or patron shakes the narrative of love and loyalty and brings the practical stakes of the relationship to the surface.

Street vendors thus started calling out the PT. At one of the meetings, a leader of a neighborhood-based association of licensed street vendors lashed out at Ordinance 38, calling it a "trap." He railed against a district administrator under Kassab who, in a videoconference, was asked by her bosses how many "heads she had cut," referring to the number of licenses she had canceled. He then called the head of SCS under Haddad "the best lawyer for Kassab" and concluded by saying: "We want this administration to honor the ideology of the Workers' Party." Others complained that Kassab was still in power and that the PT was living up to its reputation of "scheduling a meeting to schedule the next meeting" or called the whole process a "joke in poor taste."

The idea of a breach of contract was explicit in a tirade by Tina, the female leader of a neighborhood association of licensed street vendors, who expressed a sense of betrayal. "I'm indignant!" she shouted at a meeting. "All you need to do is issue an ordinance saying these people can go back to [work on] the streets. Why don't you do that?" As an association leader, she had acted as a political broker during campaigns: "I've given my life to the PT! I gave everything to the secretary [who had previously run unsuccessfully for councilman]. I even gave my granddaughters. I've helped in your campaigns for more than thirty years. I've made my granddaughters work for you. I'm indignant!"[9] While other participants called on the PT to honor its stated values, Tina was holding it accountable for breaking a deal. None of that changed the broader dynamics in the room, which Rigoberto orchestrated with poise and savvy.

WISHFUL PROTESTS

To cope with their helplessness and the awareness of being played, street vendors' representatives uttered threats of protest. At a meeting, the Union vice president talked about the licensed vendors who "are now unemployed" (i.e., unable to work). He wanted the city to take a stance. "If nothing is done," he suggested, "everyone [every street vendor with a terminated license] should set up their stall and force the city's hand."

On one occasion, some street vendors' representatives began to leave the room in protest, and the situation seemed to be getting out of control. Without losing his temper, Rigoberto read a list of licensed vendor concentrations (bolsões) that were revoked under Kassab. He spoke about the need for an agreement on policing standards (padrão de fiscalização), because, he said, the MP would continue to patrol street vendors. Senior vendors in the room showed some interest, which created confusion among those pushing for a walkout. A debate about bolsões ensued, then someone asked a question about the autonomy of district administrations. Rigoberto answered with his usual phlegm.

In a dramatic moment, a young lawyer who was a relative of a street vendors' leader burst out: "Is this a working group or is this a therapy group? We are being fooled. Rigoberto is here in good faith but he is being used by the city. Let's walk out of here. Let's make our own proposal and lay it on the table of the secretary, so he can tell us whether he agrees or not." The audience cheered.

Helena chimed in, "Let's demand an answer from the city and set a clear deadline. This has lasted for too long. Nothing has been done in eight months [since Haddad's inauguration]. We've had enough. If they don't solve this, we—"

A street vendors' leader jumped in: "If the city doesn't solve this, we'll fight them on the streets!" People applauded. At this point, the Union vice president stepped forward. Recalling the proposal made earlier that street vendors get together and craft their own list of demands, he said, "Let's do that, then give the city one week to respond. If they don't, we'll make every single worker whose license was terminated go back to his spot. Then the city will have to deal with it." The meeting between Helena and other representatives of street vendors took place in a room made available to them by the SCS. They drafted a list of demands that were mostly ignored by Rigoberto in subsequent meetings, and the protests did not take place. As time ran out, pleas replaced threats.

"There are people enduring hunger," the Union president reminded the audience virtually every time he spoke. At the end of one meeting, under pressure from Union members, he demanded that "at least one ordinance be published, so as to show we are making progress. People are calling, asking for answers. And I give them hope. I can't tell them everything we've done so far has been in vain. This is a democratic, working-class government. But it's shattering everything [*arreventando tudo*]." The vice president echoed the sentiment: "This is not fair. Those people suffer from diabetes and they are unemployed. They are experiencing hardship."

THE NEW EDGE

Two weeks before the end of the negotiations, the city finally took a stance on the licenses. Claiming that a census of license holders was conducted in 2009, Rigoberto said the city was willing to reinstate licenses revoked and canceled in or after 2010, but they would not go further back in time. Those who were not registered in that call, he said, were "nonexistent." The city was thus drawing a tentative boundary based on the date of the license termination. This proposal pushed the boundary of legality beyond what the judge had determined when she set the 2012 cutoff date but did not go far enough to encompass all those vendors targeted by the eviction campaign that began in 2005. Rigoberto was careful to place this announcement toward the end of the meeting so it could not be discussed in depth. Two participants raised questions about license holders whose licenses had been canceled before

2010. However, the conversation veered toward other issues, and the meeting ended shortly thereafter.

At the following meeting, the city shared a written proposal. It offered to reinstate, by June of the following year, licenses revoked or canceled since 2010. It also contemplated restoring the district-level deliberative bodies on street vending policy, improving the legislation, and setting new policing standards—but did not offer any specifics on any of these items. All the issues not solved by the negotiating group were to be tackled down the road by a street vendors council, the creation of which had been proposed by the NGO. Helena insisted that the structure and competences of the council be included in the settlement agreement, but Rigoberto and Henrique (another high-ranking SCS employee) balked at the idea. "The council does not exist yet. It has not been created. There is no point in regulating something that does not exist," one of them said.

One of the street vendors' recurring grievances was that the secretary never attended the meetings of the working group nor agreed to meet participants separately. Referring to the city's proposal of only restoring the licenses revoked in the last two years of the Kassab administration, the president of the Union noted, "But we are talking about those who are already working. Doesn't the mayor have the possibility to—"

Not finishing his sentence, he turned to Rigoberto and said, "You are our spokesman with the secretary. It's easier for you to reach him than for me. Those who are not working don't come here because they can't, and even if they did they wouldn't be listened to. Any government with good will could solve this problem in a second."

The list of official participants in the negotiating group did not include vendors who lost their licenses before 2010. However, the most poignant appeal to state officials' compassion came from Valdira and her friend Maria, both female vendors whose licenses had been revoked before 2010 and who came to the talks after finding out about them at the Street Vendors' Assembly.

When Rigoberto announced the proposed 2010 cutoff date, Maria complained: "What about those who were affected before [2010]? We should have the same rights. This is not fair. You forgot us."

An association leader told her, "From what I understand, that discussion will take place in the council."

"But we don't have time for the council. The goal is to include everyone. It must be decided here, in this group," Maria responded.

As others rallied around her, she went on, "It was the government who created this problem. I always made my living in the streets. I have much respect for the inspector, as much respect as he wants me to have. But my license was taken *from my bag* on December 22, 2006, and then [the cancellation] was published on January 17. That's not even a month. I've worked in the streets for forty years, under all mayors. It won't be Haddad who kicks me out. I can't take this anymore."

Valdira, who was in a similar situation, added: "The same thing happened to me. It was a civil servant who refused to renew my license [in 2006]. They kept tossing me around from one spot to another. I need to work. The inspector asked me to take down my stall, and I will, but I need to work. I have diabetes."

"If we were younger," Maria added, "we would go walk the sidewalks on the Rio Branco [a well-known red-light district street]. Now we can't even do that."

The room fell silent. Commotion was palpable. A high-ranking official, visibly moved, told Valdira to come talk to him at the end of the meeting and gave her his contact info—but then never responded to her attempts to reach him. This was the final meeting of the negotiating group.

Besides, Rigoberto's latest stance was that he could not make any decision himself; he would refer all decisions to the city's legal department, who, according to him, were to meet with their counterparts in the lawsuit on November 11. Helena, who represented the plaintiffs, said that she was not aware of any such meeting being scheduled. In the end, the meeting never took place, a settlement was not reached, and, three years later, at the end of the Haddad administration, street vendors who lost their licenses prior to 2012 were still unable to work, while those protected by the injunction remained in a legal limbo.

The Appeal of Legality

At some level, the settlement talks tell the story of a disempowered constituency confronted with a disingenuous, stonewalling government. Licensed street vendors are a social category whose demands the ruling party has few incentives to satisfy. While their few thousand votes can make a marginal difference in a race for a seat at the city council, they pale in comparison to the electoral clout and financial wherewithal of constituencies who dislike them, including the urban middle classes, in mayoral elections. "I've never seen anyone defend street vendors," a former civil servant and longtime PT insider said in an interview, "except for street vendors themselves."[10]

The pariah status of street vendors explains part but not all of what happened at the negotiating table, however. For one, while threats of demonstration did not materialize, leaders did wield sufficient authority to organize a protest. One and a half years later, when plans to evict downtown vendors protected by the court order surfaced, the Union and the DVA organized a protest that reached its goal of forcing the city to back down. More importantly, the marginal position of the group does not explain why its members kept coming back to the table despite the manifest pointlessness of the talks. Street vendors seemed not only powerless but "trapped." They saw through the government subterfuge, and they wittingly participated in the charade. The fact is that vendors lacked any imaginable alternative. A favorable settlement was their only hope.

In a passage about squatters on the outskirts of Kolkata, Roy points to the efficacy of uncertainty in the government of informal sector groups: "Colony residents do not have regularized land titles. As one young man from Mukundapur observed, 'They will never give us *pattas* [i.e., titles]. If they did, we would no longer have to depend on them for everything, every single day. . . . If they gave us pattas, the game would be over.'"[11] Comments by a licensed street vendors' leader from the neighborhood of São Miguel, in São Paulo, pointedly echoed this view: "It's in the city's interest to leave things undefined, not to resolve anything. If it's solved, then the dude will never get involved in [electoral] campaigns again. He does it for his livelihood."[12] The pull of legality was even stronger during the settlement talks, as uncertainty surrounded an acquired status, now under threat, instead of a hypothetical future state of affairs.

If uncertainty is the baseline, hope is the active ingredient. What paralyzed street vendors during the negotiations was not only the precariousness of their circumstances, as they hung by the thread of the lawsuit, but the prospect, however unrealistic, that the city would change its attitude. City officials, for their part, savvily exploited this disposition. Elusive as Rigoberto and his colleagues were on the question of the reinstatement of licenses, they cultivated hope in small ways by raising issues of concern to street vendors and entertaining the prospect of a decision. City officials thus kept street vendors on (the) edge.

To be sure, other factors also undermined collective action and resistance during the negotiations. Those representing licensed vendors were divided into different camps that were both ideological and political in nature. The actors who filed the lawsuit and obtained the court order were committed to broad ideals of expanding the "right to the city" and promoting decent work for all marginalized categories, licensed and unlicensed, disabled and able-bodied alike. The plaintiffs' goal was not, by any means, to protect only the interests of licensed vendors, let alone to preserve the dominance of the Union and the DVA. In fact, Helena and her NGO saw the established leadership of licensed street vendors as self-serving power brokers in a clientelistic political system that did not genuinely represent the interests of most informal workers. Those views were shared and expressed more explicitly by another NGO worker with ties to the CIW who coordinated an effort to build a coalition of informal workers at the national level. When I asked her if she had invited the Union and the DVA, she replied, "No, we want people who believe in solidarity, in associationalism. Not the guys who just want their licenses and screw everyone else."[13] In turn, the traditional leaders of licensed street vendors saw the CIW as neophytes impinging on their turf and luring away followers. Hence, whatever conflicting interests actors on both camps may have had, they also had different worldviews and conceptions of the rights worth fighting for. Street vendors shot themselves in the foot by discussing peripheral benefits while their right to work was still on the line. Helena, who had an academic training, put forward an abstract, normative vision that was impossible to realize in this setting.

The clash between these two sides echoes some of the debates around trade unionism in the age of precarity, specifically the accusation that union leaders defend the interests of workers who already have better working conditions than those in the precarious segments of the labor market, for whom unionization is an elusive prospect. Union representatives responded, in this case, by raising questions about the motives and legitimacy of those who claimed to speak for street vendors as a whole. Beyond the CIW's key role in filing the lawsuit, which everyone was forced to acknowledge, Helena staked her claims to speak on behalf of street vendors on the Street Vendors' Assembly set up by her NGO. As the negotiations dragged on, however, attendance at the Assembly meetings fell sharply, and a few habitués monopolized speech. Moreover, NGO workers clearly influenced the Assembly's decisions. Once, after Helena cited the Assembly at the talks to make her case, the president of the Union challenged her: "But who is the Assembly? Who?" She remained silent, seemingly unable to respond.

Had both camps committed to fighting for the restoration of as many licenses as possible—the only goal of relevance realistically attainable in this setting—their qualms about each other might not have been so damaging. Yet both the NGO and the established leadership of street vendors seemed to have their own conflicts of interest, which compromised a push for the organization of protests and the reinstatement of all licenses.

Most street vendors' leaders, who were themselves street vendors, had their licenses revoked in 2012. (Vendors in this situation were sometimes referred to as the "2012 crowd.") Hence, they were protected by the court order.

If faced with the tragic alternative, they preferred that the city reinstate their licenses than none at all. Aware of this latent cleavage, Rigoberto drew on it. One time, he floated the possibility that even the status of those in the group of 2012 could be subject to review, which put the leadership in a vulnerable position. "We thought those rights were guaranteed," the Union vice president said warily.

Here again, Roy points to the role that selection plays in the informal politics of hope and uncertainty: "Which hawkers will be rehabilitated? Which squatters will be the chosen few? The selection of a small group of hawkers and squatters, the indeterminacies of exclusion and inclusion, ensures political support, consolidating informalization as a mode of accumulation, and patronage as a mode of legitimation."[14] Selection had a disarming effect on licensed vendors and their representatives, not only because the risk of finding themselves on the wrong side of the line may have discouraged the leaders from pushing for a more encompassing arrangement, but also because selection benefits established vendors, provided they survive. While the topic was never explicitly raised, fewer vendors meant less competition. Until the final week of negotiations, the vice president of the DVA—a senior vendor considered "the boss" of downtown street trade—insisted that the 2012 crowd, to which he belonged, was distinct and should have its licenses restored right away. Tristan's chief of staff was present at the first meeting I attended, and he forcefully endorsed that view. "Restore the legality of the broken licenses! If you want to solve all problems at once you don't solve any problem. Let's go from the simple to the complex, let's follow a Cartesian method. Let's separate this matter in two, the 2012 crowd and the others," he said before leaving the room. The president of the Union, for his part, was inconsistent, at times making appeals to reinstate all licenses and at times seeming to be ready to settle for the city's proposal to limit restitution to those who lost their licenses from 2010 onward, provided that the names of the Union and the DVA figured more prominently on the announcement.

At first sight, the problem with Helena's agenda was that it was too ambitious and abstract. She seemed to care more about general principles of participatory urban planning than street vending licenses. She advocated for a comprehensive approach. "We have presented a roadmap in three stages with six pillars, which include transparent management, urban planning, participatory channels, and trade promotion. We also want the city to lay out the principles for the regulation of street vending," she said at a meeting. When the president of the Union interrupted her to point out that so long as the problem of the revoked licenses was not solved, the other matters were moot, she agreed but asked that the other items be included in the discussion.

Her reluctance to even ask for the reinstatement of all licenses, however, raised suspicions of a deeper conflict of interest. At the separate meeting between the parties representing street vendors, where the definitive list of demands to the city was to be drawn, the vice president of the DVA favored focusing on the group of 2012. But other street vendors in attendance protested, claiming all revoked licenses should be included in the proposal. Helena, however, seemed reluctant to do so. "This is like asking your dad for a Ferrari," she said, implying that an excessive bid would undermine their bargaining position. The Union president replied that five thousand licenses in a city of twenty million was not a Ferrari. At Helena's behest, however, the group eventually agreed on a plan to reinstate licenses in phases, with revocations for each year prior to 2012 being discussed at the CPAs—which also needed to be restored.

Helena had voiced the same demand for a gradual reinstatement of licenses earlier, at a meeting attended by the secretary's chief of staff. Seeing the confusion in the negotiation group, the chief of staff noted: "If you are going for an administrative review of license cancellations, you run the risk that the decision be upheld and then there is nothing you can do about it. I wouldn't take that path. Now, if what you want is for this administration to rescind every decision made under Kassab, all the cancellations and revocations, just say so. I can take that demand to the mayor." This was the first and only time that such an offer would be on the table. Yet the room fell silent. Astonishingly, no one seemed willing to seize the opportunity. After a while, Helena said: "You can do that for those [terminated in] 2012, and then we can set up a timeline for the others." Addressing her by her name, the chief of staff replied: "But that means those people [with licenses terminated before 2012] will have to wait. They will have to wait," meaning they would not be able to work until their cases were reviewed. Helena remained silent.

Helena's attitude upset Maria, a street vendor whose license was canceled in 2006 and who felt Helena had made a "terrible mistake" by not pushing for the reinstatement of all licenses revoked since 2005 when the opportunity arose. Echoing the complaint of other Assembly participants who had grown disillusioned with the CIW as well as criticism by leaders of the established vendors organizations, she implied that the CIW's priority was to receive income from abroad and satisfy its donors. "They are using us," said Luiza, another street vendor. "The only thing that's sacred for them is our signatures," which the NGO collected at the meetings of the Assembly. About the fact that nothing was done to include those with licenses revoked or canceled prior to 2012, she said that it could be due to a lack of experience. "Or maybe they wanted us to hang loose, so they could keep their jobs. Don't you see that those who are covered [by the injunction] have deserted the Assembly?"[15] Later, in an interview, Helena denied having opposed the reinstatement of licenses, though she admitted to making many mistakes.

The Day After

Much contemporary thinking about citizenship emphasizes the collective dimension. Individualism has hollowed out modern societies. The assertion of liberties and sometimes privileges that the individual is or feels entitled to undermines the collective construction of a body politic based on communal values. A commonwealth in which individuals form self-contained worlds and see themselves as the sole and sacred repository of rights ceases to be a commonwealth.

These critics have a point—so long as the basic rights of each member of the polity are established and secure. Indeed, the struggles of informal citizens put a caveat on our collectivist ideals of citizenship. What went down in that room belies the fact that street vendors barely exist as individuals in the political process or in the eyes of the state. While policy decisions that affect everyone's lives are often made out of sight, the exercise of rights remains an individual experience. Not so for licensed street vendors, who were beholden to a group of actors with conflicting, confusing, and sometimes dubious interests and agendas—and, potentially, no power—to recover their most basic right. That dependence continued to shape their fate after the negotiations.

Following the failure of the negotiating group to reach a settlement, the judicial process was put on hold during the Christmas break, and the city asked for various extensions thereafter, which the judge granted. Three years after the end of the talks, the case had not been ruled or settled. The public defender who cofiled the lawsuit received a medal for his deed at a public ceremony sponsored by Tristan at city hall and then moved out of town, withdrawing from the lawsuit. In an interview with the author, the president of the Union lamented the lack of action by the city, but in a more subdued way. At the same time, he complained about the impatience of Union members who continued to call and ask for an answer. "What [vendors] don't understand," he said, intriguingly, "is that to make an omelet, you have to break the eggs."

Given their inability to shape the policy debate—let alone the policy toward street vendors—the CIW decided to pursue a "judicial strategy" that consisted of building evidence that the city had no interest in addressing the issue. This evidence, they figured, could be used at a later point, if the case went to trial. Hence, the CIW lawyer wrote the template of a letter for vendors deprived of their licenses, which they could fill out with their name and info, and encouraged them to take those letters to city hall and request proof of delivery. Some vendors complained that they were being charged by the clerk at city hall for the procedure, which the lawyer said was a mistake. Luiza, a street vendor, also complained that some people were charging to provide the same document that the CIW lawyer had prepared and distributed for free. Upset, the lawyer said he would not allow anyone to profit from his labor. As often happens when a document or a piece of information enters the realms of informality, his template had taken on a life of its own, and no one could control how it was presented or used.

The judicial strategy echoes, in an intriguing way, the everyday practices of informal workers. Official documents such as administrative forms, stamped letters, receipts, and the like hold value in the liminal world of informality. Street vendors look for them, pay for them, and hold on to them. It is a way of asserting their rights and documenting violations thereof, such as a confiscation or eviction. Many of these documents are useless, and some—including licenses—are fake. Nonetheless, they provide a sense of existence and institutional recognition elusive in their trade.

But documenting endemic police violence crossed the line. After Helena and the lawyer left the CIW, young recruits, apparently distancing themselves from the lawsuit, suggested documenting all the abuses committed by the police against vendors. Addressing the Assembly, they said: "Can each of you bring the dates, times, and if you have the pictures of those abuses?" A street vendor whispered to his neighbor, "If you do that, you are dead. It's obvious."

Valdira raised her hand and spoke: "If, without saying anything, you can be called a snitch, to do [what you are suggesting] is to stick your neck out." The new CIW employee smiled. But the point was serious. Only outsiders with a formal understanding of the law and little practical knowledge of the street vending economy could suggest such an endeavor. The same NGO whose work had proved providential in saving the rights of street vendors through the lawsuit was now helplessly shut out of the political game, unable to redefine its purpose.

A STRAINED RELATIONSHIP

The precariousness of the situation was wearing not only on those vendors whose licenses had been terminated before 2012 and who were unable to work legally, but also on those protected by the court order who craved a return to normality and the renewal of their—now expired—licenses.[16] As the political patron of many of these vendors and a member of the ruling party, Tristan was taking part of the blame. In June 2015, the rumor spread that the city was about to remove all vendors, including those protected by the court order. The leaders of street vendors associations, including the Union and the DVA, organized a demonstration in front of city hall. The mayor eventually agreed to meet with them and called off the removal plans.

Despite the growing alienation of his electoral basis of licensed street vendors from the PT, Tristan continued to organize events at city hall to rally his followers during and after the settlement talks. At one such meeting, he introduced a bill that he was sponsoring, which added a minor provision to ML 11,039. The text required that cancellations be motivated by the district administrator. Tristan himself recognized that the bill was "symbolic" and noted that "all it does is make abuse against the street vendor a bit more difficult."[17]

The meeting and the measure extended the theatrics of the talks. Compelling bureaucrats to motivate license cancellations did little to help street vendors whose licenses were already suspended. But the ritual of enacting laws sent the message that street vendors and their patrons still exerted a degree of control over the political process. The symbolisms of legality, and lawmaking in particular, carry some weight in the liminal space of informality where licensed vendors operate.

At another ceremony, Tristan made a speech, intended to be emotional, about the disabled licensed vendor considered the boss of licensed street trade downtown. Even though he lacked formal education, Tristan said, Artur was a deep thinker who brought him the proposals for municipal bills all ready. "I don't even need to revise them," Tristan said. "[It's] as if [they were] written by a lawyer." He claimed that the street vendor's wife had written them for him and was a good writer. "As a journalist," he said, alluding to his professional background before going into politics, "I care about those things." He even shed some tears, which another vendor described the next day as "crocodile tears."[18]

Yet the councilman could not conceal the fact that the city was not doing much for his followers. At a meeting he attended in May 2014, a longtime, well-known vendor claimed vendors were not being told the truth and that the city wanted to do away with them. "I don't know who to vote for anymore," the vendor concluded to a round of applause. Frustrated, the councilman told the crowd, "Very well, as far as I'm concerned, you are now free. You hear me? I set you free. You don't have to vote for me anymore."

The Weight of Time

The law can be viewed as an instrument that both shields from abuse and subjugates, but rights are usually counted on the side of protection, as a limit to the authority of the state. The politics on display during the settlement talks, which followed the extensive and pervasive criminalization of street vendors in São Paulo, shed light on how rights under threat become an instrument of state power. The hope of seeing their rights restored neutralized licensed vendors. City authorities cultivated and exploited that hope, along with the divisions among those representing street vendors, over nine months.

The time dimension is implicit in Roy's work, too, when she writes that informal settlers are "a poor electorate which is *continuously* mobilized because land is *always* promised, but *never* secured. In this way, the territorialized uncertainty of informality guarantees political obedience [emphases added]."[19] The politics of hope play out over time, but time also sets limits to their efficacy. The manifest idleness of the talks, the agony endured by street vendors, and the pointless drama playing out in the negotiating room effected over time an exhaustion of hope. The rebellion Tristan faced, and to which he responded by "freeing" his clients, epitomizes the backlash. In 2017, Haddad ran for reelection as mayor of São Paulo—and lost. Licensed street vendors did not have much impact on the outcome, but their disenchantment with the party that had once championed their cause and offered them security was palpable. Their outrage and their agony, futile as they proved at redirecting policy, echoed the sentiment of voters who felt abandoned and betrayed in the neoliberal age. As I left São Paulo in the summer of 2014, Gabriel, a licensed vendor, told me that he would campaign for the PT because he had to, but his heart was not there anymore.

In their painful aimlessness, the talks bring out another paradox of informal citizenship. A common stereotype opposes citizens—who construct the polity by shaping its laws—to clients, who lack autonomy and power as the weaker link of unequal arrangements. Tristan's dramatic statement—"I set you free!"—and Gabriel's resignation reinforce the view of street vendors as clients. However, the debate at the talks revolved around the distribution of street vendors' rights, not the reciprocal obligations of unequal partners—notwithstanding Tina's claims about everything she had given to the party. To be sure, the empty threats and desperate pleas of street vendors were a far cry from any substantive exercise in civic participation and seemed to have little bearing on the policy process. Yet the suffering vendors experienced came not only from the dread of finding themselves out of work but also from the feeling that something that belonged to them—their rights—was being withheld, or deceitfully laid out in front of them, only to be withdrawn at the next meeting. The attachment they felt to those rights—and the emotions that stemmed from their being denied or used as bargaining chips—was a legacy of a time in which they felt they owned those rights, like citizens do.

7

The Empty Promise

In June 2014, Brazil hosted the soccer World Cup—the most popular sports event in the world. When FIFA, the world soccer governing body, awarded the 2014 World Cup to Brazil in 2007, the news was met with elation. A mecca of *futebol* and the country with the largest number of World Cup titles, Brazil had waited more than half a century to host the event after the national team lost the final to Uruguay in 1950 at Rio's iconic stadium. But the stakes went beyond soccer and the lure of winning a championship on home turf.

As David Black and Janis Van Der Westhuizen point out, sports mega-events impinge on geopolitics.[1] They provide a platform through which emerging nations seek status recognition on the world stage. It is their moment of arrival. China hosted the 2008 Summer Olympics in that spirit, as did Russia with the Sochi Winter Olympics in 2010 and the World Cup in 2018. Brazil was brimming with optimism in 2007; its economy was booming, and the Brazilian government under Lula, who was extremely popular, saw an opportunity to assert the country's global standing. It made a successful bid to host the 2016 summer Olympic Games that same year.

While hosting a sports mega-event is a logistical feat that attests to the host's managerial capacities, efficiency is not the only source of prestige. An underlying narrative of joy and communion animates an event that brings together people from around the world in a colorful festivity, where nations compete peacefully and fans act as one in support of their team. These ideals of modernity and irenic internationalism glamorize the place that hosts it. At the same time, the inclusive discourse of a global community spanning social classes and borders has faced reality checks at various editions, from dramatic surveillance and security operations to protests denouncing unnecessary public spending and social exclusion. To reconcile the practice with the narrative in the face of loud criticism, organizers in Brazil engineered a superficial, mostly cosmetic form of inclusion that involved street vendors and casts doubts on the value of their rights.

An Image Problem

The optimistic narrative was cracking well ahead of the June 12, 2014, kickoff. By the summer of 2013, when Brazil hosted a smaller tournament considered a trial run for the World Cup, the public mood had soured. The massive expenditures of taxpayer money required for building stadiums—including overcapacity stadiums in cities with little in the way of a soccer fan base—as well as other infrastructure projects of dubious long-term utility added fuel to the fire of a roiling corruption scandal shaking the ruling PT at the federal level. Meanwhile, serious issues with public services such as health care and education galvanized public anger. Hence, in June 2013, Brazil witnessed the largest demonstrations since the return to democracy. In São Paulo alone, over one million people took to the streets, denouncing corruption, affirming national pride, and demanding schools and hospitals that also "meet FIFA standards." While attendance at demonstrations fell sharply over time, partly due to violent incidents that received intense media coverage, protests against the World Cup continued sporadically through the beginning of the tournament, with chants and slogans like "a World Cup of social exclusion" (*a copa da exclusão*), "a World Cup of social inequality" (*a copa da desigualdade*), or a more defiant "There will be no World Cup!" (*Não vai ter copa*).

Despite efforts in the media to paint anti–World Cup protesters as violent radicals, the movement caused concern and embarrassment for both FIFA and the government. FIFA had to defend its corporate identity and the image of its flagship event as a friendly and harmonious coming-together of nations. The Brazilian government, on the other hand, had to show that it cared more about its people than about its commitments to a foreign organization. Faced with public backlash against the massive hidden costs of hosting the World Cup and accusations of it being undemocratic and exclusionary, organizers took remedial steps.

As part of the impression management campaign to address these reputational troubles, the government dropped the discredited line of a big opportunity to fast-track the country's economic development in favor of a patriotic appeal to host "the best World Cup ever" (*a copa das copas*). Organizers also reached out to grassroots groups and sought to include some disadvantaged categories at official events. Their efforts led to the participation of street vendors as commission sellers at World Cup sites in São Paulo.

There was more than a little irony in the choice of street vendors as a token of the World Cup's commitment to social inclusion. Most of them were barred from exercising their trade following the mass eviction campaign. And World Cup legislation itself contributed to their criminalization through monopoly rules benefiting sponsors and harsh penalties against violators that explicitly targeted street vendors. But the policy of incorporating street vendors was symbolic in character. Symbolic policies are, according to Sandra Suarez, "policies that are not designed to accomplish their purported goals."[2] They are meant to convey the impression that state officials are addressing an issue they do not intend to address, either because they cannot or because they do not want to.[3]

This chapter focuses on the making and outcomes of the street vendors' official World Cup participation program. It analyzes how organizers solved the contradiction between the normative imperative of projecting an image of inclusion, on the one hand, and the concentration of commercial rights inherent to the economic organization of the World Cup, on the other. It argues that they did so by granting street vendors shallow rights. If property rights are institutionally embedded claims on resources, then rights vary not only in the scope of the claim (e.g., *usus*, *fructus*, and *abusus*) but in terms of their embeddedness, which ranges from constitutionally embedded to enshrined in municipal law to granted by decree to stated on some kind of official document to verbal agreements. The rights street vendors received were narrow and shallow.

Making Nonpolicy

Studies of symbolic policies share a strategic premise. Policymakers confronted with a problem they are unable or unwilling to solve and facing pressure from their constituents to take action will pretend to solve the problem. However, a gap between statements, actions, and outcomes is not, in itself, a mark of symbolism. Most policies do not achieve their stated goals, and those in charge have good (political) reasons to deny shortcomings or failure. For a policy to be properly symbolic, its framers must know from the start that they are not committing the necessary resources—whether such resources are available or not—and claim to be doing what it takes to solve the problem. An element of strategic duplicity is at the core of symbolic policymaking, which resonates with the view of the public sphere as a reign of appearances.[4]

Participatory initiatives like the one described in this chapter are a common symbolic policy device.[5] Caroline Lee and Zachary Romano show how, in the wake of Hurricane Katrina, authorities set up participatory forums with survivors to discuss plans to rebuild New Orleans, the true purpose of which was to "disciplin[e] stakeholders by demobilizing dissent and reorienting action on contentious issues."[6] In that case, as in the case of street vendors during the World Cup, the policy spoke to various audiences: the direct "beneficiaries," who are likely to see through the symbolism, and the broader public, who may not be aware of the outcomes or lack thereof.

Leaving aside the question of whether symbolic policies actually fool their audiences, there is more to the enterprise than the proverbial lip service. The scarcity of ethnographic studies of symbolic policymaking contributes to the conventional view of a ploy from above. Direct observation brings out a more nuanced picture, however. Participatory forums have to be organized and run. Symbolic policy implementation mobilizes a host of actors, including state agents, not all of whom exhibit the same inclination or aptitude for hypocrisy. While some agents may be indifferent or even hold disparaging views toward the fictitious beneficiaries, others may have good intentions and push for wider benefits—yet encounter resistance within the state and discover that their hands are tied. The policy outcome is a forgone conclusion, but the process is riddled with contingency and conflict. A host of material interests surround design and implementation. And resource transfers do occur—insufficient as they may be—which, in a context of disengagement by authorities, create opportunities for graft.

As an act of symbolic policy, the distribution of rights to street vendors during the World Cup was never meant to achieve its stated goal of helping street vendors benefit from the event in a substantive way. But the shallowness of rights reflects more than the lack of political will; it also speaks to the power and pressures of corporate sponsors. And the policy process was less symbolic than informal, conducted without any institutional framework, which opened the door to profiteering. When they do not pose a threat to the state, public order, or the interests of powerful groups, a casual approach suits the government of informal citizens. This was the case for participants in the program.

FRAMING VENDOR PARTICIPATION

When Tonio, a city official and a member of the local World Cup organizing team in São Paulo, set out to look for options for a collaboration with civil society that would restore the event's tarnished image, street vendors were not on his radar. He contacted one of the local activist groups that were protesting against the World Cup. After a couple of meetings, however, the activists walked. One of the leaders accused the government of leading them on. "And she was right," Tonio acknowledged. "At that time, we didn't know what to do. We were indeed leading them on."

The outreach was not altogether unfruitful. At a meeting with the group, Tonio met Helena, the CIW worker. Helena was more receptive to Tonio's fledging proposition, and she invited him to a meeting of the Street Vendors' Assembly. In August of 2013, a little less than a year before the start of the World Cup, Tonio and another employee of São Paulo's city government made their pitch for some form of official street vendor participation during the World Cup, under terms yet to be determined, to Assembly attendants. They faced immediate pushback. A heavy-built Black leader of street vendors stood up and pointed out that Coca-Cola and other big brands wanted good-looking young women to tend their stands, not street vendors. Others complained as well. Tonio's response was surprisingly candid. Alluding to the mass demonstrations the country and the city had experienced in recent weeks, he said street vendors should fight for their rights on the streets. "That's the only way you'll get something. But we'll try to help out." Despite their misgivings, Assembly members agreed to participate in a working group to design the policy with city officials.

Defining the content of the street vendors' participation program and the rights of those who signed up was not an easy task. Most vendors are used to selling their own products on their own terms and cherish that independence. Yet organizers imposed tight limits on what products could be sold, where, and at what prices. Instead of being defined within the working group, moreover, the rules were, by and large, communicated to street vendors during the meetings through announcements or updates. They belied the power that FIFA and its sponsors wielded behind the scene.

The city thus made it clear that only products from FIFA's commercial partners would be allowed and that a designated private contractor would supply the merchandise to registered vendors. Damian, a CIW worker who participated in the working group, protested, saying he thought the city government would be in charge of running the program. "If it's not managed by private firms," a top city official replied, "the alternative is to let any street vendor go around and sell his own products. . . . I don't think that's cool." Stunned, Damian shot back: "Oh, so you don't think that's cool?" Trying to strike a conciliatory note, Tonio said that letting vendors sell their own product was "not a lost cause" but that FIFA was entitled to all official World Cup sites, and "you can't introduce products in those areas."

From a legal standpoint, of course, FIFA had the upper hand. Brazil had signed a contract and passed the General Law of the World Cup, which gave FIFA and its partners exclusive rights. They did not participate in the working group meetings, however, so city officials had to carry out parallel negotiations with them. While I did not directly observe those negotiations, officials sometimes conveyed the difficulties they were having. "FIFA kills its competitors," a city employee said. "You can't put Pepsi for instance [in World Cup spaces]. But what we are trying to do is for every sponsor to prioritize street vendors [as their sellers]."

"[The sponsors] want everything for themselves," Tonio told me at the end of a meeting. "But, of course, you can't tell that to the street vendors." A higher-ranking official was more blunt: "These guys are vampires. They don't care how much they sell. They just want that [to be the] price."

Despite the favorable terms, food giant Nestlé was not interested. In fact, city officials quickly abandoned the idea of including food sales in the program after "FIFA asked for a prohibitive price." In the end, only two sponsors, beer giant AB InBev and Coca-Cola, came on board. Participants could only sell these two companies' beverages, which had to be supplied by the designated contractor and sold at fixed prices: four reals for water and five for beer. Vendors made a 30 percent margin, which came to 1.5 reals per beer can, down from an original offer of 1.75 reals. Neither the street vendors nor the commercial partners were happy with the arrangement. Street vendors found the set prices too high and the margins too small. According to city officials, corporate sponsors thought the margins were outrageous.

Emerging information about the regulatory framework also restricted the geographical scope of the street vendors' program. Aside from the stadium, each host city had a public broadcasting site called Fan Fest. Both the Fan Fest and the stadium were surrounded by areas of commercial restriction (ACRs), where businesses must abide by strict FIFA-mandated regulations. The municipal government in São Paulo was hoping to organize a number of other public broadcastings in parks across the city, and officials in the working group saw those sites as providing additional opportunities for street vendors registered in the program to work. However, at a policy meeting, an employee of the downtown district administration recognized that, contrary to what members of the local organizing team had originally thought, any public gathering that broadcast games or was related to the World Cup in some way fell under "FIFA's jurisdiction." The stadium and the Fan Fest—an enclosed space (perímetro fechado) where FIFA "can do whatever it wants"— were off-limits. Hence, the only areas allocated to street vendors under the program were the ACRs around the stadium and the Fan Fest. In terms of benefits, this framework did not amount to much. Not only were expected profits low under these conditions, but the program set tight limits on the freedoms that street vendors are used to having and that make their trade appealing, despite the violence and other adversities they face on a daily basis.

WHAT THE LAW SAYS

The role of legality in shaping this policy was as ambiguous as the motivations of its agents. Throughout the negotiation process, task force members made references to "the law" to prop up the points they were making. "We have to act according to the law," Rodrigo, a top city official, once said. "The law forbids the sale of alcoholic beverages. We are going to have to adapt the law [for the World Cup]."

As Rodrigo himself acknowledged, however, finding the legal tool to support the participation of street vendors during the World Cup was a challenge. Street vending licenses were all suspended at the time, a settlement had not been reached, and licensed street vendors still working lawfully were working thanks to a court order. "The law now in force is bad," Rodrigo said. "It's taken most people off the streets. But we have to respect the law." At the same time, the recently passed street food law, which organizers considered using as a framework at some point, had yet to be implemented (see chap. 2).

At another meeting, after Rodrigo insisted that any street vendor allowed in the areas of commercial restriction would have to be "*ambulante*" in the literal sense of itinerant vendor, Damian, the CIW employee, pointed out that according to ML 11,039, the term *ambulante* applies to all street vendors, including fixed-spot ones. Contradicting his own claims about the need to act within the law, Rodrigo replied, confusedly, "It's not about a simple law. You have to be realistic. . . . And we can't pass another bill."

When the CIW worker asked about the publication in an official outlet of the criteria for the participation of street vendors at official World Cup sites, Tonio answered: "Well, that has to come out of the city council. There's a municipal law for the World Cup. That's what will determine the rights of street vendors." None of the decrees and ordinances issued on the World Cup alluded to the participation of street vendors in the end, however. And when Luiza asked about workplace accident insurance and protections in line with the decent work agreement signed by the city with the ILO ahead of the World Cup, her queries were essentially ignored.

The program to let street vendors work at official event sites during the World Cup thus granted them rights that were not embedded in legislation, with the final product looking more like an informal agreement. These rights had no judicial value, nor did they carry the same historical weight as, for example, licensing rights. They were, in that sense, shallow rights. As a result, the "pull" of the program on potential beneficiaries—a diffuse crowd to begin with—was nothing compared to the power city officials held over disaffected licensees with the promise of reinstating their titles. But some vendors and leaders managed to take advantage of the policy nonetheless.

Looking for Workers

As the project of letting street vendors work at official events was taking shape, several city officials expressed sympathy for the idea of giving unlicensed vendors a chance. The contractor supported the view: "We don't care who has a license and who doesn't," he said at an informational meeting. "What matters is that you follow the rules of the business." The problem with enrolling unlicensed vendors, however, is their invisibility. If keeping track of licensed vendors was already a challenge that the city seemed unable to meet, any prospect of doing a census of unlicensed vendors for the purpose of selecting participants for the World Cup program was beyond utopian.

Foucault uses the term *population* to describe the object of government in the age of biopolitics, when the exercise of state power relies on knowledge instruments—variables that signal trends in a population, upon which rulers act, such as inflation, school enrollment, or life expectancy.[7] While Foucault contrasts this mode of government with a previous regime that sought to penetrate the individual soul and control the self from within, individualized information in its bureaucratic form still matters a great deal for the making of policy. Repressing an informal population on the streets, outside the field of legality, is a matter of manpower; the target remains largely anonymous. But inclusive policy efforts like the distribution of welfare call for civil registries, social security numbers, centralized databases, and other such technologies that produce individualized knowledge and, in the process, constitute the population. From this perspective, informality is characterized by the absence or murkiness of governmental knowledge, which is even more pronounced in the case of unlicensed vendors.

None of this seemed to matter, however, as organizers did not care much about who enrolled in the program. After the number of available slots was set at six hundred, down from an initial offer of a thousand, Tonio delegated recruitment to street vendors: "All right. The Street Vendors' Assembly is our partner. We'll let you bring the list [of participants]," Tonio said at a meeting. "A little more than eight hundred [candidates] so that firms [i.e., FIFA's partners] can choose. If we make an open call, you [those street vendors in the room] will lose." Street vendors seemed to agree.

By then, however, attendance at the Assembly meetings had shrunk. There had never been more than a few dozen participants, but the great interest spurred by the lawsuit waned as settlement talks dragged on and the CIW, which had filed the lawsuit, seemed unable to extract any meaningful concession from the city. Those protected by the injunction had fewer reasons to attend, and those who did not enjoy judicial protection had grown disillusioned with it. As a result, only a handful of hardcore activists or loyalists remained, licensed and unlicensed. At the same time, disagreements among CIW employees and internal strife, which eventually led to the dismissal of Helena and the resignation of other workers, further weakened the NGO and the Assembly it hosted.

Hence, when Tonio called on street vendors to take care of recruitment, Claudia, one of the vendors' representatives, confessed they could not cope. And Luiza was afraid. She did not want to "shoot herself in the foot," she explained. "We could bring people who cause trouble," she said at a policy meeting. "It's a huge responsibility. . . . We want this to be a decent thing." Besides, she found little interest among some vendors she approached in her neighborhood. "They've been selling underwear for years," she said. "They don't want to deal with beer."

As far as I could gauge, Tonio's intentions were good, and his hope of setting a lasting inclusive policy precedent was genuine, but some of his colleagues were prejudiced. One of them once commented after a meeting: "[Vendors] are going to bring their cousins. They are little mafias. They make a lot [of money]." Referring to the registration process, he said: "They won't be able to present [the ID card], since many of them are screwed," meaning afoul of the law, according to him, due to delinquency with child alimony. Tasked with the paradoxical mission of implementing a symbolic policy, Tonio himself was ambivalent and sometimes cynical about the process. "I threw the responsibility [of recruitment] to them," he told me after a meeting. "It's going to be a mess." And when his colleague pointed out that many street vendors would be reluctant to register if they had to show their ID, he said: "If there's only one that gets in, it's not my problem." In the end, there was no official registration procedure.

THE RISK OF CAPTURE

The aloofness of the government created opportunities for other actors to take advantage of the program. When Lucia found out that she and her fellow street vendors were in charge of recruitment, she got excited, saying she would bring people from the housing movement, in which she was also

involved, regardless of their trade. A few weeks later, at an information session, the contractor addressed the crowd and validated her plans: "You can
bring whoever you want [to the registration desk], your brother, your father.
We don't even need them to come. All we need is the documents and I'll give
you the pass, which will allow you to sign up and work."

Even political actors within the city government saw an opening. At the
district of Itaquera—where the stadium is located—a top city official seemed
to have struck a deal with the leader of a local neighborhood association
named Roberto. I attended a town hall meeting in Itaquera, and the com-
plicity between the two was on full display. The district administrator introduced Roberto as the representative of the Assembly, even though Roberto
had never attended an Assembly meeting. The administrator then noted that
Roberto was in charge of registering street vendors for the World Cup. A
woman asked: "So, if Roberto is the representative, are we all subordinated to
him or are we going to divvy this up among the other associations?" (None of
the other associations had anything to do with street vending.)

The district administrator replied that "it is the role of us all to identify the
people who could benefit, reach out [to them] and tell them about this [pro-
gram]." Threading the needle with diplomacy, he then proposed what he called
a "gentlemen's agreement" in which everyone could invite other people to register. "Don't mess with it," he warned. He also said that the city could provide a
locale for registration and committed to making sure there was no favoritism.

Despite these noble gestures, the registration process in Itaquera remained in the hands of Roberto, whose wife, Nora, was the dubious leader of
the street vendors cooperative at a park where Valdira worked on weekends. I
asked Valdira if the street vendors at the park, whom the district administrator had said should have priority in the program, knew about it. She told me
that people were not signing up because it's in the hands of "Roberto, Nora,
and that crowd."

In short, the well-connected leadership co-opted the distribution of rights
around the stadium. The policy was symbolic not only in its purported goal
of allowing disenfranchised constituencies to benefit from the World Cup but
also as a governmental device for exerting control over and channeling resources toward a population. Policymakers were so detached from their own
policy that well-positioned players took advantage of it. This form of policy
capture is different from associations of licensed street vendors lobbying to
limit the expansion of licensing rights. In one case, interest groups build on
the assets they have accumulated thanks to their long-standing rights; in the
other, opportunistic players exploit the fluidity of an informal policy. And
capture did not even happen behind the scenes.

When the contractor told the crowd they could bring whoever they wanted to the registration desk at an information session open to the public and with significant media presence, a street vendor leader and close ally of Roberto quickly intervened: "We are the Cool Guys association, we are in charge of doing this registration, and we already have a list of four hundred [candidates]. All the slots are taken by members of the Assembly and the Cool Guys association. There might be some outstanding spots for those who want to participate because of dropouts, so you can come and ask us, but we have a list that is almost full."

As this leader spoke, Roberto and the contractor exchanged some words on stage. The contractor then took back the mic, saying, "Maybe we can cancel the meeting at [the registration desk] and I'll centralize all the documents through Roberto. He'll be in charge of handing them to me. Does that sound good, Roberto?"

Roberto responded "That's fine," and the contractor told the audience: "So, I take back what I said earlier. I'll leave it in his hands."

As I left the meeting, I spoke with another attendant who worked for the local newspaper. He said, "You have to be a part of the Cool Guys association if you want to work [at the stadium]. Otherwise, there's no way. It's the only way to get in. And they will charge you thirty reals. They didn't charge me because they know me, and they know I'm a journalist."

City officials had made clear from the outset that participation in the program would be free. When I asked Tonio if Roberto was charging, he responded, "Of course, all unions need to charge." I then asked if he thought Roberto was charging people to participate in the program. "I don't know," he replied. "And I don't want to know."

The Story of Fernando

The flip side of shallowness is access. In its lack of substance, the program was open to a much larger and more diverse group than the—at least on paper—tightly regulated and socially closed licensing program. Among the unlikely participants was Fernando, an unlicensed street vendor from Ecuador whose life sometimes looked like a long chain of missteps and misfortunes but whose easygoingness and free spirit allowed him to get through the most trying of circumstances.

Fernando's niche was headphones. A few weeks before the World Cup, the police confiscated his merchandise. Some unlicensed vendors had a local safety net or support system that allowed them to factor confiscations into their budgets, but for Fernando, a lone traveler and broke immigrant, a

confiscation meant losing everything he had. Even when the encounter with
the police went smoothly, as it usually did, given Fernando's meek character,
the inherent violence of losing one's livelihood had a traumatizing effect, he
told me. Assuming repression would only increase during the World Cup, he
decided not to try to borrow money or wares to replenish his stock. Shortly
thereafter, he was sleeping on the streets. I tried to help him out.

At the end of a "training session" about the World Cup street vendors'
participation program at which a city official told the audience that selling is
mostly about "that magical touch"—"some have it, others don't"—then took
off, leaving the driver in charge of the meeting, I approached Donald, the
contractor, and told him I had a friend who was out of work. He took down
Fernando's name and told me to bring him over to the stadium the following
week. Two local teams were playing, and vendors would be allowed to work
inside the stadium in a trial run of sorts for the World Cup (even though
vendors could only work in the ACR during the tournament).

Following Donald's advice, I took Fernando to the stadium. I left him at
the vendors' registration stand, kept his things—which he carried with him
since becoming homeless—and wished him good luck. When we met again, a
few hours later, he had not made much money. It turned out participants had
to bring their own coolers, which I hadn't known, and purchase the product
from the contractor in advance. Fernando had neither a cooler nor money to
buy the products. Inside the stadium, the bartender had been kind enough to
let him sell beer on credit in plastic cups. He tried for a while, then sat down
and watched the game.

I had met Fernando, a short, thin man in his mid-forties with graying hair
and wrinkles, a few months earlier on the downtown bridge of Santa Ifigênia,
while he was selling headphones showcased on top of a cardboard box. What
began as a casual—if, on my end, not entirely disinterested—conversation
evolved into genuine friendship. Our shared national origins contributed to
our bond.

As a migrant, Fernando embodied a common figure among street traders
in the squares and sidewalks of large cities. His first trip abroad took him to
Colombia, where he worked at a restaurant owned by a Middle Easterner,
then to Syria (before the war), where he followed his boss, and from there to
France and Spain. He was deported back to Ecuador when he attempted to
cross back from Spain into France by land. After a couple of weeks of trying
to sell handcrafts in his home country, for which he made no more than twenty
bucks, he was back on the road, across Latin America.

Fernando arrived in São Paulo by bus after spending some time in Chile
and Bolivia. He had been a street vendor in Santiago, Chile, where he paid

a small fee to sell ice cream. After he complained to a policeman that other vendors who had not paid the fee were selling next to him, the officer replied, "The streets are tough, aren't they?" and did nothing to sanction the trespassers. Now, in São Paulo, Fernando was the one working on the run as an unlicensed vendor.

While his childhood experiences of coming from a broken household, not feeling loved, and escaping echo those of Valdira and many others who end up etching out their living on the streets, Fernando had some cultural pursuits that were foreign to his environment. At thirty-one, while living in France, he learned to play chess. It became his passion, and he carried books as well as a small laptop on which he practiced until it got stolen at one of the downtrodden hostels where he was staying when he arrived in São Paulo. "I feel good," he told me once. "When I play chess, I feel good. . . . It helps me forget about all the things I need." He also spoke French and enjoyed reading literature.

Being a foreigner was a liability at various levels, beyond the lack of a local support system. Fernando said of Brazilian street vendors: "You can't say anything to them. One of them came and told me: 'Get out of here. That's my spot.' I said: 'What, you are selling here and there?' We had an argument. But you can't raise your voice because the others are watching. And they'll always side with the locals. You have to be careful." He was also bullied by Brazilians where he slept. And, by early 2014, the atmosphere was fraught. "There's a crisis coming," he said. "People are not selling. And when sales are not happening, you feel the tension. You know it's there. You see it in the way that [other vendors] look at you. They are not selling and you are not selling. Tension rises. I think I'm going to look for another square to work."

And yet, for all the layers of marginalization he endured as an unlicensed street vendor and an undocumented immigrant, Fernando kept a friendly attitude with those around him, from the waiter at the small restaurant where he drank coffee with a raw egg (for protein) to the guy who sold cigarettes next to him at the square outside a subway station. His attitude was an expression of his personality, but it served a survival function, of which Fernando was aware. One day, around midnight, as he was leaving his workplace, a gang of drug addicts robbed him of his wares at a nearby park. The next morning, the cigarette seller asked Fernando why he was not working; after Fernando reluctantly shared his story, his coworkers teamed up to confront the gang. According to Fernando, the street vendors told the thugs: "It's hard enough to be running from the police all day long, you are not going to screw us on top of that."

Not long after Fernando recovered his headphones from the gang, the police confiscated them. On the eve of that confiscation, Fernando was having trouble paying for the bed at the hostel where he was staying. He spoke with the landlady and worked out an arrangement. "I was relaxed," he said. "[The police] got me because I was relaxed from solving my housing problems." Not long after that, he ended up sleeping on the streets.

Fernando also had to deal with competition from other migrant workers. Headphones were the niche of African vendors, especially Senegalese, who carried large boards with foldable legs to showcase their wares. "You have your little pile of twenty headphones and these guys come and set up a huge table full of phones right next to you. There's no way you can compete with that. And you can't tell them to fuck off, either. What do you do?"

And yet, for all the adversities Fernando was facing, the roots of his end-less setbacks came, in his view, from within. Fernando hated São Paulo like he hated Ecuador, his home country. "I've never taken so much thrashing as I have in my own country," he once said. He compared the dingy skyscrapers in São Paulo to the bars of a prison cell. The first time I asked him if he had any plans for the future, his answer was "to stay alive." However, I realized in some of our conversations that his dream was to go back to Europe. He missed the quality of food. He missed the time when he used to work as a waiter in a res-taurant on the coast in Catalonia. And he missed a house where he had lived in France, by the sea. As he saw it, these memories and feelings were messing with his work. One time, when I insisted that the Senegalese must have a good supply system to carry larger inventories, he said he could have it, too.

"It's not so hard to get that. If you work constantly. If you accumulate. I could have the same volumes."

"So what's the difference?" I asked him.

"The mood. These guys came straight from Senegal. This is everything they know. . . . I've been in France. I've been much better than this. I've lived a good life. That's why I can't get to work straight. I can't stop thinking about it. I lack the motivation. But I'll get over it. I just need to accept where I am."

When I asked him what job he would like to have, he said being a waiter. He had worked ten-hour shifts as a waiter in Catalonia. But he wouldn't take that job in Brazil. "There's too much pressure, from your bosses, from your colleagues. For what? Seven hundred reals, eight hundred reals. No thanks. I'd rather be running all day from the police."

"You mean you prefer running from the police all day long?"

"Oh yeah, a thousand times. South America is good for those with money. Others are trapped. These are prison countries. There's no life here."

"But you've been a worker yourself," I pointed out.

"Oh yes, I picked coffee, cacao, figs."

"Did you like it?"

"No. It was a subsistence system. Just like this [street vending]. That's what you do in Latin America. You just work to survive. It's shitty. . . . Here, if you are poor, you are not a . . . [looks for the word] a citizen."

On June 12, kickoff day, I accompanied Fernando to the distribution point in the vicinity of the Fan Fest, where participants in the program were to receive their wares. The program was off to a bad start. The contractor was late. Since I wanted to conduct observation in the area, I gave Fernando some cash in case he had to pay for the product up front and went on to do some fieldwork.

A Poor Showing

On the opening day, inspectors went on strike, so vendors in the program faced competition from unlicensed street vendors who sold beer by their side at lower prices while making larger margins (see chap. 7). Poor logistics delayed the operation, moreover. It later transpired that the contractor had passed on distribution in the Fan Fest ACR to another company, leading one of the program participants to describe their status as "double outsourced" (*quarterizados*).

Even though the number of participants around the Fan Fest never reached the projected figure of two hundred, the roughly ninety vendors present on the first day were far too many, considering the size of the ACR; they ended up selling within feet of one another. And sales were low throughout the event. Large crowds only gathered when Brazil was playing or in the final rounds of the tournament. Even after the crackdown that followed the free-for-all of the opening day, registered vendors competed with the bars in the area, which were allowed to continue operating normally and offered a larger variety of beers at a better price. They also competed with sales inside the Fan Fest, where vendors were not recruited through the program. Inside, where the original contractor was in charge, vendors received a much smaller share of the price of each item (about 12%, according to one vendor), but prices were higher, the market was captive (since spectators could not bring their own beverages), and sales volumes were much larger. Under these conditions, the contractor and the sponsors had few incentives to promote business in the ACR, which might explain the sponsors' reluctance to lower the prices during the negotiation process.

As a result, many participants deserted the program after the initial days, including Fernando. Those who continued coming complained that it was not worth it. Valdira, who by that time had few sources of income, took part, even though selling beer went against her religious beliefs. Some days vendors sold only one or two drinks, some days they sold nothing; on a good day, Valdira said she made about fifty reals (US$22). The only vendor who reported making a profit, Mateo, broke the rules by buying the merchandise underhandedly at lower prices, from a store, instead of from the designated provider. Other registered vendors who played by the rules complained that the practice was common. The contractor, on the other hand, complained that some vendors had taken off with merchandise, leaving behind a debt of two thousand reals, which the city agreed to cover.

The vendors I interviewed at the stadium had a better experience, despite some supply problems and the limited number of game days. Luna—a woman who used to work as an unlicensed street vendor at the subway station near the stadium until the small marketplace was shut down by two police officers two weeks before the World Cup (see chap. 7)—made 120 reals one day. Not all of those who participated in the program at the stadium were street vendors, however. And the leadership of the Cool Guys association charged participants an extra thirty reals after the event.

A Critical Assessment

The program to incorporate street vendors at the World Cup fell far short of its stated goals. While some vendors made a profit, earnings were meager on the whole. Around the Fan Fest, income from sales was far lower than what unlicensed vendors could make a few blocks away, at 25 de Março, on a normal day while selling merchandise of their choosing at a price they set themselves. These shortcomings did not prevent FIFA from citing the experiment in São Paulo as part of the positive impact of the World Cup and as a testament to its commitment to holding a socially responsible event. In a leaflet, FIFA used the official figure of six hundred participants stated on the agreement signed ahead of the World Cup, which was much larger than the actual number of participants during the tournament. The program failed to gain traction among street vendors, most of whom deserted it and some of whom took advantage of it in illicit ways, but street vendors were not the main audience anyway. At the same time, it did not seem to have much of an impact on public opinion.

Tonio, who had expressed hope that the program would become a blueprint for street vendor participation at other large-scale events, acknowledged afterward that policymakers pursuing the same goals in the future would have to start from scratch. Unlike licensing, which left a legacy of protective legislation and consolidated rights that both defenders and opponents of street vendors had to reckon with, the transient World Cup initiative created shallow rights that left no traces.

Under this policy, street vendors were brought into the field of legality, but in symbolic fashion. The legal status of workers participating in this program was shallow, with little in the way of benefits, protection, or recourse. The settlement talks described in the previous chapter also had a symbolic element, since the city had little intention of reinstating licenses. From the street vendors' standpoint, however, substantive rights were at stake, and state officials strategically entertained their hopes of recovering them. By contrast, the kind of informal policy implemented during the World Cup—a symbolic incorporation of informal workers—offered neither substantive rights nor hope. Most participants expected little to begin with, and many street vendors who learned about the program had not bothered enrolling. When I asked Fred, an unlicensed vendor who worked at 25 de Março, if he planned to register, he smiled: "I prefer to stay on the wild side [*na clandestinidade*]."

There are several reasons behind the shallowness and symbolism. The fact that street vendors were not a top priority for World Cup organizers at a time of straining demands undoubtedly contributed to the underwhelming outcome. At one of the meetings, a candid civil servant shared with street vendors that they were "falling by the wayside" in the policy discussions as "more central topics" captured the government's attention, and "we forget street vendors." However, the main obstacle to a more substantial distribution of rights seemed to be resistance from FIFA and its commercial partners. The discourse of inclusion contrasted with actual restrictions imposed by the legal framework as well as with the attitudes of corporate sponsors who sought to relinquish as little as possible of the exclusive commercial and marketing rights for which they had paid dearly.

The complacent attitude of the Brazilian government toward FIFA did not help. Whereas German courts ruled that a beer monopoly was unconstitutional when Germany hosted the World Cup in 2006, Brazil amended its federal law, which forbade the sale of alcohol inside stadiums, to meet FIFA requirements. As Tonio put it at a meeting, "The rules imposed by FIFA were accepted, there's nothing we can do about it. They were accepted when the [hosting] contract was signed. Let's focus on the opportunities."[8] Those opportunities were scarce and unappealing, however, except for those who co-opted the policy by monetizing access, as the Cool Guys did, or for those who subverted it, either by taking off with the merchandise or, as Mateo did, by sourcing it from an unauthorized supplier. Defiance of the World Cup legal provisions was even more widespread on the streets, among licensed and unlicensed vendors who did not participate in the program, as the next chapter shows.

Together, the working group meetings, the negotiations that took place within it, the negotiations with sponsors, the deals with association leaders, the qualms of policymakers, and the behavior of program participants during rollout all flesh out the underlying drama of symbolic policymaking. These elements paint a complicated picture and nuance the cynicism behind conventional narratives. The city government did not have much flexibility to set the rules, and some city officials may have granted street vendors more substantive rights had they had that power. The study of the World Cup program shows how the distribution of rights is constrained by material interests outside the state and how it becomes a spectacle under the circumstances.

LEGAL FICTIONS

At some level, all institutions are fictitious. They have no material essence. But some carry more weight than others. The unbearable lightness of rights, as McCann puts it, paraphrasing Milan Kundera, lies in that paradoxical state of ideas acquiring material force through institutional embodiments. The concept of a field of legality, with its contested boundaries and shades of citizenship, suggests not only that people do not have equal rights but that rights themselves do not have equal force or value. Those at the margins do not have as many rights, or their rights do not carry the same weight. As the key agent in the construction of the legal order, the state institutionalizes privilege. Echoing a common critique of rights as emancipatory devices, and a broader tradition in the sociology of the state, McCann thus writes, "As historical contests over rights become settled for periods of time, dominant groups and their official representatives routinely police the boundaries of prevailing rights constructions to sustain status quo relationships, limiting the possibilities of practical rights claiming to the terms of what is legally permissible."[9]

The broader story of São Paulo's licensed street vendors' struggles echoes this political economy of legality, with a caveat: The city government undertook to deconstruct their rights under Kassab, not just to preserve the status quo. The story of the efforts to ensure street vendor participation during the World Cup also echoes these principles, since dominant players (i.e., FIFA and its corporate sponsors) made sure participants enjoyed fairly limited commercial rights. The symbolic concession of shallow rights speaks to a different logic, however. The state is not trying to extend its control nor simply to protect the interests of a few influential actors. It is producing a very thin form of legality, under which no one really controls—or even knows—what is happening, for the sake of giving the outside world an impression of inclusiveness.

8

The Making of Lawlessness

A única coisa permanente na minha vida é fugir.[1]
STREET VENDOR

Behind the concerns about image that inspired the street vendors' participation program during the World Cup were not only political considerations but a host of material interests that, as the previous chapter shows, curtailed the scope and depth of the rights bestowed on street vendors. Geopolitics aside, sports mega-events represent a massive business opportunity. FIFA may be registered as a nonprofit, but its aim is to maximize revenue, and its commercial partners seek returns on investment. The sources of their profits, however, are mostly intangible. In a way, mega-events epitomize the logic of postindustrial capitalism. The product is an experience—an embodied experience for those who watch the games amid a cheering crowd, be it at the stadium or a public broadcasting like the Fan Fest, and a spectatorial experience for those watching in private on a screen. What makes the experience profitable is not only what consumers are willing to pay for it and spend during the games but the imprints advertisers can make on them. According to Tariq Panja, "global sponsorship income from the 2014 [World Cup] was $650 million higher than the $1 billion generated at the 2010 World Cup."[2]

Sponsors are buying commercial and marketing rights in virtual (e.g., television screens) and physical spaces associated with the World Cup.[3] In the 1980s, the firm ISL Marketing worked with FIFA and later linked up with the International Olympic Committee to establish a model based on selling exclusive broadcasting, marketing, and merchandizing rights to a limited number of sponsoring partners.[4] As with any property rights writ large, the value of these rights depends on their exclusivity. At an informational meeting, a lawyer representing FIFA used the hypothetical example of someone dressed up in a condom costume showing up at a game to hand over promotional material. If a camera turns toward him, he's getting millions of viewers—for free. It is incumbent on organizers in the host country or city to guarantee and enforce the exclusive rights of commercial partners. To this end, sports mega-events are preceded by significant legislative action.

A Legal Monopoly

The intellectual property and commercial rights of FIFA and its partners are enshrined in ad hoc legislation that FIFA requires host countries and cities to enact. On June 5, 2012, President Rousseff thus signed the General Law of the World Cup (Lei Geral da Copa) in compliance with FIFA hosting requirements. As a result, FIFA trademarks—including symbols, emblems, and phrases either registered by FIFA or recognized as FIFA property—were protected by federal law, overriding previous legislation that forbade the trademarking of event names. Across Brazil, during the World Cup, commercial restrictions applied to trademarked symbols, names, or slogans that appeared on fan gear, such as "2014 World Cup" or "Brazil 2014." As a FIFA representative told an audience in South Africa, "all that belongs to FIFA."[5]

Restrictions are far stricter at official event sites and their surrounding areas, known as ACRs or exclusion zones, wherein sponsors held legal monopolies. The World Cup law established ACRs around official venues—in particular, the stadium and the Fan Fest—setting a maximum radius of two kilometers around each site, although the actual scope and contours were determined in negotiations between local authorities and FIFA representatives in each host city.

Inside ACRs, rules were stricter and more straightforward. The law stated that the federal government would cooperate with all other levels of government as well as other competent authorities to secure for FIFA and its partners the exclusive right to conduct marketing activities and street commerce. Violators would be liable to civil and penal sanctions including prison terms of up to one year and fines. In São Paulo, registered businesses present in those areas before the event were allowed to stay open, but informal activities like street vending were barred under severe penalties. According to Ilda Lindell, Maria Hedman, and Kyle-Nathan Verboomen, "the FIFA by-laws, which targeted mainly [street] vendors, became the legal instrument to exclude them from income-generating opportunities related to the [2010 World Cup in South Africa]."[6]

By forbidding street vending in specific areas and for a range of products as well as by increasing penalties on infringers, World Cup legislation criminalized street vendors in the legal sense of turning activities that were common and widespread into punishable offenses. Even though the main threat to the interests of sponsors resided in marketing stunts rather than retailing, as the lawyer suggested, the provisions applied to any unauthorized vendor within the foreclosed areas and to anyone selling unauthorized products beyond them.

Notwithstanding the symbolic efforts to incorporate informal workers discussed in the previous chapter, the legal framework both concentrated property rights among formal businesses and heighted penalties on (informal) transgressors. It drew boundaries around official events and sites and, in those spaces, restricted the field of legality to a small number of corporate actors. Neil Fligstein describes markets as battlefields divided into incumbents and challengers.[7] Incumbents seek to curtail competition through their shaping of the rules of the game and conceptions of control, whereas challengers try to carve out a niche for themselves. Their strategies sometimes comply with and sometimes disrupt the institutional order. During the World Cup, incumbent control was total. Ad hoc legislation created legal monopolies, leaving little room for legal challenge.

Legal Resistance

Studies of monopolization and other forms of extreme market concentration point to several avenues of resistance available to those marginalized or displaced from the marketplace. The first is legal challenge. To the extent that high levels of concentration or the tactics employed by incumbents to achieve them contravene existing antitrust legislation, small businesses can call on regulators—and, if unheeded, courts—to enforce competition. Oftentimes, however, the struggle also requires lobbying to secure new laws that protect the interests of small businesses, which face countervailing efforts from their powerful rivals. The "store wars" that pitted independent shopkeepers against store chains in the United States revolved around the "enactment and repeal of anti-chain-store legislation."[8] Independent store advocates "sought to establish laws designed to tax chain stores out of business," while chain store associations pushed for favorable legislation at the state and federal level, eventually winning their case in the Supreme Court.[9] Likewise, the Grange movement fought for antitrust laws after "modernizers and corporate forces mobilized institutional support, including general incorporation laws, the recognition of the corporation as a legal person," and other means to pursue combination and consolidation.[10]

New laws are not easy to secure, however. According to Marc Schneiberg and colleagues, "anticorporate movements can pursue economic organization as an alternative to using the state against corporations," as in the case of microbrewers or agricultural producers who "opt for economic self-organization as an alternative to politics [or] turn to cooperatives with particular force if political access is blocked."[11] Even then, legislative action is sometimes required. Low-power FM radio stations developed in reaction to a series of regulations issued by the Federal Communications Commission (FCC) that enabled corporate ownership of multiple stations, leading to a twofold increase in the rate of market concentration between 1995 and 2000.[12] Local radio advocates lobbied for some channels to be allocated by law and "succeeded in extracting the right to broadcast from the FCC and Congress."[13] Whether or not they enter the political arena, small players rely on, and are protected by, the existing institutional framework. Challengers strive to uphold an accommodating market structure or attempt to remain in the game under new organizational forms, but their right to participate in the market is seldom in doubt.

The circumstances facing street vendors in São Paulo during the 2014 World Cup differed from other instances of small business countermovements in that, as workers operating at the margins of legality in a hostile policy environment that criminalized them, street vendors had no legal power to claim a share of the market. The monopolistic tendencies of the mega-events industry are enshrined in legislation, the content of which is difficult to change, especially in a short period of time. Licensed vendors protected by the injunction had a few fragile rights to pursue street trade but no political leverage. Unlicensed vendors had neither. This chapter examines what informal workers did to score a profit against the odds and characterizes some of their actions as economic subversion.

Selling Colors

In May 2014, one month before kickoff, I conducted a small survey of forty-five street vendors—most of them licensed—to capture their mood and expectations. An overwhelming majority said that they did not think their economic circumstances would change as a result of the World Cup. Some expressed fear of not being able to work due to FIFA's strict regulations, around which there was much speculation. "They say it's forbidden [to sell World Cup merchandise]," a vendor said. "They say you can even lose your license. I'm just going to close shop and leave for Bahía [his home state, during the tournament]." Another authorized vendor said that he could not take advantage of the tournament because, as a licensed vendor, he was not allowed to sell "pirated goods," meaning knockoffs of official jerseys, soccer balls, and the like.

Licensed vendors are stakeholders in the field that marginalizes them. They have a modicum of rights, and they are afraid of losing them if they break certain rules. That reluctance most likely increased in the wake of the criminalization campaign, when vendors realized that small infractions they were used to committing without sanction could have dramatic consequences on their livelihoods. Still, about a third of respondents said they planned to take steps to tap World Cup activity, mostly by switching to World Cup–related products or adding them to their stock.

Authorities themselves were uncertain about the rules. At a policy meeting, the downtown chief of inspectors conveyed a question put to him by the Union and DVA leadership about whether authorized vendors would be allowed to sell official World Cup items if they could produce evidence of legal procurement. No one really knew the answer. Another question about the sale of fan wares came up at a different meeting. Whenever the Brazil national soccer team plays, demand for fan gear increases nationwide. Such gear includes items like flags, T-shirts, scarves, vuvuzelas, and rearview mirror covers bearing the green and yellow colors of Brazil. In line with local street vending parlance, I refer to this merchandise generically as World Cup merchandise (*mercadoria da copa*). Materials with the colors of national teams did not fall within the purview of the World Cup statutes so long as they did not display any official symbol. But the law was ambiguous enough to offer law enforcement substantial leeway, especially in an informal environment where norms are not always enforced to the letter and where most actors ignore the letter of the law. Insisting that green and yellow items were fair play, a civil servant who was involved in conversations with FIFA stated assertively: "FIFA does not own the Brazilian flag."

"Yet," said one of his colleagues.

"What do you mean yet?" asked the first speaker, annoyed by the insinuation.

Accurate information is a scarce resource in informal economies. Not everyone is bothered or hindered by its absence, however. About a month before the World Cup, a woman with a licensed stall downtown, who was probably an illicit tenant, sounded very optimistic. Her stall was covered with Brazilian paraphernalia. She sat relaxed and smiling, clean and well dressed. I asked her if she believed that the event would bring money to street vendors. She replied without hesitation: "Oh, for sure, it's already bringing me more money." When I asked her whether the World Cup would be good for Brazil, she said: "Many people are complaining, but I don't like that attitude. They expect the government to bring things on a tray [*de mão beijada*]. You need to go after what you want."

"Is that what you are doing?"

"Yes, within the *esquema do Brasil*."

She was one of the first to enter the fan market in earnest, but she was by no means the only one. In a survey of licensed vendors conducted immediately after the tournament, half of respondents reported selling World Cup merchandise. The decision to do so was not completely random. On 25 de Março, where revenue per stall was said to be several times above the city average, all stalls offered World Cup merchandise. But not everyone made a profit. Because the volume of sales was large at that location, the vendor had to buy wholesale ahead of the event. According to Sephir, by the time most vendors realized there would not be a crackdown, wholesale prices had risen and retail sales had slowed down.

In fact, about a quarter of the 241 respondents in the survey reported an increase in income, while two-thirds said they lost money. Yet 72 percent did not experience an increase in police repression, and a tenth claimed it went down. The main driver behind the drop in income thus seems to have been a shift in consumer demand. A leather belt vendor whose income dropped during the World Cup explained, "The only thing people cared about was soccer. Soccer, soccer, soccer." Echoing this view, a seller of wooden cooking utensils said he broke even, but only because the sale of Word Cup merchandise compensated for the drop in sales of his usual wares. A few licensed vendors did sell garments with falsified logos, and those whose license was not for garments broke the rules by selling jerseys, but the general mood was one of tolerance, and the sale of World Cup merchandise among authorized vendors was not perceived as an act of defiance. What stood out was the uneven distribution of information about rights ahead of the tournament and the resulting inequality in the ability of these vendors to take advantage and profit from the boost in demand. In a post–World Cup interview, Helena, the NGO worker, complained that, on the opening day, the stall of one of the leaders, whose license was for packaged food, stood alone near the Fan Fest with green and yellow jerseys hanging from it. Its owner had accurately explained to me which products would be authorized and which would be forbidden in an interview ahead of the tournament. Unlike the rank and file, licensed street vendors' leaders had access to officials and were aware of the rules. Information is not just scarce, it is unequally distributed.

FURTHER AFIELD

Unlicensed vendors, who work in the outer margins of legality, had fewer rights but, paradoxically, more freedom; they did not have to worry about whether the merchandise they sold violated FIFA's legal standards. On the 25 de Março, the sale of World Cup products was widespread among the unlicensed. The following notes from fieldwork describe some of the trends.

> On the morning of the first game, the 25 de Março was bustling as usual. For the last two weeks, virtually all licensed and unlicensed street vendors had been selling World Cup merchandise, especially green and yellow air horns, which they sounded to attract customers, turning the place into a deafening mayhem. When I arrived, at around ten in the morning, I ran into Leila and Fiona, a lesbian couple in their early twenties who had moved in together and supported themselves by selling children's toys on the streets without license. They were not working and looked concerned while chatting with other peddlers whom I did not know. They asked me if I had seen Kevin, a mutual friend, who also worked as a vendor in the area. Even though they were not working and were technically not subject to confiscations, we moved into a nearby shopping mall where they felt safer and, from there, reached Kevin by phone. He joined us at the mall carrying a huge Brazilian flag—at least five feet by three—for which he was asking fifty reals [US$22]. They chatted. He agreed that the place was "wet" [*molhado*], the slang term for tightly policed. For a while, the small group remained in silence. Then Kevin said, "Alright. I need to work. I can't stay idle [*ficar parado*]." I asked the girls if they were also going. "In these conditions?" Fiona told me, "We can't."

Despite the tense atmosphere of the opening day, post–World Cup interviews suggest there was not a sustained hike in repression. In fact, Leila herself said that she did not think repression had increased significantly during the World Cup. And only a few vendors did not substitute World Cup merchandise for their usual wares. One of them was Blondine, the single mother in her forties who sold battery-powered massagers for anywhere between eighteen and forty-four reals (US$8 to US$20). When I asked her why, she replied that she felt repression was harsher on those selling World Cup products and that she was afraid. Besides, massager sales had improved, as there was less competition. By contrast, her friend Ana was not only selling World Cup merchandise but had brought her teenage son along to help. Sounding the air horns was exhausting, and his youth came in handy.

Sales of World Cup merchandise, which began in earnest about two weeks before the event, went on for one week after kickoff, then fell sharply. Two unlicensed vendors, Fred and Kevin, filled out a log at my request. It shows that Fred switched to selling flags on May 30, almost two weeks before the start of the World Cup, and continued through June 21, before going back to his usual products. Only once did he suffer a confiscation—on May 24, before he began selling World Cup merchandise—and the value of the loss was less than

5 percent of the profits he made on that day. His earnings more than doubled from June 7 to June 14, as the value of sales rose sharply while profit margins remained stable at around 60 percent. Profits also doubled for his brother Kevin during that week, which was the only period in which he carried World Cup merchandise. Kevin, however, had his wares confiscated three days in a row after he began selling World Cup merchandise, then again six times before the end of the tournament; this was far more often than in normal times. He later estimated that his income increased by about two thousand reais (US$800) during the World Cup, about a 50 percent bump at that location. Other street vendors at 25 de Março also reported that their income was higher than average thanks to the World Cup. On the other hand, Will, whose earnings went up, said he had worked longer hours, at various locations, to clear his stock of World Cup merchandise.

Beyond 25 de Março, street vendors also changed their inventory, though the bump to their income was probably less significant. A destitute vendor selling cheap, used plastic accessories on a sidewalk added a few green and yellow bracelets to the corner of the ragged tarp on which he showcased his wares. Street artists, who were allowed to keep working, incorporated the national colors to their craft. Matilde said she added green and yellow threads to the bracelets she knitted and they sold well. However, another street artist complained that many of his colleagues broke the rules. They offered manufactured World Cup products instead of handmade items, which is the requirement to obtain a street artist permit. "They became peddlers," he said dismissively.

While unlicensed street vendors' marginal position on the field of legality afforded them more freedom in choosing the merchandise, for they had less (rights) to lose, they also lacked protection, and the hardest hit were also unlicensed vendors. At strategic points, where police deployment increased, longtime vendors had a hard time. At the historic square of Santa Cecília, two elderly vendors said patrols increased, as did the number of apprehensions, to the point where they barely worked during the World Cup. They managed to cope through a system of rotating loans.

In the survey I conducted one month before the World Cup at the subway station of Itaquera, next to the stadium, I found around thirty street vendors at the station, including one who had been there "since the subway opened" almost thirty years ago. By the end of the tournament, there were only twelve street vendors left. In a survey conducted one week after the World Cup, I found only seven vendors, five of whom said that their income had significantly decreased during the tournament. All of them conveyed stories of increased hardship. According to those still present, their absent colleagues had deserted the venue or the trade.

The Logic of Subversion

Whether economic action that breaks the law on a daily basis constitutes re-sistance, subversion, or another kind of politically charged stand against the state or social order is a subject of much debate among students of urban in-formality. Most agree that the scope of economic informality far exceeds the realm of survival. In their creativity, their dynamism, and even their wealth-creation capacities, informal economies belie survivalist interpretations. But the extra step of attaching political meaning or value to their workings re-mains problematic. After all, in their daily lives, most informal workers are just trying to make a living or, at best, increase their income; they are not pur-suing regime change. Several authors thus opt for terms that convey trans-gression without challenge, such as Asef Bayat's "quiet encroachment of the ordinary" or Saskia Sassen's notion of "presence"—that is, a spatial and physi-cal mark in the city that upsets the (social) order of things but does not imply dissent.[14] The sale of fan gear during the World Cup fits this pattern. It is a way of nibbling at the edges, in some cases without even breaking the law.[15]

However, other actions undertaken by street vendors in the context of the World Cup constitute direct acts of defiance to the barriers imposed by organizers. Coupled with cynical views that cast those in power as criminals, these practices transcend the realm of passive resistance or organic illegality. I conceptualize them as economic subversion: a deliberate breaking of rules, for economic gain, coupled with an understanding of the social order as op-pressive and corrupt. Economic subversion contrasts with legal resistance, which uses the law to fend off, or defend oneself against, big players.

THE BEER MARKET

Some adventurous street vendors changed not only their wares but their workplace and routines during the World Cup. Demand for fan gear in-creased nationwide, but demand for drinks also rose at fan gatherings. The largest fan gatherings in each host city were at the stadium and the Fan Fest, along with their surrounding areas of commercial restriction, all of which fell under FIFA's strict exclusive marketing laws.[16] Some experienced and some first-time vendors took their chances in those spaces.

Fan turnout at the Fan Fest varied sharply depending on what countries were playing. Vendors only showed up when the plaza was crowded—during the games of the Brazilian national team and in the final rounds of the tour-nament. On the opening day of the World Cup, when Brazil faced Croatia in São Paulo, a strike by the association of street vending inspectors created a free-for-all situation in the ACR, which filled up with street vendors of all sorts. After that day, however, the strike ended, and policing tightened dramatically. But trade went on for both licensed and unlicensed vendors.

On June 17, the day of Brazil's second game, the municipal guard carried out raids of street vendors, which began two hours before the game. Because the streets were cluttered, street vendors did not have to constantly run from law enforcement as they do in their daily work. Instead, they blended with the crowd while discreetly offering merchandise to people around them. They carried the merchandise concealed in their backpacks, in large plastic bags, or, occasionally, in buckets or coolers.

On the margins of the ACR, near the exit of the northern subway station, a small cluster of vendors formed but disbanded in a stampede when the police approached. A teenager who was selling manioc pancakes (*tapioca*) with a food cart did not take off, however. He was caught, and his cart was confiscated. As it turned out, he had no previous experience with street trade. He had been there on the opening day to hand out religious leaflets for his church and, seeing unlicensed vendors work freely all around him, decided to try his hand on the next big game day.

Other unlicensed vendors stationed themselves at strategic spots with access to large flows of pedestrians and less exposure. Thus, on the stairs leading to a bridge on the way from the main subway station to the entrance of the Fan Fest, a woman sold drinks from an open backpack. She was sitting on the stairs, about halfway up, leaning against the wall. The flow of fans going up and down the stairs protected her from view by police officers in the plaza. Lookouts stood at the top and bottom of the stairs. If police approached by either side, the lookout would tip the seller, who would then close the backpack, put it on, and exit the stairs by the opposite end.

As the tournament advanced and policing increased, the number of unlicensed vendors in the ACR declined. During a walking survey around the ACR conducted a half hour before Brazil's second game, I counted forty-four unlicensed street vendors. On the day of Brazil's following game, with a crowd of similar proportions, I counted only twenty-four street vendors. Toward the end of the tournament, the police would cordon off an area containing the Fan Fest and some adjacent space, making it harder for vendors to cater to fans on the waiting line. Short interviews revealed that there were both long-time street vendors and opportunistic neophytes like the teenager mentioned earlier. But several experienced vendors I spoke with on 25 de Março did not see the point. Carrying drinks and ice in plastic bags is exhausting, Lucas pointed out, and you only sell well when you are among the customers, not at the margins.

He had a point. Big business lay inside the Fan Fest. There, the market was literally captive, as fans were checked by police at the entrance and forbidden from bringing in any beverages. Prices reflected this state of affairs. Whereas in the ACR, a can of beer from an unlicensed vendor went for three reals (US$1.33),[17] inside the Fan Fest, where official sponsor AB Inbev had a legal monopoly, the going price for the same can of beer was six reals (US$2.65), and the volume of sales was much larger.

The Fan Fest was enclosed with high metal fences and guarded by private security guards. Not only was access harder for vendors as a result, but circulating with a backpack inside the Fan Fest made you an immediate suspect, and the expected sanctions were much heavier. As Lucas explained in an interview, "When you get caught in an open space, on the streets, that's fine. But in an enclosed space, it's different. You are way more vulnerable." Entering the beer market inside the Fan Fest thus required overcoming both material and psychological barriers.

And yet, a minority of unlicensed vendors did sell beer inside the Fan Fest. In an interview conducted after the tournament, an experienced unlicensed vendor explained how he proceeded. After filling up his backpack with cans of beer, he would pay a bribe to one of the security guards—fifty reals (US$22) per passage—to let him jump over the fence. A confederate—his girlfriend— stood on the line to enter as a regular fan. Once inside the Fan Fest, they met at an agreed-upon location. She would then keep the backpack full of beer cans at her feet while pretending to watch the game. In the meantime, he would go around selling one can at a time. When the stock sold out, the cycle began anew: he exited normally, through the gates, with his empty backpack, filled it with beers, and jumped over the fence while she waited for him inside.

Unlike the daily routines of these workers at the edge of the law, these practices required planning and coordination. They involved entering forbidden spaces. Some of these vendors were not simply dodging security forces or running away from them; they were actually engaging them (e.g., paying a bribe) to access the foreclosed site. There is a subtle but important distinction between informal labor that disregards the rule of law, as the concept of encroachment suggests, and informal labor that challenges it. The views that (some) street vendors held about "the system" support the description of their acts as subversive.

Subversive Views

Many of the informal workers I interviewed expressed some form of political awareness. They may not have seen their own work as a challenge to the state, but they saw the powers that be as actively preventing them from earning an honest living. Unlicensed vendors' reactions to news of stricter enforcement ahead of the World Cup at the Itaquera subway station illustrate this sentiment.

On Sunday, May 25, 2014, two police officers approached the informal marketplace of about thirty street vendors. The older one addressed the small crowd to let them know that police presence was going to increase, which meant vendors would no longer be able to work in that area over the next two months.

"I don't like doing this," the policeman said. "I know this is how you make your living. These are tough times, for you, for us, for everyone."

"That's fine," a street vendor replied. "You are doing what you were told."

But curiosity soon dissipated, and dejection took hold. "I'm going home to watch a movie," one of them said. "Let's get out of here." Another one asked: "Why do they do this? This is not right. Where do they expect us to get our food from?" Pointing to a coworker, she went on: "Her husband suffered a stroke recently. This is her only source of income. She sells coffee in the morning, then works here in the evening. What are we going to do now? They are doing all this for the tourists. And what are we, trash?" Then, alluding to vandalism during anti–World Cup protests, she said, "If there is some destruction, I'll join. Mark my words, I'll be among them. And I'm an honest person. But no one can put up with this. At least one stone I'll throw."

A coworker who had just arrived inquired what happened. "They just broke our legs," another street vendor replied.

I had approached these same workers earlier that month to inquire about their prospects for the World Cup. The most pessimistic respondents predicted that the World Cup would only bring "more misery." One of them spoke of "the end of the world." Another one wished a bomb would go off and invite death and chaos on the entire party. Many of them said it would only benefit "the big guys" or the "higher class." The themes of crime and insecurity, which were not part of the questionnaire, came up in some of the answers, coupled with complaints that the police should "let honest people work" or keep them safe instead of running after them.

The assertion of their moral worth, as honest people and workers, contrasts with the moral condemnation of the political establishment, which was a recurring theme, especially (but not only) among unlicensed vendors. The most vivid expression of the latter came from a street performer known as the *cantante gaúcho*, or gaucho singer, whom I approached one morning on the streets of downtown São Paulo. His was a cheerful, jumpy act with *yippee* shouts and a merry guitar accompaniment. I had heard from a street vendor that the gaucho singer had been a street vendor himself in the southern district of Santo Amaro. I asked him, and he denied it fiercely. "I don't know who told you that. Never was." His attitude was aggressive and defensive at the same time. He went on:

> I'm not a parasite, I work on the streets. Brazil is on the loose. There's these criminals, *vagabundos*, who sit on their chairs all day long and get paid sixty thousand [reals], or thirty, or forty, to do nothing. You know who I'm talking about? And we, in the streets, barely make it. They don't care if it rains or not, they get out of their offices in their big, nice cars, straight out of their parking lots, they don't see the people. And they pay these other vagabundos [the police] to run after us. Not to let us work. They threaten us, beat us, because they see themselves in a position of power . . . [correcting himself] because they are in a position of power. What can we do? You think you speak well? But what difference does that make? Don't take offense. Anyone can speak. The drug addict can talk. Even the bird sings. You don't have power. These guys [the higher-ups], they have those diplomas that they don't even earn. Most of them buy them. You know how the son of a normal person prepares himself to apply for a job, he may have a fine CV, has studied hard, took all the exams. He may even harbor some hopes that he will get the job, submits the file long before the deadline. And then the *filinho de papai* [daddy's son] is pushed through with a phone call. So the guy ends up trying to make a living on the streets. And they throw the police after him. That's Brazil.

The man moved constantly while he spoke, as if wanting to leave, but he could not bring himself to stop his rant. His alienation reached far beyond what law and society scholars call legal cynicism—that is, the lack of belief in the fairness of the legal system. It extended to the economic and political order as a whole, and he expressed profound hostility toward the people who benefited from or enforced that order, whom he described repeatedly as "criminals" (*vagabundos*). And he was not alone in using this language. Another street vendor described the political party behind the eviction campaign as "a gang" (*quadrilha*), while Fred alluded to the sway actual drug lords—especially São Paulo's all-mighty Primeiro Comando da Capital (PCC)—hold, in his view, over the political system. Through these statements, informal workers reversed the logic of the policy of symbolic and material criminalization that targets them. Branding those in power as criminals seemed a more empowering coping strategy for members of a group targeted by criminalization than the frequent alternative of dehumanizing oneself with terms like *nobodies*, *trash*, or *dogs* or statements such as, "Come election time, we are all citizens. But afterwards, we can go to a veterinarian and she won't see us."

The intensity of these subversive views varied across categories of street vendors, with licensed vendors expressing more frustration with the ruling party than disaffection with the system, but cynicism was pervasive. "Everything that poor people enjoy is forbidden," Kevin once said, referring to a ban on kites. Even when devoid of bitterness or resentment, as in the case of Ernesto, an unlicensed vendor in his sixties who suffered from a host of illnesses, the understanding of society as fundamentally unfair and biased against the poor colored many street vendors' views. Echoing a theme from the cantante gaúcho's tirade, Ernesto described a hypothetical situation in which the nephew of some big shot cuts in front of the line while the son of a poor person who studies hard to get his degree is doomed in his search for employment.

As far as I could tell, there was no direct correlation between the level of cynicism and the level of deviance. The street vendor who broke into the Fan Fest was not the most politically aware or radical. Yet cynicism and deviance coexisted among the street vendors, especially the unlicensed. Economic subversion differs from political subversion in that it does not intend to overthrow those in power or capture the state. But the economic order is also a legal order that institutionalizes inequality through an unequal allocation of rights, and street vendors consciously defy that order. Using the term *subversion* indicates that there is more political significance to the praxis of street vending, at the margins, than prevailing theories allow for.

On the other hand, the specter of a fall—or leap—into a life of actual crime haunted unlicensed vendors. During the preliminary World Cup survey, a street vendor near the stadium said, unprompted, that in Brazil, "If you want to live well, you got to live like a criminal [*bandido*]." Fernando also told me that he felt tempted to become a thief, and he occasionally pilfered at supermarkets. Life choices aside, the pressures these workers endure in an oppressive environment sometimes push them over the edge. When I returned to Brazil one year after finishing fieldwork, a street vendor I knew well shared that, in a moment of distress, he had attacked a fellow street vendor, who had provoked him, with a knife. Another vendor I had interviewed, sweet and affable in character, was reportedly on the run after coming close to killing his romantic partner in an argument.

Informing Struggles

The winner-take-all structure of postindustrial markets threatens small businesses and pushes them to the sidelines. Small business owners respond differently, depending on their legal status and political influence, to the threat of being forced out of the market by high-power players. Some challenge the legality of the process. Others—or the same ones, after the first route fails—go on trading at the margins under new organizational forms. Inside the field of legality, when avenues for judicial or legislative action are shut, small businesses use the protections afforded by existing laws, along with opportunities embedded in the market structure, to organize privately and carry on with their economic activity, thus preventing the advent of a full-fledged monopoly.[18] Street vendors during the World Cup had neither option. Instead, they subverted the legal framework with its monopolistic tendencies and attendant enforcement system in order to enter fan markets. Their experience suggests that legal restrictions against informal workers breed more deviance, not less. To the extent that these actors concomitantly hold critical views of the social order and of the forces that limit their life chances, their action may be characterized as economic subversion. In the context of the World Cup, it was an informal way to overcome the monopolization of access to consumers.

Not everything street vendors did to take advantage of the World Cup broke the law. As the Union vice president noted ahead of the tournament, selling green and yellow jerseys from your stall, as an authorized vendor, did not constitute an offense, especially if the license was for garments, nor were such practices targeted by authorities. Only three respondents in the survey of licensed street vendors reported having their wares confiscated during the World Cup. The most subversive act was the sale of alcoholic beverages around and inside the Fan Fest, in defiance of multiple legal provisions as well as a sophisticated surveillance and security apparatus set up to enforce them.

As a strategy premised on breaking the norms rather than shaping them, subversion carries risk. For this reason, subversion is limited in scope, meaning that only a few challengers can successfully engage in it. The exception to this was unlicensed vendor participation in the World Cup merchandise market, which seemed to be widespread. According to a street vendor, the police did not "dare" to confiscate items bearing the colors of Brazil, "out of respect for the national flag."

Moreover, economic subversion is, by and large, an individualistic enterprise. Coordination within small groups of two or three individuals took place and seemed profitable, but there was not a movement of solidarity among challengers, contrary to instances of legal opposition to market concentration or political insurgency. Economic subversion during the World Cup was based on individualistic planning and actions rather than large coalitions or even cooperation. As a result of the risk involved and the illegality of the actions, there was even less solidarity than I had observed in the daily practice of unlicensed peddling. Individual success or failure did not foster within-group solidarity.

Finally, the most successful individual cases of subversion I observed during the World Cup suggest that the strategy was especially rewarding for those already immersed in the informal economy, as they had both the know-how and the disposition to take substantial risk. Effective vendors drew on preexisting expertise as well as other assets (status, information, risk-taking habits, etc.) developed by participants of an economy characterized by routine infringement of legal norms.

It is also noteworthy that those further at the margins of the legal order—that is, unlicensed vendors—had fewer misgivings about engaging in economic subversion and taking advantage of the event. Indeed, a street vendor with a license is a stakeholder in the legal and economic order that marginalizes her. That position sets boundaries on her ability to challenge the rules of protected markets. While virtually all licensed vendors practice some form of routinized transgression, they are less willing to take new or further steps toward illegality in unknown circumstances. Being outside the field of legality, unlicensed street vendors are freer to break the rules and challenge new measures of exclusion. But they are also more vulnerable. A majority of licensed vendors saw their income decline during the tournament; however, the vendors who lost their livelihood as a result of the World Cup were all unlicensed.

A potential drawback to the concept of economic subversion is the misleading impression that those involved are only one step away from subversion in its full, political sense. This is not the case. Subversion in its conventional sense entails not only a defiance of the state and its laws, which informal workers practice, but a political agenda, which informal workers lack. Paradoxically, some of the small business movements that pursued a legal challenge against monopolies had such an agenda. When US shopkeepers were resisting chain stores in the 1930s, the National Retail Druggists Association journal thus denounced "masses of Americans wholly at the mercy of the despotic power of a monopolistic class."[19] But shopkeepers resorted to legislatures and courts, not arson. Despite street vendors holding deeply critical views of the political system, the relentlessness of repression they endure and the inherently individualistic logic of their work routines and economic subversion, among other factors, prevent the emergence of a social movement.

Paradoxically, too, a social movement decried the repressive and exclusionary character of World Cup legislation at the time. The legal monopolies conceded to FIFA and its commercial partners became an object of public scrutiny and criticism. And subgroups within that movement, such as the Black Blocks, engaged in the violent destruction of property during protests as an expression of their anarchist views. The exclusion of self-employed informal workers was just one plank in a larger critique of the legal framework as well as the security and enforcement practices surrounding mega-events, however.

While street vendors echoed some of the themes from the anti–World Cup movement in their everyday conversations, especially those relating to lavish infrastructure spending, few of them participated in demonstrations, and, when they did, it was not always for political reasons. Lest we forget, protesters are consumers, too. At an anti–World Cup march to which he was invited, Ernesto showed up with a basket of candy, hoping to score a few bucks on the side.

At the same time, vendors regretted that the general mood of discontent with the event—along with the disappointing performance of the Brazilian national team—depressed consumer spending. Ironically, at every World Cup edition, Brazil's games are broadcast on public squares with far less police presence. Some of the street vendors interviewed in this study sell beverages and snacks without a license at these showings. As Kevin noted, "The World Cup is good for our business, so long as it is held abroad."

*

People who study those in the informal sector and interpret their activities as acts of resistance tend to base their claims on what they see rather than what they hear. Whatever the metaphor—encroachment, invasion, occupation, and so on—the meaning of informal behavior often lies in the eye of the beholder. There's no doubt that street vendors, shantytown residents, and underground workshop owners defy the rules of a skewed sociopolitical order on a daily basis as well as a host of legal norms and rights that preserve inequality. Whether they do it on purpose, or at least consciously, is another question, which studies of informality seldom address. I submit that illicit behavior constitutes economic subversion to the extent that it is associated with a critique of the social order in thought or in speech. Economic subversion is a spontaneous but conscious assault on the distribution of rights.

Those who engage in subversion exit the realm of citizenship. They renounce the field of legality, which they understand as biased, and they abandon the struggle to achieve or retain legal status and the rights that come with it. Their goal is not to change the content of legality. Theirs is not a revolutionary struggle. But they generate or appropriate wealth playing by their own rules. The cost of that independence is a daily experience of violence.

Conclusion
The End of Citizenship?

The ability to regulate social life through abstract codes and ritual enactments thereof—in a word, through secular symbols—is one of modernity's shining features. Yet that feat comes with its own bag of ambiguities and paradoxes. Legality is the institutional order that modern states build for their citizens—even as their own agents violate it or fail to enforce it. Informal economies epitomize the limited reach of states that Portes and Centeno describe as "frustrated."[1] But the gap between the law on the books and on the streets is not filled with thin air; it has its logics and texture. In practice, the construction of legality involves a host of fractious interests, unequal in their capacity to make and break the laws, clashing over the enactment and rescinding of rules or the interpretation thereof. On this contentious process, *The Edge of the Law* sets its focus.

By framing legality as a space in which people have rights, key dynamics of citizenship come into relief, including the discursive tools and practical methods used in the drawing of boundaries. If citizens draw boundaries to protect their rights and preserve their assets, so too do informal workers. To the nationalist rabble-rouser, the problem of citizenship is a straightforward matter that revolves around enforcing borders and ethnic boundaries. For the informal worker trying to make ends meet on the streets of an unequal city, citizenship is a constant struggle. I have used the concept of informal citizen to capture her fight and its tensions.

Framing legality as a field under (permanent) construction also makes the dynamics of labor regulation at the edge of the law easier to grasp. For those who are still admitted on the field of legality—that is, licensed street vendors—the politics of defining the rules, often at the expense of aspiring players, gave way to the more rattling politics of trying to stay on the field while authorities sought to push them out. Playing on the edge had subjective implications for vulnerable workers, including emotional attachment to their threatened legal status, which authorities drew upon. It also had mental health implications and material repercussions on the lives of those pushed to the sidelines.

A classist stereotype in the vein of the culture of poverty points to informality as evidence that poor people do not obey the law. Events that came to light around the time of the World Cup and in connection to it indicate that informal workers were not the only ones breaking the rules, however. Less than a year after the tournament ended, Swiss authorities arrested seven FIFA officials at a luxury hotel in Zurich, ahead of FIFA's annual congress. FIFA's long-serving and recently reelected president, Sepp Blatter, stepped down within days. Revelations of a dubious two-million-dollar transfer to another top-ranking official, Michel Platini, who was considering running against Blatter, led to both men being charged with fraud—and eventually acquitted. Meanwhile, the US Department of Justice indicted the FIFA officials arrested in Zurich along with a host of other soccer officials and media executives. According to the *New York Times*, "The Justice Department's indictment describes a corrupt system in which news media and marketing executives regularly paid bribes to secure the lucrative rights to broadcast and advertise international soccer."[2] Blatter had faced other allegations of wrongdoing in the sale of marketing rights to sports media companies in the past. Corporate trends thus seem to mirror what went on in the streets. As Jan Breman and Barbara Harriss-White both note, the informalization of business parallels the informalization of labor.[3]

In São Paulo, where public advertisement is forbidden under the Clean City ordinance, a major World Cup sponsor painted its logo on the wall of a shop facing the above-ground subway line leading to the stadium. The shop owner was fined, and the company agreed, under pressure, to paint over its emblem.[4] The financial shenanigans surrounding the construction of the stadium, which was completed only one month ahead of the World Cup and hosted the opening game, reverberated long after the tournament was over. Odebrecht, the Brazilian construction giant that built the stadium, was at the heart of a massive corruption investigation that shook the entire political system. In a plea deal, two of its former executives reported paying 2.5 million reals to the president of the club that owns the stadium to secure the contract. Emilio Odebrecht, the company's former CEO, denied the payment of bribes and said the stadium was built as a "present" for Lula.

The receding of legality as a space of protection for workers thus parallels its thinning as a mechanism for the regulation of organizations, including big business and state agencies. The result is resentment at the bottom, which informal workers expressed forcefully, calling politicians criminals, and a volatile social landscape that favors the spread of actual violent criminal activity such as drug trafficking or mugging. Some vendors also expressed a paradoxical form of nostalgia over a "life of crime" that they may or may not have already experienced.

An Impossible Policy

Against this background, the prospect of a large-scale legal incorporation of informal workers—either in De Soto's business-oriented version of securing property rights or along the lines of the ILO's decent work agenda, which calls for filling "rights deficits"—comes across as wishful, if not delusional.[5] Even under conditions of political openness, as observed during the Erundina administration (1989–1992), the regulation of street vendors—and especially of those who benefit from a minimum of legal protection—was caught in what a former district administrator aptly described as *a politics of retailing*. This book shows that rights are part of the retail shaping the government of informal citizens, along with other goods and services, including law enforcement.

The distribution of rights takes a variety of forms, from the over-time, self-reinforcing structuring of licensing rights to the symbolic, institutionally disembedded granting of commission seller rights for the length of a tournament. Like the politics of enforcement, the distribution of rights can be effective when it occurs in exchange for political support or quiescence, even in its tentative, allusive shape—the promise of rights, if carefully managed, keeps would-be recipients in check.

As a governing tool, the distribution of rights is constrained not only by larger political and economic forces but by the social and legal structures that evolve *within* the informal economy and inform the practice of retailing. "Their everyday life revolves around the inspectors," an official noted, suggesting licensed vendors only cared about petty regulatory issues, over which they bargained with authorities. Echoing this view, a top official who took part in the initial negotiations over licenses under Erundina regretted that "all those meetings were about the size of the stall, whether the fruit could be cut or not cut, and if cut how it should be wrapped. There was never a debate over what I call the regulation of the informal economy."[6] The negotiations for a settlement to the lawsuit described in chapter 6 confirm informal labor representatives' focus on piecemeal rights.

The fact that state officials do not want to deal with the process of organizing street vendors or ensuring the representativeness of their leadership compounds the problem. Several policymakers in São Paulo expressed a preference for a scenario in which vendors organized themselves, selected their own leaders, and even inspected (*fiscalizar*) themselves. In this regard, too, informal citizens differ from actual citizens, who are taken more seriously by state officials—or ought to be—because the state embodies their project.[7] A consequence of such detachment is that, as a former administrator of the downtown district pointed out, the representatives of licensed street vendors have been the same for twenty years. "But you have to deal with them because that's all there is," he said.[8] And what they want is simply to "secure what they have."

What they have, however, is shrinking. The rituals of exchange at the heart of the old populist form of government, variants of which persist or recur through political cycles, combined the distribution of material resources with a sense of belonging performatively instilled in the masses by the leader. Economic restructuring and accompanying trends in neoliberal governance limit the volume of resources available to political machines while favoring targeted poverty reduction programs. "Brazil is parceled out [*loteado*]," a street vendor said, expressing the rarefication of economic opportunities in spatial terms, according to the natural conception of value in his trade. In the past, the vendor suggested, there had been room for distributive policies such as licensing. Now, everything had an "owner"—from street corners to district administrations—and rights were handed out with parsimony.

Valdira captured the essence of the politics of retailing and their limits as she walked out of a policy meeting after someone raised the question of the unlicensed vendors' predicament: "I was upset with [the CIW lawyer]. He lets Ana, Luiza, and Claudia speak. They don't know anything about this [matter]. That one, Ana, saying that there are 138,000 peddlers in the city. If the city doesn't want to fix things as they are, how would they agree to grant that many permits? It's ridiculous. I want things that are real, mine. We want them to give back the five thousand [licenses] that were unfairly taken from us." A prescient street vendors' leader complained about the lack of foresight that the traditional leadership showed in simply trying to secure what they have. Licensed vendors are aging, he noted, and when they die, "there won't be room for street vendors anymore," because licenses are not transferable and the city was unwilling to issue new ones.

These liminal workers-cum-citizens face the threat of extinction, which raises the stakes in their exchanges with policymakers. Existential crises like "the massacre" and its agonizing aftermath brought the content of their basic rights to the forefront and called into question the state's prerogatives. But points of detail continued to haunt the settlement talks, the city's disingenuousness precluded any progress, and the outcome was a prolongation of a fragile and degraded status quo.

Reflecting on the roots of what feels—to both sides—like a permanent impasse, a former district administrator decried the lack of political will. "For the government, street vendors are a headache," he said. They are "a social issue that has not yet risen to a political issue." He added, "The only way to reach beyond [a policy of retailing] would be with a broad-based initiative, but there's no will for that."

He was not alone in holding this view: "It's been a problem since I was born," a street vendor said at a meeting, referring to street vendors.

"Before you and I were born," replied a top city official.

"That's because the government doesn't want to solve it," the street vendor said.

"You think so?" the official asked, thoughtfully, before moving on to more pressing matters.

Except the lack of will is structurally embedded. The PT's nonpolicy toward licensed street vendors caught in a judicial limbo reflects as much a lack of courage and commitment as the impossible politics of a postindustrial city that is both wealthy and ridden with poverty.

Likewise, the techniques of control and repression deployed against street vendors in the age of criminalization are also embedded in the economic structures of an aspiring global city. Vendors and other marginalized members of the growing informal labor force who spill onto public spaces undermine the ideal of the shiny metropolis as much as they disrupt in physical and symbolic ways the processes of postindustrial capital accumulation. Stricter laws and stronger enforcement contribute to the making of a utopian urban space adapted to the needs and requirements of high value–added service industries such as finance or mass entertainment. The violence that the state inflicts upon street vendors thus expresses the gap between a conceptual space that is functional to a range of influential urban interests and the actual grinding city in which people try to get by.

The concept of the city as a playground offering powerful but safe emotions is an extension of this urbanistic project, the implementation of which wreaks its own share of havoc. The World Cup brought a small number of workers in the fold of legality, mostly for the benefit of an (inattentive) audience, without granting them much in the way of entitlements. At the same time, it restricted the range of legal behavior for informal workers as a whole, dramatically increased penalties for infractions, and—quite literally—built walls around the main sites of "play" (i.e., the Fan Fest). Some informal workers broke in all the same, while others lost their livelihood.

In short, the macro processes of economic restructuring and institutional decay coupled with the culture and structure of licensed street vending and its often corrupt political economy undermine broad-based enfranchisement projects. Along with the electoral politics of a highly unequal, exclusionary city, they threaten the residual rights of workers once covered by protective arrangements. The cynicism prevailing among unlicensed vendors and the exhaustion of hope among the licensed few reflect a collective realization of this state of affairs.

In the hopeful edifice of modern political philosophy, when citizens face injustices that rulers commit or dismiss, tackling the task of redress is incumbent upon civil society. The epics of the lawsuit that "saved" licensed street vendors hint at the potential of the so-called third sector. It was, after all, an NGO that filed it on behalf of street vendors. Toward the end of my fieldwork, however, the NGO lawyer who cofiled the lawsuit looked back at the experience with disenchantment. "The street vendors' problem will not be solved by the ACP [lawsuit], it will not be solved by an official petition, it will not be solved by an ordinance," she said. Describing the policy of Haddad as sweeping the rubbish under the carpet, she acknowledged that "all the ACP did was to stem the bleeding."

The head of a charity that ran a shelter where Fernando and other homeless people could spend some time during the day had an even more damning assessment of the role of civil society: "This is all a big circus. The way it works, you go ask the government for money. They'll give it to you, but they'll set their conditions. Then you hire your friends . . . for laundry services, for private security."[9] He saw NGOs as "worn out by corruption" because of the difficulty of finding donors, which forces them to play politics. A friend of his was fired from her NGO because she refused to support a congressman. As for the prospect of bringing about some kind of systemic change, he said, "We don't change anything." He saw his role as offering the disenfranchised a respite from the brutal life of the streets. "Without us," he added, "there would be more violence [on the streets]."

Cycles of Violence

Despite the constant tension and its huge social costs, the system of government described in this book, which rests on the management of informal citizenship through the increasingly fictitious distribution of rights, seemed to "hold" during my time in the field. Most alternative political projects—like the one put forward by the NGO worker during the settlement talks—came across as unrealistic. Increasing alienation among the governed and other stakeholders around them raises the question of its sustainability, however. In other parts of the world, where similar trends of informal labor exclusion and criminalization are taking place, social explosions have followed.

On December 11, 2010, thousands of miles away from where research for this book was conducted, a policewoman approached a street vendor named Mohamed Bouazizi in the small Tunisian town of Sidi Bouzi. Bouazizi, who supported his siblings through street trade, did not have a license to sell the fruits and vegetables he had procured that morning on credit from distributors, so the officer confiscated his produce as well as his weighing balance. How exactly the interaction between the police officer, her aides, and Bouazizi went down is a matter of some controversy. The officer denies allegations that she slapped Bouazizi in the face, but there are reports that her aides may have kicked him.

The street vendor headed to the governor's palace to try to recover his balance, but the palace doors were shut. The governor refused to see him. Shortly thereafter, Bouazizi purchased a gallon of gasoline, poured it on himself, and set himself on fire. He is reported to have shouted "How do you expect me to make a living?" before his self-immolation on Sidi Bouzi's central square.

Bouazizi's story resonated with his fellow town residents and countrymen, who took to the streets in outrage. The protests grew and eventually brought down Zine el Abidine Ben Ali, Tunisia's dictator of thirty years, who fled by plane to Saudi Arabia with a gun in his hand. The protests even spread across borders in what came to be known as the Arab Spring. They resulted in the ousting of another long-standing dictator, Hosni Moubarak, in neighboring Egypt on February 11, 2011.

A narrow reading of what started this transnational political drama is that the governor made a strategic mistake when he refused to meet with the disgruntled street vendor who had come knocking at his door. The politician failed to engage in the politics of retailing that underpins the fragile balance that keeps a growing population of workers living on edge, at the edge of the law, under control. A more encompassing view sees the general trend toward the criminalization of informal labor in a context of economic restructuring with limited income-making opportunities as erasing the space for these politics to happen, even in their abstract form of shallow rights and empty promises, and considers some kind of social and political backlash as inevitable.

In Search of a Trend

How did the upward movement of civic (self-)construction that swept Brazil at the turn of the century devolve into the bare land of precarious hope for some and widespread cynicism for others documented in this book? Did the miseries of informal citizenship edge out the dignity of James Holston's insurgent citizens? Did Holston look at the same people through a romantic lens? Place (and, by extension, sector) accounts for some of the difference, but time is an essential factor.

Leaving aside the optimism underlying Holston's theory, street trade differs from housing in important respects. The looseness of rights is common to all informal situations, but the levels of political awareness and organization, along with the ideologies inspiring social actors, vary widely. São Paulo's housing movement is historically strong, with nationwide activist networks like the Movimento dos Trabalhadores Sem Teto (Roofless Workers Movement) pushing for access to housing. Some of the neighborhoods in São Paulo's impoverished Southern Zone attracted a flurry of civil rights groups and left-wing activists during the dictatorship, which helped build legal and political consciousness among residents. By contrast, the economy of street vending is fragmented, perceived by its opponents and some of its participants as a zero-sum game, and, for those who have rights, organized in clientelistic fashion.

However, the contrast between the narrative of civic insurgency and the vanishing of rights documented in this book also stems from a difference of historical period. Marshall's famous theory of ascendant citizenship—from civil to political to social rights—came under fire for its Eurocentric inspiration and teleological assumptions, notwithstanding Marshall's caveats.[10] The story of street vendors further shows that the distribution of rights is reversible. In the wake of Brazil's transition to democracy, under Erundina, street vendors enjoyed an expansion of rights. While there is no extensive ethnographic account of their feelings and worldviews, it is probable that licensed vendors at the time came close in their outlook to Holston's self-empowered shantytown residents. As the tide of urban policy shifted in response to global economic trends in the neoliberal era, licensed vendors in São Paulo found themselves—quite literally—begging for their rights.[11]

Time gives more meaning and solidity to rights, but structural trends also erode institutions over time. It may be that, in other spheres of life, some survivors of the mass eviction campaign remained assertive through the ordeal, but the campaign definitely shook their certainties and convictions as workers. Even some informal homeowners with long-standing ties to the land they lived on suffered eviction and displacement during the Olympics, which sowed division and restlessness among them.[12] Other developments in society at large, from government corruption to economic crisis and gang violence, further undermine the experience of citizenship and the exercise of rights for a majority of low-income Brazilians.

It is ironic that participatory mechanisms such as the settlement talks or the community-based design of the World Cup street vendors' participation program would be used to quell or manage disaffection. Brazil is the birthplace of participatory budgeting, a policy tool that the PT introduced in the southern city of Porto Alegre in the late 1980s and that became a beacon of inclusive policymaking around the world. According to Michael Touchton and colleagues, "leftist political governments and civil society activists created [participatory budgeting] during a rejuvenation of Brazil's democracy and civil society as a way to complement representative democracy and redress its many noted inequities."[13] Participants from "underserved communities and groups that have been historically excluded from the perspective of representative democracy" get a chance to "learn about decision-making processes in development policy and can organize to pursue their communities' interests beyond the [participatory budgeting] process."[14] In the words of another longtime student of participatory budgeting, Gianpaolo Baiocchi, the policy device breeds civically engaged agents that are concurrently "militants and citizens."[15] Touchton and colleagues go so far as to suggest that it "potentially empowers participants to demand access to basic constitutionally guaranteed rights,"[16] while Leo Avritzer and others note a range of institutional conditions participatory initiatives have to meet to deliver their expected benefits.[17] Even the most nuanced or critical accounts fall short of capturing what happened to street vendors in São Paulo, however, where, after Kassab all but ignored the participatory tools embedded in street vendors' legislation, the PT orchestrated a charade of dialogue and participation. Instead of breeding empowered citizens, instrumental or cosmetic participatory initiatives revealed the subjecting bonds and weaknesses that plague informal citizenship.

How deep and how steady the trend toward disenfranchisement is, and whether it is bound to result in social upheaval with political salience, are hard to determine. Several street vendors died in São Paulo, either at the hands of the police or running from them, without sparking any large-scale movement. In places like New York and Los Angeles, some programs have sought to provide certain guarantees to peddlers, notwithstanding widespread and lingering insecurities. At the same time, criminalization proceeds apace on the legislative front. Following the mass demonstrations of 2013, a bicameral commission introduced Bill 449, which "defined the crime of terrorism," previously absent from federal legislation. The government claimed the law was necessary for the World Cup, despite Brazil not facing any serious terrorist threat. Lawyers, NGOs, and activist groups warned the law could be used to crack down on dissent and denounced the criminalization of protest.[18] Then, on March 16, 2016, five months before the start of the Olympic

Games, President Rousseff, a former guerrilla fighter who was imprisoned and tortured during the military dictatorship, signed another antiterrorism bill into law. Rousseff was ousted from power two months later through an impeachment procedure that her followers regard as a coup, given its tenuous legal basis. And two years later, far-right populist Bolsonaro won the presidential elections on an anticorruption platform steeped with nostalgia for the military dictatorship. Political violence rose on his watch.

It may be that the space of legality is both shrinking and fading. Perhaps, in this new era, the police are the face of the state for disenfranchised workers, and withholding enforcement the method of appeasement. Through electorally determined cycles of laxism and suppression, the politics of rights considered in this volume, which concerned a minority of vendors to begin with, may become a thing of the past. But if the story of street vendors in São Paulo teaches us anything, it is that the institutions of legality are resilient. Looking at their workings, as we have, is important; many lives still depend upon them.

Acknowledgments

It takes a cohort, for starters. I am grateful to all the friends I made during my years as a doctoral student in Austin, especially Jorge Derpic, Katherine Sobering, Caitlin Collins, Yu Chen, Omar Awapara, Katherine Jensen, and the Zacapas. I am also grateful to the people I met there and who accompanied me later on, during part of the journey. I thank Eva—for her words. And Marta Ascherio for her love, laughter, and encouragements.

The Denis family took me in when I landed, then looked after me in every possible way during all my time in Austin. I see their house on Greenway Street as a second home. Despite having four children, Laurence and Jérôme treated me like a son. I could never have accomplished this work without their support. I will never forget the delicious meals, the movies watched together, and our lively dinner table conversations.

As if having one family near me during graduate school was not enough, my aunt and uncle in Houston also provided a haven. I miss the concerts and the bike rides. Their visits to Austin were a source of joy and entertainment. I'm sure *la tía* Guadalupe misses the chance to visit Mozart Café every few weeks.

Several mentors and protectors, whom I am now lucky enough to be able to call my colleagues, also carried me forward on the long road to publication. At the University of Texas at Austin, Javier Auyero, my adviser, supported me from our first encounter in Paris almost fifteen years ago, when I entertained the vague and unlikely prospect of doing a PhD in the United States, to the day I defended my dissertation in Austin several years later, and afterward, as I applied for academic positions. His support defined my career as a scholar. Ari Adut brought light, irony, erudition, and crisp cross-cultural insights into academic life, all of which made the PhD experience bearable—and, at times, even fun. His advice on how to submit a book manuscript for review was determinant. Mary Rose read some chapters and suggested, rather casually, a novel interpretation of the story that came to occupy a central place in the final version of this book. The courses on Latin America by Bryan Roberts and Peter Ward shaped my academic worldview.

I never took a class with Nadya Guimarães at the University of São Paulo, at least not in the conventional sense of class attendance, yet she contributed more than anyone else to the thinking and research behind this book. As my academic *madrinha* during my fieldwork in São Paulo, Nadya gave me access to crucial resources—from libraries to experts to a sharp understanding of local institutions—and, most importantly, invited me into an outstanding community of scholars. The Oficina de Sociologia Econômica e do Trabalho (OSET) workshop that she founded and ran is among the most stimulating scholarly forums I have ever taken part in. I am grateful to all its participants, especially Rogério Barbosa, who introduced me to Brazilian academia, and Flávio Carvalhães, whose lasting friendship was a gateway into the field on my first trip to Brazil. I owe whatever expert knowledge I have managed to build on Brazil to his early efforts to put me in touch with the right people.

My year and a half as a scholar in residence at McGill University enabled me to work on the research on which this volume is based following a painful turn in my personal life. I am forever grateful to Phil Oxhorn for providing that opportunity and to Erik Martinez-Kuhonta for welcoming me so warmly, introducing me to his family, and offering pointed advice on career moves and strategies.

The meanders of postdoctoral academic life took me to Switzerland, where I spent over three years at the University of Neuchatel, and the London School of Economics (LSE), where I was a visiting fellow participating remotely in talks and seminars in the midst of the pandemic. At the University of Neuchatel, I am thankful to Philip Balsiger for his friendship and advice as well as to Ola Söderström, whose caring and generous stewardship allowed me to stay in, and even succeed at, the academic game. All the people I met and befriended in "Neuch" own a share of this book, including my coconspirators in the push to make Swiss academia more welcoming to young scholars under the helm of our *condottieri*, Nicola Cianferoni. Ibrahim Soysüren, Dennis Pauschinger, Ophélie Bidet, and Ramazan Hakki Öztan deserve special mention. At LSE, I am grateful, in particular, to Jonathan Jackson, Elizabeth Hochstetler, and Tine Hanrieder. When I presented the research on which this book is based in the seminar series of the Department of International Development, which Tine co-organized, I promised to share news about the book "if and when" it came out. Tine corrected me, saying,

"Not if, but when." It was a touching expression of faith from someone who barely knew me. Well, Tine, now!

"I'm writing my book!" became a running joke with my friend Carla in Neuchatel. She saw it, rather perceptively, as an excuse not to go out on days when I was not feeling sociable or felt stressed about work in general. Whenever we met, Carla would ask me about "the book" with a smile. The book thus began to take on a mythical quality. I can finally produce proof that it was real.

Too many colleagues at my current academic home, the Université libre de Bruxelles (ULB), where I brought this manuscript to completion, helped me settle in Brussels and navigate a new institutional environment. Some of them deserve much more than the few lines I have room for. Laurence Roudart took me under her wing. She provided crucial advice as well as kind support. She also enabled me to travel abroad in the fall of 2022. The time I spent in Brazil and at home in Ecuador proved crucial to rethinking the argument and rewriting much of the manuscript to make it fit for review. Gani Aldashev shared his insights into academic life in Europe as well as his native knowledge of central Asia while treating me to delicious cross-cultural recipes. Sasha Newell and his family made me feel at home in Brussels while nurturing the connection to the US academic world. His counsel on book publishing was both strategic and reassuring. The company of Martin Deleixhe and Joël Noret make my everyday professional life more pleasant. I thank Thomas Berns for his fairness and Jean-Benoît Pilet for his helpful ear. However nothing brings more joy and meaning to my work than the time I spend with our graduate students and alumni at the Centre d'Etude de la Coopération Internationale et du Développement (CECID): Jonathan, Laura, Raffaele, Romane, Veronica, Yansa, Andrea, Lou, Claudia, Fadia, Myriam, and Rélex.

With some coworkers, I have developed bonds that go far beyond whatever the expression *friend and colleague* can begin to capture. Giovanni Esposito is the light of the fifteenth floor at the bâtiment S. I have distracted him way too many times with random questions or coffee-break entreaties; he has always welcomed me with a smile. His friendship and enlightened companionship as well as that of his partner form the center of my social life in Brussels. I see Antoine Roblain as a brother who has helped me grow and lighten up at the same time, and I see Frédéric Louault as an angel of sorts who, when he learned that I had gotten a job at ULB, offered to host me at his home with his family for as long as I needed, even though we had never so much as exchanged emails before. And that was only the beginning. Finally, I am grateful for the friendship of Marc and Bérengère as well as Gabriela and Michel, who, among many other necessities of academic life and life more broadly, helped me get the wooden desk on which I wrote or revised much of this volume.

Other family and friends across the Atlantic also took part in this adventure and contributed to its happy denouement. I am grateful to all of them, including my father, my stepmother Paula, my sister Manuela, my brother Josh, the Cathébras family, Víctor Bretón (who inspired me to follow a scholarly path), and, of course, my mother, to whom this book is dedicated. They know what a journey it has been—thrilling and grueling at the same time. It would be delusive not to acknowledge the losses and sacrifices. I'll mention one. In the same week that I signed the contract for this book, I met someone. By then, the project had been ten years in the making. My trepidation overwhelmed her. I hope that if she sees the final product, she'll understand.

My deepest feelings of gratitude are of course with all the people who participated in this study and from whom I learned more about life and politics than in all my years at university. I met, talked with, and befriended dozens of street vendors. I hope that this book does justice to their struggle. Two of them allowed me to use their real names: Fernando and Valdira. I also met and talked with dozens of other people whose work shaped in some way what happened on the streets, even though they did not draw their income directly from selling on the sidewalks. I am grateful to them, too, for the access and insights they provided. I hope they understand that whatever criticism they may find in this book about the actions of the institutions they belong to or the decisions they made are based on my analytic appraisal of a social dynamic and by no means entail a judgment on their person. During my last month of fieldwork, I was lucky to have Calla Hummel as a research partner. I am thankful for their patience and graceful handling of my fledging researcher's anxieties over intellectual property.

As my first academic mentor, Yves Surel gave me the confidence I needed to pursue this line of work. Hélène Combes at Sciences Po helped me get ahead at various critical junctures while always inquiring about the book project. Ashley Mears at the University of Amsterdam offered some useful tips in the final stretch.

This project benefited from funding from the National Science Foundation, the Swiss National Science Foundation, and the IJURR Foundation (formerly the Foundation for Urban and Regional Studies). Some chapters in the book draw on previous publications. Chapter 4 includes research previously published in "The Peddlers' Aristocracy: Social Closure, Path Dependence, and Street Vendors in São Paulo," *Qualitative Sociology*, 42(1), 117–138, 2019, Springer Nature. Chapter 5 incorporates data and analysis presented in "The Politics of Field Destruction and the Survival of São Paulo's Street Vendors,"

Social Problems, 63(3), 395–412, 2016, Oxford University Press. Chapter 8 contains material discussed in "Symbolic Capital, Informal Labor, and Post-industrial Markets: The Dynamics of Street Vending during the 2014 World Cup in São Paulo," *Theory and Society*, 48(2), 217–238, 2019, Springer Nature. I acknowledge the publishers' permission to reuse.

Finally, I cannot close the acknowledgments without thanking my editor at the University of Chicago Press, Elizabeth Branch Dyson. This book is my first book. Halfway through its writing, I realized I had no idea what a book was. Other editors lost interest, but Elizabeth gave me a second—then a third—chance. She pushed me to clarify the argument and shepherded the manuscript through all the revisions. If the proverbial phrase *This book would not have been possible without* . . . applies to anyone, it's her.

Appendix: Fieldwork

This book is mostly based on qualitative fieldwork. The bulk of field research took place over the course of one year, from August 2013 to August 2014. It was preceded by two preliminary research trips in the summers of 2011 and 2012 and was followed by a one-month follow-up trip in June 2015. During a total of fifteen months spent in São Paulo, I collected data through observation, interviews, document analysis, and questionnaire surveys.

My initial entry point was an NGO working with street vendors, the Center for Informal Workers (CIW), and a forum it organized to discuss inclusive policy for street vendors, the Street Vendors' Assembly (hereafter the Assembly). I was invited to its meetings by the lead organizer, an NGO worker named Helena, and I contacted those street vendors present at the meetings. Among them were leaders of street vendors associations, including the Union and the DVA, whom I subsequently interviewed at their offices. Invitations to attend other meetings followed, from political rallies to government-sponsored settlement talks regarding a lawsuit, and I requested interviews with attendants at each event, whenever possible. I also met street vendors either by approaching them directly and introducing myself as a researcher from a university in the United States or, on a couple of occasions, by purchasing something from them and striking up a casual conversation on a random topic before disclosing the true motives behind my query and requesting the person's informed consent to ask research-related questions.

Reactions from vendors ranged from enthusiastic to offensive, with various shades of discomfort and apprehension in between, occasionally tempered by curiosity toward a foreigner who spoke Portuguese with an unidentifiable accent. My sense is that I was perceived as a curious but discrete outsider and something of an oddity in a setting where white foreigners are few and fewer still display any interest in street vendors. Over time, I developed personal ties with several vendors, and I repeatedly visited their stalls or spent time with them after their work hours at restaurants, public events, church, my house, or their homes. I grew especially close to fourteen street vendors, seven of whom held or had held a license and five of whom were disabled.

Since conversations with some actors occurred repeatedly, in formal and informal settings over weeks or months, and key insights sometimes came from casual interactions (e.g., a joke in an elevator), any clear-cut estimate of the number of interviews and interviewees is bound to be arbitrary, if not misleading. With this caveat, it is safe to say that I met and talked to more than eighty street vendors. Included in this are thirty-four interviews on the impacts of the 2014 World Cup conducted with a collaborator. The latter interviews followed an interview guide. The other interviews were more free-flowing, and I recorded them through simultaneous or subsequent note-taking.

With state officials, I used referrals from previous interviewees as well as formal requests for an interview submitted by email or in person in which I introduced myself and explained the purpose of my research. I targeted people who played a crucial role in policymaking toward street vendors. Most interviewees with institutional positions were friendly and open, and I was fortunate enough to get access to key players who shaped street vending policy and legislation at critical junctures. I carried out semistructured interviews with ten high- and mid-ranking city officials, nine leaders of street vendors associations, six NGO workers, four police officers of various ranks, three current or former city councilmen as well as three aides, two leaders of storeowners associations, two storeowners, two lawyers, and a judge. In some cases, I conducted standard interviews that lasted between ten minutes and several hours at the interviewee's office. These were tape-recorded. In other cases, interviews extended over lunch or drinks, and I recorded their content afterward in writing. The high frequency of interrupted conversations, lasting chats, and other casual but instructive interactions led me to adopt a more flexible attitude toward the structuring of interviews. That said, one of the book's strengths lies, I believe, in my ability to establish relations of trust and familiarity with informants on different sides, especially policymakers in the city government and street vendors or their representatives.

Documentary evidence, on the other hand, runs the gamut from newspaper articles, handouts, letters, and flyers to official memos to a book written by a councilman about his experience investigating a network of corruption within the city government that involved street vendors, among others. Aside

from the digitalized archives of the city council—which contain bills, hearings, vote tallies, motivations, and so on going back to 1892 and from which
I extracted and analyzed some 180 files—the collection of documents was
embedded in the general logic of fieldwork, driven by its contingencies, constraints, and serendipities.

Of particular import to documentary analysis was getting access to the
lawsuit filed by the NGO and a public defender against the city. I am grateful
to the judge for authorizing my taking a look at the case. Another important
source of data was the *Diário Oficial*, the newspaper of public record of the
city of São Paulo, which contains all legislative and administrative decisions
adopted by the city or the city council regarding both the legal framework
governing street trade and the fate of individual license holders. The analysis
of all these documents involved careful reading and interpretation, sometimes informed by inquiries with stakeholders, but I did not use software or
special coding methods.

Toward the end of my time in the field, Brazil hosted the 2014 World Cup.
The question of its impacts was central to the heated public debate surrounding this mega-event, which imposed a highly restrictive legal framework on
small businesses hoping to benefit from it. Street vendors sat high on the list of
potentially affected groups, yet studies of their experiences during sports mega-
events were scarce. Thanks to doctoral dissertation funding from the National
Science Foundation, a collaborator and I were able to run a survey that comple-
mented document analysis and direct observation during the event.[1]

These research efforts benefited from my embeddedness in the field over
the course of ten months prior to the tournament, which ran from June 12
to July 13, 2014. Thanks to previous ties to street vendors and city officials,
I was able to attend policy meetings in the run-up to the World Cup. I also
drew on those ties and information to design the survey, which focused on
licensed street vendors. In May 2014, I conducted a short pilot survey containing questions about expectations for the World Cup in three areas of the
downtown district of Sé.[2] The larger survey took place immediately after the
World Cup. Calla Hummel, a collaborator and fellow graduate student at
the University of Texas at Austin, planned the logistics of survey administration
to ensure randomization. A list of all authorized vendors in the district of Sé
was publicly available, and we used it as a sampling frame. We also contacted
all other districts to find out whether they had any authorized vendors. Then,
from mid-July to early August, Calla and I administered the questionnaire to
all stalls in three districts—that is, Sé, Lapa, and São Miguel Paulista—which
together contained about half the population of licensed vendors. We approached vendors at 741 licensed stalls and obtained, in total, 241 responses.

Rather unexpectedly, this mega-event also offered an opportunity to examine the scope and logic of policies that extend rights to informal workers. Local organizers launched a program to let street vendors work as commission sellers in response to widespread criticism about FIFA's stringent—and, according to critics, discriminatory—hosting requirements. I attended most of the meetings with street vendors in which the program was designed and conducted observations of program participants during the tournament.

Notes

Chapter One

1. International Labour Organization (ILO), "Decent Work and the Informal Economy," International Labour Conference 90th session, Report VI (Geneva, 2002), 3.

2. The phrase *informal politics* is the title of John Cross's classic on street vendors in Mexico City, which focuses on enforcement and informal exchanges.

3. ILO, "Decent Work and the Informal Economy," 3.

4. Patricia Fernández-Kelly and Jon Shefner, *Out of the Shadows: Political Action and the Informal Economy in Latin America* (Penn State University Press, 2006).

5. Henry Dietz, "Urban Squatter Settlements in Peru: A Case History and Analysis," *Journal of Inter-American Studies* 11, no. 3 (July 1969): 353–70, https://doi.org/10.2307/165418.

6. Janice Perlman, *The Myth of Marginality: Urban Poverty and Politics in Rio De Janeiro* (University of California Press, 1976).

7. Dietz, "Urban Squatter Settlements in Peru"; Samuel P. Huntington, *Political Order in Changing Societies* (Yale University Press, 2006).

8. ILO, "Decent Work and the Informal Economy."

9. ILO, "Decent Work and the Informal Economy," 15, fig. 2.2.

10. Miguel Angel Centeno and Alejandro Portes, "The Informal Economy in the Shadow of the State," in *Out of the Shadows: Political Action and the Informal Economy in Latin America*, ed. Patricia Fernandez-Kelly and John Shefner (Penn State University Press, 2006), 40.

11. ECLAC/CEPAL, *Preliminary Overview of the Economies of Latin America and the Caribbean 2019* (United Nations, 2020).

12. Juan Pablo Pérez Sáinz, "The New Faces of Informality in Central America," *Journal of Latin American Studies* 30, no. 1 (1998): 157–79.

13. Diane E. Davis, "The Political and Economic Origins of Violence and Insecurity in Contemporary Latin America: Past Trajectories and Future Prospects," in *Violent Democracies in Latin America: Toward an Interdisciplinary Reconceptualization*, ed. Daniel Goldstein and Desmond Arias (Duke University Press, 2010), 56. See Bruno Nazim Baroni, "Spatial Stratification of Street Vendors in Downtown Mexico City" (master's thesis, Massachusetts Institute of Technology, 2007).

14. Maxwell A. Cameron, "Political Parties and the Worker-Employer Cleavage: The Impact of the Informal Sector on Voting in Lima, Peru," *Bulletin of Latin American Research* 10,

no. 3 (1991): 293–313, https://doi.org/10.2307/3338672; Cameron, "The Politics of the Urban Informal Sector in Peru: Populism, Class, And 'Redistributive Combines,'" *Canadian Journal of Latin American and Caribbean Studies* 16, no. 31 (January 1991): 79–104, https://doi.org/10.1080 /08263663.1991.10816655; Kurt Weyland, "A Paradox of Success? Determinants of Political Support for President Fujimori," *International Studies Quarterly* 44, no. 3 (2000): 481–502, https://doi.org/10.1111/0020-8833.00168.

15. Wendy Hunter, *The Transformation of the Workers' Party in Brazil, 1989–2009* (Cambridge University Press, 2010).

16. Manuel Castells and Alejandro Portes, "World Underneath: The Origins, Dynamics, and Effects of the Informal Economy," in *The Informal Economy: Studies in Advanced and Less Developed Countries*, ed. Alejandro Portes, Manuel Castells, and Lauren A. Benton (Johns Hopkins University Press, 1989), 11–40.

17. Rina Agarwala, *Informal Labor, Formal Politics, and Dignified Discontent in India* (Cambridge University Press, 2013).

18. John Christopher Cross, *Informal Politics: Street Vendors and the State in Mexico City* (Stanford University Press, 1998), 30.

19. See Vera Telles and Daniel Hirata, "Cidade e Práticas Urbanas: Nas Fronteiras Incertas entre o Informal, o Ilegal, e o Ilícito," *Estudos Avançados* 21, no. 61 (2007): 173–91; Sudhir Alladi Venkatesh, *Off the Books: The Underground Economy of the Urban Poor* (Harvard University Press, 2006), 8–13.

20. See, for example, Martha Chen and Françoise Carré, eds., *The Informal Economy Revisited: Examining the Past, Envisioning the Future* (Taylor & Francis, 2020).

21. Michael G. Donovan, "Informal Cities and the Contestation of Public Space: The Case of Bogotá's Street Vendors, 1988–2003," *Urban Studies* 45, no. 1 (2008): 30.

22. Karen Tranberg Hansen, Walter E. Little, and B. Lynne Milgram, eds., *Street Economies in the Urban Global South* (SAR Press, 2013); Martha Chen and Françoise Carré, *The Informal Economy Revisited*; Verónica Crossa, "Resisting the Entrepreneurial City: Street Vendors' Struggle in Mexico City's Historic Center," *International Journal of Urban and Regional Research* 33, no. 1 (2009): 43–63; Venkatesh, *Off the Books*.

23. Loïc Wacquant, *Punishing the Poor: The Neoliberal Government of Social Insecurity* (Duke University Press, 2009).

24. Cross, *Informal Politics*.

25. Quoted in Marco César Alvarez, "Cidadania e Direitos Num Mundo Globalizado," *Perspectivas: Revista de Ciências Sociais* 22 (1999), https://periodicos.fclar.unesp.br/perspectivas /article/download/2090/1712.

26. Rocio Rosales, "Survival, Economic Mobility and Community among Los Angeles Fruit Vendors," *Journal of Ethnic and Migration Studies* 39, no. 5 (2013): 697–717.

27. Henry Mayhew, *The London Underworld in the Victorian Period: Authentic First-Person Accounts by Beggars, Thieves and Prostitutes* (Dover Publications, 2005).

28. Gracia Clark, *Traders versus the State: Anthropological Approaches to Unofficial Economies*, Westview Special Studies in Applied Anthropology (Westview Press, 1998); Daniel M. Goldstein, *Owners of the Sidewalk: Security and Survival in the Informal City* (Duke University Press, 2016).

29. Crossa, "Resisting the Entrepreneurial City"; Noelani Eidse, Sarah Turner, and Natalie Oswin, "Contesting Street Spaces in a Socialist City: Itinerant Vending-Scapes and the Everyday Politics of Mobility in Hanoi, Vietnam," *Annals of the American Association of Geographers* 106, no. 2 (2016): 340–49; Turner and Laura Schoenberger, "Street Vendor Livelihoods and Everyday

Politics in Hanoi, Vietnam: The Seeds of a Diverse Economy?," *Urban Studies* 49, no. 5 (2012): 1027–44; Mitchell Duneier, *Sidewalk* (Macmillan, 1999).

30. In Zimbabwe in 2005, the government of Robert Mugabe launched Operation Murambatsvina, which means "Drive the Trash Out," to clear shantytowns and eliminate informal trade in urban areas. For Kolkata, see Ananya Roy, "Gentlemen's City: Urban Informality in the Calcutta of New Communism," in *Urban Informality: Transnational Perspectives from the Middle East, Latin America, and South Asia*, ed. Ananya Roy and Nezar AlSayyad, 141–64 (Lexington, 2004); David Harvey, "From Managerialism to Entrepreneurialism: The Transformation in Urban Governance in Late Capitalism," *Geografiska Annaler: Series B, Human Geography* (1989): 3–17; Saskia Sassen, *The Global City* (Princeton University Press, 1991).

31. Sharit K. Bhowmik, "Street Vendors in Asia: A Review," *Economic and Political Weekly* (2005): 2256–64.

32. See WIEGO, "Street Vendors and Market Traders," https://www.wiego.org/informal-economy/occupational-groups/street-vendors#size. Accessed September 5, 2024.

33. Ray Bromley, "Street Vending and Public Policy: A Global Review," *International Journal of Sociology and Social Policy* 20, no. 1/2 (2000): 1–28.

34. Alison Brown, "Street Trading in Four Cities: A Comparison," in *Contested Space: Street Trading, Public Space, and Livelihoods in Developing Cities*, ed. Alison Brown (ITDG Publishing, 2006): 175–86, 181.

35. Bromley, "Organization, Regulation and Exploitation in the So-Called 'Urban Informal Sector': The Street Traders of Cali, Colombia," *World Development* 6, no. 9 (1978): 1164.

36. John Cross and Sergio Peña, "Risk and Regulation in Informal and Illegal Markets," in *Out of the Shadows: Political Action and the Informal Economy in Latin America*, ed. Patricia Fernández-Kelly and Jon Shefner (Penn State University Press, 2006), 65.

37. Calla Hummel, *Why Informal Workers Organize: Contentious Politics, Enforcement, and the State* (Oxford University Press, 2021).

38. Cross and Peña, "Risk and Regulation in Informal and Illegal Markets," 65.

39. Wacquant, *Punishing the Poor: The Neoliberal Government of Social Insecurity*, 1.

40. ILO, "Women and Men in the Informal Economy: A Statistical Picture" (ILO, 2018).

41. ILO, "Women and Men in the Informal Economy."

42. Household data retrieved from the International Labour Organization database ILOSTAT available at https://rshiny.ilo.org/dataexplorer3/. Accessed August 26, 2024.

43. Alisha C. Holland, *Forbearance as Redistribution: The Politics of Informal Welfare in Latin America* (Cambridge University Press, 2017). Political scientists studying informal settlements in the '60s already noticed the paradoxical aloofness of the state in the face of an overt violation of its law. In *Squatters and Oligarchs*, David Collier attributes this hands-off approach to political returns in terms of social quiescence. Indeed, the permanent threat of eviction compels squatters to an otherwise orderly behavior, while informal settlements relieve the state from the obligation to provide affordable housing to its neediest citizens—whose claims consequently focus on more manageable needs such as infrastructure improvements.

44. Bromley, "Street Vending and Public Policy: A Global Review."

45. See, for example, Cross, *Informal Politics*; Hansen, Little, and Milgram, *Street Economies in the Urban Global South*; Michel Misse, "Trocas Ilícitas e Mercadorias Políticas: Para Uma Interpretação de Trocas Ilícitas e Moralmente Reprováveis Cuja Persistência e Abrangência No Brasil Nos Causam Incômodos Também Teóricos," *Anuário Antropológico* 35, no. 2 (2010): 89–107.

46. Roy, *City Requiem, Calcutta: Gender and the Politics of Poverty* (University of Minnesota Press, 2003).

47. Brodwyn M. Fischer, *A Poverty of Rights: Citizenship and Inequality in Twentieth-Century Rio de Janeiro* (Stanford University Press, 2008), 2.

48. Eduardo Yázigi, *O Mundo Das Calçadas: Por Uma Política Democrática de Espaços Públicos* (Humanitas, 2000).

49. Oswaldo Truzzi, *De Mascates a Doutores: Sírios e Libaneses Em São Paulo* (Editora Sumaré, 1992).

50. Peter M. Townroe, "Location Factors in the Decentralization of Industry: A Survey of Metropolitan São Paulo, Brazil" (World Bank Working Papers 517, 1983).

51. Kalmann Schaefer and Cheywa R. Spindel, "Sao Paulo: Urban Development and Employment," (ILO,1976), 58.

52. Townroe, "Location Factors in the Decentralization of Industry," 21.

53. João Batista Pamplona, "Mercado de trabalho, informalidade e comércio ambulante em São Paulo," *Revista Brasileira de Estudos de População* 30, no. 1 (2013): 26.

54. Pamplona, "Mercado de trabalho, informalidade e comércio ambulante em São Paulo."

55. The city council passed a municipal bill legalizing the street trade of nonpackaged foods after the 2014 World Cup.

56. Most names are fictitious.

Chapter Two

1. On the cultural implications of citizenship, see Evelina Dagnino, "Citizenship: A Perverse Confluence," *Development in Practice* 17, no. 4–5 (August 2007): 549–56, https://doi.org/10.1080/09614520701469534.

2. Hannah Arendt, *The Origins of Totalitarianism* (Harcourt Place, 1951); see also Margaret R. Somers, *Genealogies of Citizenship: Markets, Statelessness, and the Right to Have Rights* (Cambridge University Press, 2008).

3. Thomas H. Marshall, *Citizenship and Social Class* (Cambridge University Press, 1950).

4. Marshall, *Citizenship and Social Class*.

5. Marshall, *Citizenship and Social Class*, 15–16.

6. Marshall, *Citizenship and Social Class*, 29, 68.

7. Maria Hermínia Tavares de Almeida and Fernando Henrique Guarnieri, "Toward a (Poor) Middle-Class Democracy?," in *Democratic Brazil Divided*, ed. Peter Kingstone and Timothy J. Power (University of Pittsburgh Press, 2017), 175–79.

8. Gay W. Seidman, *Manufacturing Militance: Workers' Movements in Brazil and South Africa, 1970–1985* (University of California Press, 1994).

9. Ruth Berins Collier and David Collier, *Shaping the Political Arena: Critical Junctures, the Labor Movement, and Regime Dynamics in Latin America* (Princeton University Press, 1991), 7.

10. Collier and Collier, *Shaping the Political Arena*.

11. Brodwyn M. Fischer, *A Poverty of Rights: Citizenship and Inequality in Twentieth-Century Rio de Janeiro* (Stanford University Press, 2008), 93.

12. Fischer, *A Poverty of Rights*.

13. Fischer, *A Poverty of Rights*.

14. Seidman, *Manufacturing Militance*, 17.

15. Marshall, *Citizenship and Social Class*, 41.

16. Paul Singer, "Movimentos de Bairro." In *São Paulo: O Povo em Movimento*, ed. Paul Singer and Vinícius Caldeira Brant (Editora Brasileira de Ciências, 1980), 83–107.

17. Partha Chatterjee, *The Politics of the Governed: Reflections on Popular Politics in Most of the World*, Leonard Hastings Schoff Memorial Lectures (Columbia University Press, 2004); Chatterjee, *Lineages of Political Society: Studies in Postcolonial Democracy* (Columbia University Press, 2011).

18. James Holston, *Insurgent Citizenship* (Princeton University Press, 2009).

19. Holston, "Insurgent Citizenship in an Era of Global Urban Peripheries," *City & Society* 21, no. 2 (2009): 255.

20. Holston, "Insurgent Citizenship in an Era of Global Urban Peripheries," 246.

21. Holston, "Insurgent Citizenship in an Era of Global Urban Peripheries," 247.

22. Arendt, *The Origins of Totalitarianism*, 277; Somers, *Genealogies of Citizenship*, 121.

23. Catherine Perret, *L'enseignement de La Torture, Réflexions Sur Jean Améry* (Seuil, 2013), https://hal-univ-paris8.archives-ouvertes.fr/hal-02512665/.

24. Ayten Gündogdu, *Rightlessness in an Age of Rights: Hannah Arendt and the Contemporary Struggles of Migrants* (Oxford University Press, 2014), 18.

25. Anne McNevin, *Contesting Citizenship: Irregular Migrants and New Frontiers of the Political* (Columbia University Press, 2011), https://doi.org/10.7312/mcne15128.

26. Gündogdu, *Rightlessness in an Age of Rights*, 19.

27. Max Weber, *Economy and Society: An Outline of Interpretive Sociology* (University of California Press, 1978); Rogers Brubaker, "Beyond Ethnicity," *Ethnic and Racial Studies* 37, no. 5 (2014): 804–8, https://doi.org/10.1080/01419870.2013.871311.

28. Aihwa Ong, *Flexible Citizenship: The Cultural Logics of Transnationality* (Duke University Press, 1999), https://www.dukeupress.edu/flexible-citizenship.

29. Somers, *Genealogies of Citizenship*.

30. Arlie Russell Hochschild, *Strangers in Their Own Land: Anger and Mourning on the American Right* (New Press, 2018).

31. See Somers, *Genealogies of Citizenship*, for a comprehensive discussion of this argument.

32. Guy Standing, *The Precariat* (Bloomsbury Academic, 2011); Thomas Piketty, *Capital in the Twenty-First Century* (Harvard University Press, 2014), https://doi.org/10.4159/9780674369542.

33. Dagnino, "Citizenship," 550.

34. Dagnino, "Citizenship," 553.

35. Vincanne Adams, *Markets of Sorrow* (Duke University Press, 2013).

36. Paul Pierson, *Politics in Time: History, Institutions, and Social Analysis* (Princeton University Press, 2004).

37. Susana Rotker and Katherine Goldman, *Citizens of Fear: Urban Violence in Latin America* (Rutgers University Press, 2002).

38. Ong, *Flexible Citizenship*, 215–16.

39. Fischer, *A Poverty of Rights*, 128.

40. Cited in Fischer, *A Poverty of Rights*, 127.

41. Cited in Tavares de Almeida and Guarnieri, "Toward a (Poor) Middle-Class Democracy?," 175.

42. Jesse Barron, "A Homeless Man Attacked Him. But Was There More to the Story?" *New York Times*. Nov. 16, 2023. https://www.nytimes.com/2023/11/16/magazine/san-francisco-homelessness.html. Accessed August 26, 2024.

43. Chatterjee, *The Politics of the Governed*; Chatterjee, *Lineages of Political Society*.

44. Roy, *City Requiem, Calcutta.*

45. Hochschild, *Strangers in Their Own Land.*

46. José Álvaro Moisés, "Political Discontent in New Democracies: The Case of Brazil and Latin America," *International Review of Sociology* 21, no. 2 (July 1, 2011): 1, https://doi.org/10.10 80/03906701.2011.581807.

47. Michael McCann, "The Unbearable Lightness of Rights: On Sociolegal Inquiry in the Global Era," *Law & Society Review* 48, no. 2 (2014): 252.

Chapter Three

1. Interview with the author, São Paulo, October 2013.

2. Interview with the author, São Paulo, December 2013.

3. I use the going exchange rate at the time of fieldwork (2013–2014): 2.2 reals per US dollar.

4. Interview with the author, São Paulo, November 2013.

5. See chapter 2 for an analytic description of citizenship.

6. See chapters 4 and 5.

7. Michèle Lamont and Virág Molnár, "The Study of Boundaries in the Social Sciences," *Annual Review of Sociology* 28, no. 1 (2002): 167–95.

8. Andreas Wimmer, *Ethnic Boundary Making: Institutions, Power, Networks* (Oxford University Press, 2013).

9. Charles Tilly, *Durable Inequality* (University of California Press, 1998).

10. Michael Mann, *The Dark Side of Democracy: Explaining Ethnic Cleansing* (Cambridge University Press, 2005).

11. Interview with the author, São Paulo, March 2014.

12. Interview with female street vendor, São Paulo, November 2013.

13. Interview with Kid, an unlicensed street vendor in his twenties, São Paulo, August 2014.

14. Interview with the author, São Paulo, March 2014.

15. Interview with the author, São Paulo, March 2014.

16. The councilman's name is a pseudonym.

17. Clifford Geertz, "Suq: The Bazaar Economy in Sefrou," in *Meaning and Order in Moroccan Society: Three Essays in Cultural Analysis*, ed. Clifford Geertz, Hildred Geertz, and Lawrence Rosen (Cambridge University Press, 1979).

Chapter Four

1. Claudio Bertolli, "Os Trabalhadores Ambulantes Na Cidade De Sao Paulo: Aspectos Históricos," in *Os Ambulantes e Seu Trabalho: Um Projeto de Institucionalização* (Secretaria das Administrações da Cidade de São Paulo, n.d.), 83–125.

2. I have chosen to use the literal translation of the Portuguese term *ponto*—"spot"—to refer to the established location where a street vendor works.

3. Bertolli, "Os Trabalhadores Ambulantes na Cidade de São Paulo."

4. Municipal Law 5,201 adopted on May 29, 1957.

5. Official letter from mayor Adhemar Barros to the city council president motivating the bill, dated July 13, 1957. City council digital archives, Lei PL 4519/1957.

6. Douglass C. North, *Institutions, Institutional Change and Economic Performance* (Cambridge University Press, 1990); Raymond Murphy, "The Structure of Closure: A Critique and

Development of the Theories of Weber, Collins, and Parkin," *British Journal of Sociology* (1984): 547–67; Kim A. Weeden, "Why Do Some Occupations Pay More than Others? Social Closure and Earnings Inequality in the United States," *American Journal of Sociology* 108, no. 1 (2002): 55–101.

7. Interview with party member and city official during the Erundina administration, São Paulo, February 2014.

8. Interview with the author, São Paulo, January 2014.

9. Interview with party member and city official during the Erundina administration, February 2014.

10. Interview with the author, São Paulo, January 2014.

11. Interview with Aldaiza Sposati, São Paulo, January 2014.

12. Interview with Aldaiza Sposati, São Paulo, January 2014.

13. Stuart A. Scheingold, *The Politics of Rights: Lawyers, Public Policy, and Political Change* (University of Michigan Press, 2010).

14. Scheingold, *The Politics of Rights*.

15. Interview with Bruno Feder, São Paulo, November 2013.

16. Interview with Artur, São Paulo, September 2013.

17. Municipal Law 11,124, adopted November 26, 1991.

18. Collier and Collier, *Shaping the Political Arena*.

19. Pierson, *Politics in Time*.

20. Interview with Rubens Possati, chief regulator of street vending in Sé, São Paulo, November 2013.

21. Cross, *Informal Politics*.

22. Interview with the author, São Paulo, February 2013.

23. "Relatório Final Da Comissão Parlamentar De Inquérito Para Apurar As Denúncias Pertinentes À Fiscalização Do Comércio Ambulante," Câmara Municipal de São Paulo, November 28, 2002; José Eduardo Cardozo, *A Máfia Das Propinas* (Editora Fundação Perseu Abramo, 2000), 126.

24. A deal of this nature, involving Councilman Hanna Garib, was denounced on live television by Afonso José da Silva, an unlicensed street vendors' leader, in February 1999. Two weeks later, Afonso survived an attempt on his life by two gunmen. He remained a vocal critic of corruption and abuse toward street vendors until his assassination ten years later.

25. Cardozo, *A Máfia Das Propinas*.

26. Hernando De Soto, *The Other Path: The Invisible Revolution in the Third World* (Harper & Row, 1989).

27. Even the president of the city council was reported to have covered, in 1999, a debt stemming from checks street vendors had used to pay inspectors, which then bounced at a supermarket. See "Presidente da Câmara de SP é Denunciado," *Folha de São Paulo*, February 22, 2000, https://www1.folha.uol.com.br/fol/geral/ult22022000231.htm.

28. Cardozo, *A Máfia Das Propinas*, 116.

29. A DVA leader did note, however, that the previous organization representing licensed disabled vendors, ABRADEF, got involved in corruption from the 1970s onward.

30. Minutes from the earing at the city council on November 26, 1998, to discuss PL 1,017/97 and PL 806/97.

31. Cardozo, *A Máfia Das Propinas*, 72.

32. "Relatório Final Da Comissão Parlamentar De Inquérito Para Apurar As Denúncias Pertinentes À Fiscalização Do Comércio Ambulante," Câmara Municipal de São Paulo, November 28, 2002, 19.

Chapter Five

1. McCann, "The Unbearable Lightness of Rights."

2. Street vendors' leaders and champions, like councilman Tristan, would use such descriptors at public meetings.

3. Cross, *Informal Politics*.

4. Holland, *Forbearance as Redistribution*.

5. Cross, *Informal Politics*.

6. In Cross's view, state integration is a key predictor of successful policy implementation.

7. Municipal Law 11,039.

8. Interview with the author, São Paulo, September 2013.

9. Interview with the author, São Paulo, November 2013.

10. Interview with the author, São Paulo, November 2013.

11. Interview with district administrator, São Paulo, March 2014.

12. Interview with the author, São Paulo, August 2013.

13. Stuart Wilson, "Litigating Housing Rights in Johannesburg's Inner City: 2004–2008," *South African Journal on Human Rights* 27, no. 1 (2011): 127–51; Charles R. Epp, *The Rights Revolution: Lawyers, Activists, and Supreme Courts in Comparative Perspective* (Cambridge University Press, 1998); Michael W. McCann, *Rights at Work: Pay Equity Reform and the Politics of Legal Mobilization* (University of Chicago Press, 1994); Scheingold, *The Politics of Rights*.

14. Daniel M. Brinks and Varun Gauri, eds., *Courting Social Justice: Judicial Enforcement of Social and Economic Rights in the Developing World* (Cambridge University Press, 2010).

15. Somers, *Genealogies of Citizenship*.

16. Salo V. Coslovsky, "Beyond Bureaucracy: How Prosecutors and Public Defenders Enforce Urban Planning Laws in São Paulo, Brazil," *International Journal of Urban and Regional Research* 39, no. 6 (2015): 1111.

17. Coslovsky, "Beyond Bureaucracy," 1111.

18. Coslovsky, "Beyond Bureaucracy," 1112.

19. Interview with the author, São Paulo, September 2013.

20. Wilson, "Litigating Housing Rights in Johannesburg's Inner City," 141.

21. Interview with the author, São Paulo, October 2013.

22. Coslovsky, "Beyond Bureaucracy," 1114.

23. Interview with the author, São Paulo, September 2013.

24. Interview with the author, São Paulo, September 2013.

25. Interview with the author, São Paulo, September 2013.

26. Interview with the author, São Paulo, September 2013.

27. Nezar AlSayyad, "Urban Informality as a 'New' Way of Life," in *Urban Informality: Transnational Perspectives from the Middle East, Latin America, and South Asia*, ed. Ananya Roy and Nezar AlSayyad (Lexington, 2004).

28. Arendt, *The Origins of Totalitarianism*.

29. Robert D. Putnam, *Bowling Alone: The Collapse and Revival of American Community* (Simon & Schuster, 2000).

30. The injunction echoes the lawsuit in recognizing a risk of "irreparable damage." Preliminary injunction issued by Judge Carmen Cristina Teijeiro e Oliveira, 5ª Vara da Fazenda Pública da Capital, São Paulo, June 4, 2012.

31. Interview with the author, São Paulo, September 2013.

Chapter Six

1. Five years later, after losing his bid for reelection, Haddad would run for president as a surrogate of Lula, as the former president had been barred from running for public office due to an ongoing corruption investigation.

2. Stephanie Lee Mudge, "What's Left of Leftism?: Neoliberal Politics in Western Party Systems, 1945–2004," *Social Science History* 35, no. 3 (2011): 337–80.

3. Hunter, *The Transformation of the Workers' Party in Brazil*.

4. Interview with the author, São Paulo, August 2012.

5. Aside from commitment to laissez faire, Mudge (2011) measures neoliberalism by a preference for law-and-order policies and policies oriented toward financial, professional, and white-collar constituencies.

6. Interview with Helena, São Paulo, August 2013.

7. The sentence in Portuguese echoed the famous last words of Brazil's historic ruler, Getúlio Vargas, who said: "*Saio da vida para entrar na história*," which translates roughly to "I'm stepping out of life to enter history."

8. Javier Auyero, *Poor People's Politics: Peronist Survival Networks and the Legacy of Evita* (Duke University Press, 2000).

9. The head of SCS ran unsuccessfully for a council seat in the same election in which Haddad was elected.

10. Interview with the author, São Paulo, April 2014.

11. Roy, "Gentlemen's City," 150.

12. Interview with the author, São Paulo, April 2014.

13. Interview with the author, São Paulo, February 2014.

14. Roy, "Gentlemen's City," 154.

15. Interview with the author, São Paulo, March 2014.

16. They were still able to work, thanks to the court order, but the expiration date on their document had passed.

17. Meeting held at city hall on August 23, 2013.

18. Ceremony at city hall, October 18, 2013.

19. Roy, "Gentlemen's City," 150.

Chapter Seven

1. David Black and Janis Van Der Westhuizen, "The Allure of Global Games for 'Semi-Peripheral' Polities and Spaces: A Research Agenda," *Third World Quarterly* 25, no. 7 (2004): 1195–214.

2. Sandra L. Suárez, "Symbolic Politics and the Regulation of Executive Compensation: A Comparison of the Great Depression and the Great Recession," *Politics & Society* 42, no. 1 (2014): 74.

3. Ingolfur Bluhdorn, "Sustaining the Unsustainable: Symbolic Politics and the Politics of Simulation," *Environmental Politics* 16, no. 2 (April 2007): 251–75, https://doi.org/10.1080/09644010701211759; Murray J. Edelman, *The Symbolic Uses of Politics* (University of Illinois Press, 1964); Mark Hugh Leff, *The Limits of Symbolic Reform: The New Deal and Taxation, 1933–1939* (Cambridge University Press, 1984).

4. Ari Adut, *Reign of Appearances: The Misery and Splendor of the Public Sphere* (Cambridge University Press, 2018).

5. Laurie Boussaguet, "Participatory Mechanisms as Symbolic Policy Instruments?," *Comparative European Politics* 14, no. 1 (January 2016): 107–24, https://doi.org/10.1057/cep.2015.12.

6. Caroline W. Lee and Zachary Romano, "Democracy's New Discipline: Public Deliberation as Organizational Strategy," *Organization Studies* 34, no. 5–6 (May 2013): 738, https://doi.org/10.1177/0170840613479233.

7. Michel Foucault, *Surveiller et Punir* (Gallimard, 1975).

8. Meeting of the World Cup street vendors' participation program task force, March 2014.

9. McCann, "The Unbearable Lightness of Rights," 249.

Chapter Eight

1. "Escaping is the only stable thing is my life."

2. Tariq Panja, "As Sponsors Shy Away, FIFA Faces World Cup Shortfall," *New York Times*, November 18, 2017, https://www.nytimes.com/2017/11/28/sports/soccer/world-cup-sponsors-russia-2018.html.

3. Black and Van Der Westhuizen, "The Allure of Global Games for 'Semi-Peripheral' Polities and Spaces"; David Whitson and John Horne, "Underestimated Costs and Overestimated Benefits? Comparing the Outcomes of Sports Mega-Events in Canada and Japan," *Sociological Review* 54, no. 2 (2006): 71–89.

4. John Horne and Wolfram Manzenreiter, "An Introduction to the Sociology of Sports Mega-Events," *Sociological Review* 54, no. 2 suppl. (2006): 1–24.

5. See VPRO Blacklight documentary *Trade Mark Twenty Ten*, directed by Rudi Boon and co-directed by Stefano Bertacchini, produced by Pepijn Boonstra and Ymke Kreiken. Date of release: Nov. 16, 2009. As noted at min. 17, even "2010," during the 2010 World Cup, "belong[ed] to FIFA."

6. Ilda Lindell, Maria Hedman, and Kyle-Nathan Verboomen, "The World Cup 2010, 'World Class Cities,' and Street Vendors in South Africa," in *Street Economies in the Urban Global South*, ed. Karen Tranberg Hansen, Walter E. Little, and B. Lynne Milgram (SAR Press, 2013), 197.

7. Neil Fligstein, "Markets as Politics: A Political-Cultural Approach to Market Institutions," *American Sociological Review* (1996): 656–73.

8. Paul Ingram and Hayagreeva Rao, "Store Wars: The Enactment and Repeal of Anti-Chain-Store Legislation in America," *American Journal of Sociology* 110, no. 2 (2004): 446–87.

9. Ingram and Rao, "Store Wars," 447.

10. Marc Schneiberg, Marissa King, and Thomas Smith, "Social Movements and Organizational Form: Cooperative Alternatives to Corporations in the American Insurance, Dairy, and Grain Industries," *American Sociological Review* 73, no. 4 (2008): 637–38.

11. Schneiberg, King, and Smith, "Social Movements and Organizational Form," 639, 647. For microbrewers, see Glenn R. Carroll and Anand Swaminathan, "Why the Microbrewery Movement? Organizational Dynamics of Resource Partitioning in the US Brewing Industry," *American Journal of Sociology* 106, no. 3 (2000): 715–62.

12. Henrich R. Greve, Jo-Ellen Pozner, and Hayagreeva Rao, "Vox Populi: Resource Partitioning, Organizational Proliferation, and the Cultural Impact of the Insurgent Microradio Movement," *American Journal of Sociology* 112, no. 3 (2006): 802–37.

13. Greve, Pozner, and Rao, "Vox Populi," 808.

14. Asef Bayat, "Un-Civil Society: The Politics of the 'Informal People,'" *Third World Quarterly* 18, no. 1 (1997): 53–72; Sassen, "Whose City Is It? Globalization and the Formation of New Claims," *Public Culture* 8 (1996): 205–24.

15. For licensed vendors with a license for garments.

16. In São Paulo, the neighborhood of Vila Madalena, known for its vibrant nightlife, also experienced a flood of tourists who watched games inside bars or from the sidewalks. This influx caught authorities off guard, and some vendors worked there, too. Unfortunately, limited research capacities prevented me from conducting observation in that area.

17. Conversions are based on the exchange rate at the time of the World Cup.

18. Schneiberg, King, and Smith, "Social Movements and Organizational Form."

19. Ingram and Rao, "Store Wars," 446.

Conclusion

1. Centeno and Portes, "The Informal Economy in the Shadow of the State."

2. Matt Apuzzo, "A U.S. Tax Investigation Snowballed to Stun the Soccer World," *New York Times*, May 29, 2015, https://www.nytimes.com/2015/05/30/sports/soccer/more-indictments -expected-in-fifa-case-irs-official-says.html.

3. Jan Breman, "Informality: The Bane of the Labouring Poor under Globalised Capitalism," in *The Informal Economy Revisited*, ed. Chen and Carré (Taylor & Francis, 2020), 31–37; Barbara Harriss-White, "India's Informal Economy: Past, Present and Future," in *The Informal Economy Revisited* ed. Chen and Carré (Taylor & Francis, 2020), 37–44.

4. Interview with city official and World Cup organizer, June 2014.

5. ILO, "Decent Work and the Informal Economy."

6. Interview with Aldaiza Sposati, São Paulo, January 2014.

7. The fact that many of us don't feel authorities take our problems seriously might speak to a broader trend—the informalization of citizenship.

8. Interview with the author, São Paulo, May 2014.

9. Interview with the author, São Paulo, August 2014.

10. Marshall, *Citizenship and Social Class.*

11. See Somers, *Genealogies of Citizenship.*

12. This was the case for the residents of Vila Autodromo, an informal settlement in Rio torn down in the run-up to the 2016 Olympic Games. The 2017 documentary *Favela Olímpica* directed by Samuel Chalard and produced by Frédéric Gonseth documents their plight.

13. Michael Touchton, Stephanie McNulty, and Brian Wampler, "Participatory Budgeting and Community Development: A Global Perspective," *American Behavioral Scientist* 67, no. 4 (2023): 522.

14. Touchton, McNulty, and Wampler, "Participatory Budgeting and Community Development," 520.

15. Gianpaolo Baiocchi, *Militants and Citizens: The Politics of Participatory Democracy in Porto Alegre* (Stanford University Press, 2005).

16. Touchton, McNulty, and Wampler, "Participatory Budgeting and Community Development," 522.

17. Leonardo Avritzer, "O orçamento participativo e a teoria democrática: Um balanço crítico," in *A Inovação Democrática no Brasil*, ed. Leonardo Avritzer and Zander Navarro, 13–60 (Cortez Editora, 2003).

18. Jonathan Watts, "World Cup 2014: Brazil's Plans for Anti-Terror Law Alarm Rights Groups," *Guardian*, April 19, 2014, https://www.theguardian.com/football/2014/apr/19/world-cup-brazil -anti-terror-law-alarms-human-rights-groups.

Appendix

1. Doctoral Dissertation Research Improvement Grant award number 1434365.

2. I administered the same questionnaire to a small cluster of unlicensed vendors near the subway station of Itaquera, where a new stadium was being built for the World Cup.

References

Adut, Ari. *Reign of Appearances: The Misery and Splendor of the Public Sphere.* Cambridge University Press, 2018.

Agarwala, Rina. *Informal Labor, Formal Politics, and Dignified Discontent in India.* Cambridge University Press, 2013.

AlSayyad, Nezar. "Urban Informality as a 'New' Way of Life." In *Urban Informality: Transnational Perspectives from the Middle East, Latin America, and South Asia,* edited by Ananya Roy and Nezar AlSayyad, 7–32. Lexington Books, 2004.

Alvarez, Marco César. "Cidadania e Direitos Num Mundo Globalizado." *Perspectivas: Revista de Ciências Sociais* 22 (1999): 95–107. https://periodicos.fclar.unesp.br/perspectivas/article/download/2090/1712.

Álvaro Moisés, José. "Political Discontent in New Democracies: The Case of Brazil and Latin America." *International Review of Sociology* 21, no. 2 (2011): 339–66. https://doi.org/10.1080/03906701.2011.581807.

Apuzzo, Matt. "A U.S. Tax Investigation Snowballed to Stun the Soccer World." *New York Times,* May 29, 2015. https://www.nytimes.com/2015/05/30/sports/soccer/more-indictments-expected-in-fifa-case-irs-official-says.html.

Arendt, Hannah. *The Origins of Totalitarianism.* Harcourt Place, 1951.

Auyero, Javier. *Poor People's Politics: Peronist Survival Networks and the Legacy of Evita.* Duke University Press, 2000.

Avritzer, Leonardo. "O Orçamento Participativo e a Teoria Democrática: Um Balanço Crítico." In *A Inovação Democrática no Brasil,* edited by Leonardo Avritzer and Zander Navarro, 13–60. Cortez Editora, 2003.

Baiocchi, Gianpaolo. *Militants and Citizens: The Politics of Participatory Democracy in Porto Alegre.* Stanford University Press, 2005.

Baroni, Bruno Nazim. "Spatial Stratification of Street Vendors in Downtown Mexico City." Master's thesis, Massachusetts Institute of Technology, 2007.

Bayat, Asef. "Un-Civil Society: The Politics of the 'Informal People.'" *Third World Quarterly* 18, no. 1 (1997): 53–72.

Bertolli, Claudio. "Os Trabalhadores Ambulantes Na Cidade De São Paulo: Aspectos Histori-cos." In *Os Ambulantes e Seu Trabalho: Um Projeto de Institucionalização*, 83–125. Secretaria das Administrações da Cidade de São Paulo, n.d.

Bhowmik, Sharit K. "Street Vendors in Asia: A Review." *Economic and Political Weekly* (2005): 2256–64.

Black, David, and Janis Van Der Westhuizen. "The Allure of Global Games for 'Semi-Peripheral' Polities and Spaces: A Research Agenda." *Third World Quarterly* 25, no. 7 (2004): 1195–214.

Bluhdorn, Ingolfur. "Sustaining the Unsustainable: Symbolic Politics and the Politics of Simu-lation." *Environmental Politics* 16, no. 2 (2007): 251–75. https://doi.org/10.1080/0964401 0701211759.

Boussaguet, Laurie. "Participatory Mechanisms as Symbolic Policy Instruments?" *Comparative European Politics* 14, no. 1 (2016): 107–24. https://doi.org/10.1057/cep.2015.12.

Breman, Jan. "Informality: The Bane of the Labouring Poor under Globalised Capitalism." In *The Informal Economy Revisited: Examining the Past, Envisioning the Future*, edited by Mar-tha Chen and Françoise Carré, 31–37. Taylor & Francis, 2020.

Brinks, Daniel M., and Varun Gauri, eds. *Courting Social Justice: Judicial Enforcement of Social and Economic Rights in the Developing World*. Cambridge University Press, 2010.

Bromley, Ray. "Organization, Regulation and Exploitation in the So-Called 'Urban Informal Sector': The Street Traders of Cali, Colombia." *World Development* 6, no. 9 (1978): 1161–71.

———. "Street Vending and Public Policy: A Global Review." *International Journal of Sociology and Social Policy* 20, no. 1/2 (2000): 1–28.

Brown, Alison. "Street Trading in Four Cities: A Comparison." In *Contested Space: Street Trad-ing, Public Space, and Livelihoods in Developing Cities*, edited by Alison Brown, 175–96. ITDG Publishing, 2006.

Brubaker, Rogers. "Beyond Ethnicity." *Ethnic and Racial Studies* 37, no. 5 (2014): 804–8. https://doi.org/10.1080/01419870.2013.871311.

Cameron, Maxwell A. "Political Parties and the Worker-Employer Cleavage: The Impact of the Informal Sector on Voting in Lima, Peru." *Bulletin of Latin American Research* 10, no. 3 (1991): 293–313. https://doi.org/10.2307/3338672.

———. "The Politics of the Urban Informal Sector in Peru: Populism, Class, And 'Redistributive Combines.'" *Canadian Journal of Latin American and Caribbean Studies* 16, no. 31 (January 1991): 79–104. https://doi.org/10.1080/08263663.1991.10816655.

Cardozo, José Eduardo. *A Máfia Das Propinas*. Editora Fundação Perseu Abramo, 2000.

Carroll, Glenn R., and Anand Swaminathan. "Why the Microbrewery Movement? Organiza-tional Dynamics of Resource Partitioning in the US Brewing Industry." *American Journal of Sociology* 106, no. 3 (2000): 715–62.

Castells, Manuel, and Alejandro Portes. "World Underneath: The Origins, Dynamics, and Ef-fects of the Informal Economy." In *The Informal Economy: Studies in Advanced and Less Developed Countries*, edited by Alejandro Portes, Manuel Castells, and Lauren A. Benton, 11–40. Johns Hopkins University Press, 1989.

Centeno, Miguel Angel, and Alejandro Portes. "The Informal Economy in the Shadow of the State." In *Out of the Shadows: Political Action and the Informal Economy in Latin America*, edited by Patricia Fernandez-Kelly and John Shefner, 23–48. Penn State University Press, 2006.

Chatterjee, Partha. *Lineages of Political Society: Studies in Postcolonial Democracy*. Columbia University Press, 2011.

———. *The Politics of the Governed: Reflections on Popular Politics in Most of the World.* Leonard Hastings Schoff Memorial Lectures. Columbia University Press, 2004.

Chen, Martha, and Françoise Carré, eds. *The Informal Economy Revisited: Examining the Past, Envisioning the Future.* Taylor & Francis, 2020.

Clark, Gracia. *Traders versus the State: Anthropological Approaches to Unofficial Economies.* Westview Special Studies in Applied Anthropology. Westview, 1998.

Collier, David. *Squatters and Oligarchs: Authoritarian Rule and Policy Change in Peru.* Johns Hopkins University Press, 1976.

Collier, Ruth Berins, and David Collier. *Shaping the Political Arena: Critical Junctures, the Labor Movement, and Regime Dynamics in Latin America.* Princeton University Press, 1991.

Coslovsky, Salo V. "Beyond Bureaucracy: How Prosecutors and Public Defenders Enforce Urban Planning Laws in São Paulo, Brazil." *International Journal of Urban and Regional Research* 39, no. 6 (2015): 1103–19.

Cross, John Christopher. *Informal Politics: Street Vendors and the State in Mexico City.* Stanford University Press, 1998.

Cross, John, and Sergio Peña. "Risk and Regulation in Informal and Illegal Markets." In *Out of the Shadows: Political Action and the Informal Economy in Latin America*, edited by Patricia Fernández-Kelly and Jon Shefner, 49–80. Penn State University Press, 2006.

Crossa, Verónica. "Resisting the Entrepreneurial City: Street Vendors' Struggle in Mexico City's Historic Center." *International Journal of Urban and Regional Research* 33, no. 1 (2009): 43–63.

Dagnino, Evelina. "Citizenship: A Perverse Confluence." *Development in Practice* 17, no. 4–5 (2007): 549–56. https://doi.org/10.1080/09614520701469534.

Davis, Diane E. "The Political and Economic Origins of Violence and Insecurity in Contemporary Latin America: Past Trajectories and Future Prospects." In *Violent Democracies in Latin America: Toward an Interdisciplinary Reconceptualization*, edited by Daniel Goldstein and Desmond Arias, 35–63. Duke University Press, 2010.

De Soto, Hernando. *The Other Path: The Invisible Revolution in the Third World.* Harper & Row, 1989.

Dietz, Henry. "Urban Squatter Settlements in Peru: A Case History and Analysis." *Journal of Inter-American Studies* 11, no. 3 (1969): 353–70.

Donovan, M. G. "Informal Cities and the Contestation of Public Space: The Case of Bogotá's Street Vendors, 1988–2003." *Urban Studies* 45, no. 1 (2008): 29–51.

Duneier, Mitchell. *Sidewalk.* Macmillan, 1999.

Economic Commission for Latin America and the Caribbean (ECLAC/CEPAL). *Preliminary Overview of the Economies of Latin America and the Caribbean 2019.* United Nations, 2020.

Edelman, Murray J. *The Symbolic Uses of Politics.* University of Illinois Press, 1964.

Eidse, Noelani, Sarah Turner, and Natalie Oswin. "Contesting Street Spaces in a Socialist City: Itinerant Vending-Scapes and the Everyday Politics of Mobility in Hanoi, Vietnam." *Annals of the American Association of Geographers* 106, no. 2 (2016): 340–49.

Epp, Charles R. *The Rights Revolution: Lawyers, Activists, and Supreme Courts in Comparative Perspective.* Cambridge University Press, 1998.

Fernández-Kelly, Patricia, and Jon Shefner, eds. *Out of the Shadows: Political Action and the Informal Economy in Latin America.* Penn State University Press, 2006.

Fischer, Brodwyn M. *A Poverty of Rights: Citizenship and Inequality in Twentieth-Century Rio de Janeiro.* Stanford University Press, 2008.

Fligstein, Neil. "Markets as Politics: A Political-Cultural Approach to Market Institutions." *American Sociological Review* 61, no. 4 (1996): 656–73.

Foucault, Michel. *Surveiller et Punir*. Gallimard, 1975.

Geertz, Clifford. "Suq: The Bazaar Economy in Sefrou." In *Meaning and Order in Moroccan Society: Three Essays in Cultural Analysis*, edited by Clifford Geertz, Hildred Geertz, and Lawrence Rosen, 123–313. Cambridge University Press, 1979.

Goldstein, Daniel M. *Owners of the Sidewalk: Security and Survival in the Informal City*. Duke University Press, 2016.

Greve, Henrich R., Jo-Ellen Pozner, and Hayagreeva Rao. "Vox Populi: Resource Partitioning, Organizational Proliferation, and the Cultural Impact of the Insurgent Microradio Movement." *American Journal of Sociology* 112, no. 3 (2006): 802–37.

Gündogdu, Ayten. *Rightlessness in an Age of Rights: Hannah Arendt and the Contemporary Struggles of Migrants*. Oxford University Press, 2014.

Hansen, Karen Tranberg, Walter E. Little, and B. Lynne Milgram, eds. *Street Economies in the Urban Global South*. SAR Press, 2013.

Harriss-White, Barbara. "India's Informal Economy: Past, Present and Future." In *The Informal Economy Revisited: Examining the Past, Envisioning the Future*, edited by Martha Chen and Françoise Carré, 37–44. Taylor & Francis, 2020.

Harvey, David. "From Managerialism to Entrepreneurialism: The Transformation in Urban Governance in Late Capitalism." *Geografiska Annaler: Series B, Human Geography* (1989): 3–17.

Hochschild, Arlie Russell. *Strangers in Their Own Land: Anger and Mourning on the American Right*. New Press, 2018.

Holland, Alisha C. *Forbearance as Redistribution: The Politics of Informal Welfare in Latin America*. Cambridge University Press, 2017.

Holston, James. *Insurgent Citizenship*. Princeton University Press, 2009.

———. "Insurgent Citizenship in an Era of Global Urban Peripheries." *City & Society* 21, no. 2 (2009): 245–67.

Horne, John, and Wolfram Manzenreiter. "An Introduction to the Sociology of Sports Mega-Events." *Sociological Review* 54, no. 2 suppl. (2006): 1–24.

Hummel, Calla. *Why Informal Workers Organize: Contentious Politics, Enforcement, and the State*. Oxford University Press, 2021.

Hunter, Wendy. *The Transformation of the Workers' Party in Brazil, 1989–2009*. Cambridge University Press, 2010.

Huntington, Samuel P. *Political Order in Changing Societies*. Yale University Press, 2006.

Ingram, Paul, and Hayagreeva Rao. "Store Wars: The Enactment and Repeal of Anti-Chain-Store Legislation in America." *American Journal of Sociology* 110, no. 2 (2004): 446–87.

International Labour Organization (ILO). "Decent Work and the Informal Economy." International Labour Office 90th Conference Report VI. ILO, 2002.

———. "Women and Men in the Informal Economy: A Statistical Picture." (third edition). International Labour Office. ILO, 2018.

Lee, Caroline W., and Zachary Romano. "Democracy's New Discipline: Public Deliberation as Organizational Strategy." *Organization Studies* 34, no. 5–6 (May 2013): 733–53.

Leff, Mark Hugh. *The Limits of Symbolic Reform: The New Deal and Taxation, 1933–1939*. Cambridge University Press, 1984.

Lindell, Ilda, Maria Hedman, and Kyle-Nathan Verboomen. "The World Cup 2010, 'World Class Cities,' and Street Vendors in South Africa." In *Street Economies in the Urban Global South*, edited by Karen Tranberg Hansen, Walter E. Little, and B. Lynne Milgram, 179–200. SAR Press, 2013.

Mann, Michael. *The Dark Side of Democracy: Explaining Ethnic Cleansing*. Cambridge University Press, 2005.

Marshall, Thomas H. *Citizenship and Social Class*. Cambridge University Press, 1950.

Mayhew, Henry. *The London Underworld in the Victorian Period: Authentic First-Person Accounts by Beggars, Thieves and Prostitutes*. Dover Publications, 2005.

McCann, Michael. "The Unbearable Lightness of Rights: On Sociolegal Inquiry in the Global Era." *Law & Society Review* 48, no. 2 (2014): 245–73.

McCann, Michael W. *Rights at Work: Pay Equity Reform and the Politics of Legal Mobilization*. University of Chicago Press, 1994.

McNevin, Anne. *Contesting Citizenship: Irregular Migrants and New Frontiers of the Political*. Columbia University Press, 2011.

Misse, Michel. "Trocas Ilícitas e Mercadorias Políticas: Para Uma Interpretação de Trocas Ilícitas e Moralmente Reprováveis Cuja Persistência e Abrangência No Brasil Nos Causam Incômodos Também Teóricos." *Anuário Antropológico* 35, no. 2 (2010): 89–107.

Mudge, Stephanie Lee. "What's Left of Leftism? Neoliberal Politics in Western Party Systems, 1945–2004." *Social Science History* 35, no. 3 (2011): 337–80.

Murphy, Raymond. "The Structure of Closure: A Critique and Development of the Theories of Weber, Collins, and Parkin." *British Journal of Sociology* 35, no. 4 (1984): 547–67.

North, Douglass C. *Institutions, Institutional Change and Economic Performance*. Cambridge University Press, 1990.

Ong, Aihwa. *Flexible Citizenship: The Cultural Logics of Transnationality*. Duke University Press, 1999.

Pamplona, João Batista. "Mercado de trabalho, informalidade e comércio ambulante em São Paulo." *Revista Brasileira de Estudos de População* 30, no. 1 (2013): 225–49.

Panja, Tariq. "As Sponsors Shy Away, FIFA Faces World Cup Shortfall." *New York Times*, November 18, 2017. https://www.nytimes.com/2017/11/28/sports/soccer/world-cup-sponsors-russia-2018.html.

Pérez Sáinz, Juan Pablo. "The New Faces of Informality in Central America." *Journal of Latin American Studies* 30, no. 1 (1998): 157–79.

Perlman, Janice. *The Myth of Marginality: Urban Poverty and Politics in Rio De Janeiro*. University of California Press, 1976.

Perret, Catherine. *L'enseignement de la torture : Réflexions sur Jean Améry*. Seuil, 2013. https://hal-univ-paris8.archives-ouvertes.fr/hal-02512665/.

Pierson, Paul. *Politics in Time: History, Institutions, and Social Analysis*. Princeton University Press, 2004.

Piketty, Thomas. *Capital in the Twenty-First Century*. Harvard University Press, 2014. https://doi.org/10.4159/9780674369542.

Putnam, Robert D. *Bowling Alone: The Collapse and Revival of American Community*. Simon & Schuster, 2000.

Rosales, Rocio. "Survival, Economic Mobility and Community among Los Angeles Fruit Vendors." *Journal of Ethnic and Migration Studies* 39, no. 5 (2013): 697–717.

Rotker, Susana, and Katherine Goldman. *Citizens of Fear: Urban Violence in Latin America.* Rutgers University Press, 2002.

Roy, Ananya. *City Requiem, Calcutta: Gender and the Politics of Poverty.* University of Minnesota Press, 2003.

———. "Gentlemen's City: Urban Informality in the Calcutta of New Communism." In *Urban Informality: Transnational Perspectives from the Middle East, Latin America, and South Asia,* edited by Ananya Roy and Nezar AlSayyad, 141–64. Lexington Books, 2004.

Sassen, Saskia. *The Global City.* Princeton University Press, 1991.

———. "Whose City Is It? Globalization and the Formation of New Claims." *Public Culture* 8 (1996): 205–24.

Schaefer, Kalmann, and Cheywa R. Spindel. *São Paulo: Urban Development and Employment.* International Labour Office, 1976.

Scheingold, Stuart A. *The Politics of Rights: Lawyers, Public Policy, and Political Change.* University of Michigan Press, 2010.

Schneiberg, Marc, Marissa King, and Thomas Smith. "Social Movements and Organizational Form: Cooperative Alternatives to Corporations in the American Insurance, Dairy, and Grain Industries." *American Sociological Review* 73, no. 4 (2008): 635–67.

Seidman, Gay W. *Manufacturing Militance: Workers' Movements in Brazil and South Africa, 1970–1985.* University of California Press, 1994.

Singer, Paul. "Movimentos de Bairro." In *São Paulo: O Povo em Movimento,* edited by Paul Singer and Vinícius Caldeira Brant, 83–107. Editora Brasileira de Ciências, 1980.

Somers, Margaret R. *Genealogies of Citizenship: Markets, Statelessness, and the Right to Have Rights.* Cambridge University Press, 2008.

Standing, Guy. *The Precariat.* Bloomsbury Academic, 2011.

Suarez, Sandra L. "Symbolic Politics and the Regulation of Executive Compensation: A Comparison of the Great Depression and the Great Recession." *Politics & Society* 42, no. 1 (2014): 73–105.

Tavares de Almeida, Maria Hermínia, and Fernando Henrique Guarnieri. "Toward a (Poor) Middle-Class Democracy?" In *Democratic Brazil Divided,* edited by Peter Kingstone and Timothy J. Power, 175–79. University of Pittsburgh Press, 2017.

Telles, Vera, and Daniel Hirata. "Cidade e Práticas Urbanas: Nas Fronteiras Incertas Entre o Informal, o Ilegal, e o Ilícito." *Estudos Avançados* 21, no. 61 (2007): 173–91.

Tilly, Charles. *Durable Inequality.* University of California Press, 1998.

Touchton, Michael, Stephanie McNulty, and Brian Wampler. "Participatory Budgeting and Community Development: A Global Perspective." *American Behavioral Scientist* 67, no. 4 (2023): 520–36.

Townroe, Peter M. "Location Factors in the Decentralization of Industry: A Survey of Metropolitan Sao Paulo, Brazil." World Bank Working Papers 517, 1983.

Truzzi, Oswaldo. *De Mascates a Doutores: Sírios e Libaneses em São Paulo.* Editora Sumaré, 1992.

Turner, Sarah, and Laura Schoenberger. "Street Vendor Livelihoods and Everyday Politics in Hanoi, Vietnam: The Seeds of a Diverse Economy?" *Urban Studies* 49, no. 5 (2012): 1027–44.

Venkatesh, Sudhir Alladi. *Off the Books: The Underground Economy of the Urban Poor.* Harvard University Press, 2006.

Wacquant, Loïc. *Punishing the Poor: The Neoliberal Government of Social Insecurity.* Duke University Press, 2009.

Weber, Max. *Economy and Society: An Outline of Interpretive Sociology*. University of California Press, 1978.

Weeden, Kim A. "Why Do Some Occupations Pay More than Others? Social Closure and Earnings Inequality in the United States." *American Journal of Sociology* 108, no. 1 (2002): 55–101.

Weyland, Kurt. "A Paradox of Success? Determinants of Political Support for President Fujimori." *International Studies Quarterly* 44, no. 3 (2000): 481–502.

Whitson, David, and John Horne. "Underestimated Costs and Overestimated Benefits? Comparing the Outcomes of Sports Mega-Events in Canada and Japan." *Sociological Review* 54, no. 2 (2006): 71–89.

Wilson, Stuart. "Litigating Housing Rights in Johannesburg's Inner City: 2004–2008." *South African Journal on Human Rights* 27, no. 1 (2011): 127–51.

Wimmer, Andreas. *Ethnic Boundary Making: Institutions, Power, Networks*. Oxford University Press, 2013.

Yázigi, Eduardo. *O Mundo das Calçadas: Por uma Política Democrática de Espaços Públicos*. Humanitas, 2000.

Index

Page numbers in italics refer to figures.

www.ingramcontent.com/pod-product-compliance
Lightning Source LLC
Chambersburg PA
CBHW032136020426
42334CB00016B/1183